VIOLENCE IN THE MEDIA

A Reference Handbook

Other Titles in ABC-CLIO's
CONTEMPORARY
WORLD ISSUES
Series

VIOLENCE IN THE MEDIA

A Reference Handbook

Nancy Signorielli

**CONTEMPORARY
WORLD ISSUES**

A B C CLIO

Santa Barbara, California
Denver, Colorado
Oxford, England

Library of Congress Cataloging-in-Publication Data

Signorielli, Nancy.
    Violence in the media : a reference handbook / Nancy Signorielli.
        p. cm. — (Contemporary world issues)
    Includes bibliographical references and index.
    ISBN 1-85109-604-3 (hardback : alk. paper) — ISBN 1-85109-609-4
    (ebook) 1. Violence on television—Handbooks, manuals, etc.
    2. Violence in mass media—Handbooks, manuals, etc.
    I. Title. II. Series.

    PN1992.8.V55S55 2005
    303.6—dc22

                                                    2005003253

07   06   05   10 9 8 7 6 5 4 3 2 1

This book is also available on the World Wide Web as an e-book.
Visit http://www.abc-clio.com for details.

ABC-CLIO, Inc.
130 Cremona Drive, P.O. Box 1911
Santa Barbara, California 93116–1911

This book is printed on acid-free paper.
Manufactured in the United States of America

Contents

Preface

Violence in the media has been a topic of concern that increased as American society became more and more involved with and dependent upon media. In the late 1800s, there was concern that the dime novels, whose stories often featured crime and violence, would have a negative impact on young readers. In the 1930s, when the movies captured our hearts and spare time, there was concern that violent images would negatively affect children. In the 1950s, when television burst upon the social scene and quickly took over as the primary source of most entertainment and information, the concern focused on the considerable violence that was part of both entertainment and information programming. Parents, teachers, members of the clergy, and politicians wondered if watching so much violence on television would have a negative affect upon children. People consistently thought and asked: Is media violence a factor in the increase of violence in society? Is media violence related to the increase of violence in U.S. schools, tragic incidents such as Columbine, the killing spree of the Washington-area sniper, and terrorism? The concern may come down to simply discovering what role the media, particularly violent media, play in American society.

These questions do not have simple answers, and there are no simple solutions to the problems of media violence. Over the years, there have been numerous congressional hearings devoted to understanding violence on television, both in terms of how much exists and what its effects might be. The government has made funding available to study television violence several times, including the extensive set of projects commissioned as part of the Surgeon General's Television and Social Behavior project in the early 1970s and the 1982 updates of many of these studies funded by the National Institute of Mental Health. Funding has also been made available from other sources, including professional organizations such as the American Medical Association and, in the mid-1990s, the media industry, including the National Cable Broadcasters Association and four television networks (ABC, CBS, Fox, and NBC). Over the years, the Federal Communications Commission (FCC) has sponsored several Notices of Inquiry, the most recent on July 28, 2004, to gather information about television violence and its effects. Since the 1960s, most of these projects have found that there are relatively high levels of violence on television and that these violent images may have detrimental effects upon viewers, particularly children. Is the media totally to blame for the increased violence in society? Probably not, but it may be a contributing factor.

The most proactive action of Congress occurred in 1996, when a provision was added to the new Telecommunications Act that required all 13-inch and larger television sets manufactured after 1999 to come equipped with the V-chip, an electromagnetic device that would allow parents to limit their children's viewing. Moreover, along with the V-chip legislation, the industry was told to develop a ratings system that would work with the V-chip to give parents and care givers information about the age-appropriateness and content of those television programs their children might want to watch. These ratings were implemented in 1997 and today are displayed during the first fifteen seconds of a television program.

I have spent most of my academic career examining television violence. I became interested in the study of media while working on my M.A. degree in Experimental Psychology at Queens College of the City University of New York in 1966 and 1967. When I completed my degree early in the summer of 1967, I had the unique opportunity to meet and talk with George Gerbner. This meeting was a turning point in my career, and that fall I entered the doctoral program in communication research that was commencing at the Annenberg School for Communication at the University of Pennsylvania. In 1968, Professor Gerbner was awarded the grant to study violence in prime-time programs by the National Commission on the Causes and Prevention of Violence. Like most of the students at the Annenberg School, I became involved in this project. My involvement increased when I became Professor Gerbner's research assistant and began to oversee data collection procedures. My dissertation research analyzed a portion of these data, and once I completed my doctorate in 1975, I continued my involvement with Professor Gerbner and the Cultural Indicators project. Our research team and studies grew along with my continued fascination with the study of television violence and gender roles in the media. I remained at the University of Pennsylvania until moving to the University of Delaware in the fall of 1987. Although I now work in a different venue, my research and interest in these topics have continued to grow and prosper.

My interest in the study of television, particularly its portrayal of violence and gender roles, has spanned almost forty years, from the late 1960s until now. My interest in this topic reflects my love of the media, particularly television, and my work as an academic—teaching and research. I watch television frequently and when I watch I analyze, think, and wonder about the images and messages I see. As most academics, this approach translates to my teaching about media. Some of my students, however, lament that I have "ruined" their television viewing because I have opened their eyes to looking beyond the story to analyze, think, and wonder about what they're watching and why the images they see over and over are part of the landscape of television and other media. In other words, I have helped them become more media-literate.

Throughout my career, I have found that media violence has continued to be a particularly important and relevant topic. Whether looking at violence in relation to television, video games, or other media, concern about the harm that may result from seeing so many violent images continues to manifest itself among many different populations—parents, teachers, the clergy, and politicians. Even though people know much more about media violence today than they did when television was in its infancy and when I first began my studies, concern about its potential negative effects has not abated. The fact that this topic remains one of considerable interest and importance can be seen in the latest Notice of Inquiry issued by the FCC (July 28, 2004) to seek the most current and up-to-date information on the presentation of violent programming and its impact on children.

When Mim Vasan, my editor at ABC-CLIO, approached me about this project, I was immediately enthralled. This was an opportunity to focus my lifetime interest in the media, particularly television violence, in a useful volume. I knew that many books had already been written and published on this topic, but most I felt were geared primarily to upper-level undergraduates, graduate students, and scholars in the field of mass communication. There were few sources that made this interesting, extensive, and important field of study readily available to younger students and/or their parents or others not immersed in the world of academics. I saw this book as a way to reach and generate interest among high school students and those just beginning their undergraduate careers. It would also be a book that parents, teachers, and others in the lay public could read to get more information about media violence and the numerous sources and resources that exist relating to the topic. I was particularly interested in writing this book because it provided a way for me to talk both practically and theoretically about media violence.

Structure of the Book

The structure of the book reflects its dual focus on practicality and theory. It consists of nine chapters. The first three chapters provide a narrative about television violence, its history, what researchers know about it, its controversies, and how ordinary people can use television to their advantage. Chapter 1 presents the background and history of the study of media violence, as well as a description of some of the most important theories about television violence and its possible effects. This chapter gives the reader the framework to explore and understand the rest of the narrative materials and to apply when exploring resources from other sources, such as those listed in the annotated bibliography (Chapter 9). Chapter 2 presents what we currently know about media violence. It discusses the level of violence on television and the results of some of the key studies that have explored how media violence may affect viewers, particularly children. Chapter 3, then, explores some of the problems and controversies surrounding the study of media violence, such as concern about how to best define violence and how to isolate and count discrete scenes or incidents of violence. This chapter ends with a section of possible solutions for parents about how to become more media literate and how to help their children get the most out of television and develop the tools of media literacy.

Chapter 4 is a Chronology of the study of media violence, and Chapter 5 consists of biographical sketches of some of the key players in the study of media violence. These key players include academics, media advocates, and politicians. They are the people who were instrumental in the study of media violence in the late 1960s and 1970s, as well as those who are currently involved in its study. Chapter 6 gives some current facts and figures about television violence. This chapter presents new analyses of data from my ongoing study of television violence that has compared levels of violence from the late 1960s to the first few years of the twenty-first century. The chapter also includes tables reprinted from the National Television Violence Study, an important study of television violence completed during the mid-1990s. This chapter provides a narrative of how the research was conducted, definitions of the important elements in the analyses, tables of data, and a short interpretation of what the data in these tables are telling us.

Chapters 7, 8, and 9 provide resource information. Chapter 7, Organizations and Websites, outlines most of the key organizations that have been involved in the study of media violence. These entries provide organization names, addresses, phone numbers, and World Wide Web addresses, as well as the addresses of web pages that may be of particular interest. This list of organizations thus provides a starting-off point for the reader interested in learning more about media violence. Chapter 8, Video and Film Resources, lists and describes many of the videos that have been produced about media violence. Some of these videos are available for purchase, and some may be found in libraries. Watching these videos will provide yet another way to explore the topic of media violence. Chapter 9, Print Resources and Annotated Bibliography, is an annotated bibliography of some of the most important print resources. This chapter includes annotations for government publications, writings of those in the media industry, reports commissioned by organizations, scholarly works (journal articles, books, and book chapters), and trade publications (books written for the lay audience). The last section of this chapter annotates sources related specifically to video games. This chapter provides annotations for some of the classic studies but focuses upon some of the recent important sources.

Overall, this book provides an interesting perspective and look at media violence. It approaches the topic from a historical and theoretical perspective, providing a fairly comprehensive narrative in Chapters 1, 2, and 3. The remainder of the book provides practical information and facts and figures about how much violence there is on television, lists of organizations, and available videos. Finally, the annotated bibliography provides sources for the reader to explore to further their knowledge of media violence. Media violence is an intriguing topic; I invite the reader to become engrossed in its study.

Acknowledgments

There are so many people to whom I am indebted in the preparation of this book. First, I would like to thank Mim Vasan for providing me with this opportunity and for all her help along the way. Second, I thank my family for their ongoing support, particularly my daughter, Laura Jane, whose clerical and detective skills were particularly helpful in the final stages of the preparation of the manuscript. Last, and certainly not least, I am indebted to George Gerbner, mentor, colleague, and friend, for his vision of mass communication media that has had such a profound influence on my thinking and academic career.

1

History of Violence in the Media

During the past half century, the mass media have come to play a particularly important role in society. The media are so pervasive today that few can escape their influence. Media serve many day-to-day functions. They provide us with information and entertainment and have become the major source of persuasion in society. Although the mass media consist of many different outlets and technologies, including radio, books, newspapers, magazines, music, and the World Wide Web, in the past half century television has become the medium that reaches most of the people, most of the time. Television is part and parcel of everyday life. In the average home, the television set is "on" for more than seven hours a day, and the average person watches at least three hours a day. Children and older people typically watch more than three hours a day, whereas teens, particularly older adolescents, have traditionally watched less. But even today's college students are watching much more television than in previous generations because most college and university campuses attract students by providing "wired" environments—dorm rooms and/or apartment complexes with twenty-four-hour cable and Internet connections.

Television plays a unique role in today's society, serving as the primary storyteller for the United States and increasingly the world. Its stories cut across all genres—classic entertainment programs such as situation comedies, dramas, and crime-action type programs as well as reality, news, and information programs. The medium provides information and the bulk of people's entertainment. What is critical about television and other storytelling media is that its stories are now created and told, not by parents, teachers, clergy, or even peers, but by large multinational media giants whose primary concern is generating the most profits for the least expenditure. Although the newer delivery systems, such as cable television and satellite dishes, have ensured that television is no longer dependent upon the electromagnetic spectrum, a scarce public resource, broadcast (over-the-air) technology still plays a critical role in defining the media environment, and by law (Communications Act of 1934 and its updated version, the Telecommunications Act of 1996) television is still expected to operate in the "public interest, convenience, and necessity." It is in this framework that the potential consequences of television's violent messages on society have been under scrutiny since television entered most American homes in the 1950s.

Although violence has always been a part of society and human nature, at no other time in history have people of all ages and walks of life been exposed to as many violent images and messages as they are today. Media messages about violence, whether in the news, movies, music, video games, or television's entertainment programming, pervade day-to-day life and are almost impossible to escape.

This chapter first discusses media violence from a historical perspective, focusing particularly on the numerous congressional hearings and the implications of these hearings for programming. The chapter then examines why television violence is such an important topic, describing some of the most important theories of the potential effects of television violence. Chapter 2 considers the prevalence of media violence, particularly on television, and some of the specific effects of media violence, and Chapter 3 explores some of the problems and controversies surrounding the study of media violence and presents possible solutions to help reduce the negative consequences of living with media violence.

Concern about media violence has had a long and interesting history. At the turn of the century, attention focused on the effects of dime novels (detective stories). As movies became more widespread and popular, so did concern. In the early 1930s more than a dozen studies were conducted as part of the Payne Fund Studies. One study examined the content of 1,500 films produced in 1920, 1925, and 1930, and found that more than three-quarters of these films focused on three topics—crime, love, and sex (Dale 1935). Moreover, even though alcohol use was forbidden because of prohibition during the years these films were made, the films nevertheless openly portrayed its use and that of tobacco. Other studies investigated what movie-goers learned from watching films. Peterson and Thurstone (1933) found that children's attitudes toward war, prohibition, crime, the treatment of criminals and other topics were changed by the movies. Similarly, Blumer and Hausner (1933) found that some children (those in reform school, ex-convicts, delinquents, and those living in high crime areas) committed acts of delinquency after going to the movies. Overall, Charters (1933) in summarizing this set of studies found that movies in general had an adverse effect on children, particularly adolescents. In the 1950s, comic books were criticized as a bad influence on children (Wertham 1954). In short, the question of violence on television emerged in the very early days of television and has remained a hotly debated issue.

Congressional Hearings and Legislation

During the 1950s, television entered most households and became the major source of family entertainment. In 1950 roughly 2 percent of U.S. homes had TV sets, and by the mid-1950s, over 64 percent of U.S. homes had sets. The rapid growth and expansion of television continued, until by 1960, television was in about 90 percent of U.S. homes. Television viewing became the national pastime. Not surprisingly, there were concerns ranging from the amount of time people, especially children, watched television, to its influence on school performance, detrimental effects on eyesight, and content, particularly violence.

Following in the footsteps of radio and the movies, numerous television programs revolved around crime and violence. As early as 1933, parents had expressed concern that violence in radio programs had a negative emotional effect on their children (Cooper 1996). Similarly, violence was an early concern about motion pictures. W. W. Charters reviewed the findings of the Payne Fund Studies and noted that crime movies influenced delinquents: "minor delinquencies are aggravated by these pictures in many cases; cues for criminal actions are presented and are sometimes copied by young delinquents" (1933, 54).

By the mid-1950s, complaints about radio and movies transferred to television. Many parents, politicians, government officials, and educators thought that television was a factor in the increase in crimes committed by American youngsters. Recently there has been concern that media violence is one of the factors responsible for outbreaks of violence in the schools, including attacks at Columbine High School in Littleton, Colorado (1999), and Santana High School in Santee, California (2001), and the killings by the Washington-area sniper (2002).[1]

Hearings during the 1950s

In the 1950s, complaints about television violence and fear about the relationship between television violence and juvenile delinquency grew. In 1952 the Commerce Committee of the House of Representatives (chair, Oren Harris, D-AR) held the first congressional hearing, seeking to determine whether radio and television programs contained offensive or immoral content or emphasized violence, crime, and/or corruption. In 1954 the Senate Subcommittee to Investigate Juvenile Delinquency (Chair, Robert Hendrickson, R-NJ) held hearings to ascertain if television's crime and horror programs were related to the rise in juvenile delinquency. These hearings consisted of presentations by staff investigators and industry representatives. The former used this platform to state their concerns, and the latter described how they operated and their view of television's effects. The representative for the National Association of Radio and Television Broadcasters (now the National Association of Broadcasters) clearly stated that no research suggested a relationship between television and juvenile delinquency (Rowland 1983).

Testimony before the Hendrickson committee indicated that children watched between three and four hours of television each day—almost as much time as they spent in school—and that the programs they watched contained an average of 6.2 acts of violence each hour. Interestingly, the California Youth Authority reported that in two years there had been a 10-percent increase in juvenile crime and that the majority of those involved in these crimes said television crime programs contributed to their criminal behavior (Cooper 1996). At the same time, testimony by television executives indicated that they were dedicated to providing entertaining and quality programming but that there was no relationship between televised violence and criminal behavior and that they would consider any attempt to regulate program content as censorship.

In April 1955 during the 84th Congress, the Senate Subcommittee to Investigate Juvenile Delinquency (Chair, Senator Estes Kefauver, D-TN) turned again to the question of television violence. Kefauver was particularly interested in the testimony of social science researchers Eleanor Maccoby and Paul Lazarsfeld, who indicated that there was not much information about the effect of violence on television because it had not been studied extensively. They could, nevertheless, discuss how films influenced children and believed that there were parallels between the two media.

Maccoby (1954), for example, noted that children, including the very young, found television very attractive. Her interviews with more than 300 mothers indicated that children had higher levels of aggressive behavior after watching violent programming. Testimony by Dr. Ralph Banay, a U.S. Bureau of Prisons psychiatric consultant, noted that emotionally disturbed children could be harmed by television violence. He "analogized that as prison was often described as a college for crime, television was a preparatory school for delinquency" (Cooper 1996, 31). Lazarsfeld (1955), however, testified that the research about television violence was inconclusive and that it was not possible to say there was a causal relationship between juvenile crime and watching violence on television.

The Hendrickson-Kefauver hearings substantiated the need for long-term social science research. Willard Rowland (1983) notes that even though numerous studies and theories were available, researchers were reluctant to make definitive claims. Moreover, the way the hearings were held made it almost impossible to reach firm conclusions (Cooper 1996). First, the scientific evidence was inconclusive and conflicting. Second, despite thorough questioning, Kefauver and the committee did not question the validity of testimony and made no attempt to reconcile conflicting statements. Third, the hearings indicated the need for continued research. Network executives, although admitting that some risk existed, promised to examine the impact television violence might have on children (Rubinstein 1980). Last, the industry agreed to modify the Television Code to discourage presenting violence and illicit sex in an attractive manner (NARTB 1956).

Hearings during the 1960s

The early 1960s brought more attention to television violence. Most programming was devoted to entertainment for mass audiences, with an abundance of action-adventure programs. In 1960, for example, an extremely violent program, *The Untouchables*, was the most highly rated and successful program. Newton Minow, the new chair of the Federal Communications Commission (FCC) and the other commissioners generally agreed that television programming lacked quality but did not advocate that the FCC take a more proactive or regulatory stance. Minow, however, was particularly outspoken about the lack of quality programming; his most famous speech, given before the National Association of Broadcasters in May 1961, described television as a "vast wasteland" (Cooper 1996).

During 1961 the Senate Subcommittee to Investigate Juvenile Delinquency (Chair, Senator Thomas Dodd, D-CT) held year-long hearings that relied extensively upon social science research. Prior to the hearings, the subcommittee staff found that between 1954 and 1961 the percent of programs with violence, particularly those broadcast when children were watching, had increased. The hearings called upon social scientists who testified that television influenced viewers, particular teenagers, and children. Dr. Peter Legins, a professor of sociology at the University of Maryland, for example, noted how broadcasters touted television's advertising appeal, particularly for children, and asked whether it would have the same level of influence in other realms of behavior. These hearings also called television writers and producers to testify, some of whom admitted that they had been asked on occasion to add more violence or action to their programs. Nevertheless, as was true for Kefauver's hearings in 1954, testimony was rarely challenged, and the hearings had little impact on legislation (Cooper 1996). These hearings, once again, revealed little completed research, indicating that the industry had not kept its promise to do more studies (Liebert and Sprafkin 1988).

The reaction of the FCC was tempered. FCC chair Minow, in an address to radio and television executives, noted that he did not agree with some of the witnesses that television violence was a specific cause of juvenile delinquency. Rather, Minow, indicated that he was in agreement with the testimony of Wilbur Schramm (Stanford University) who said that television may be harmful to some children, some of the time, but that for most children television is neither harmful nor beneficial (Cooper 1996).

In 1964, Senator Dodd held another round of hearings. Although Dodd began with praise for the industry, positive statements were quickly replaced with talk of the network's broken promises about reducing the amount of violence on television. Dodd and his committee cited their current study showing that network violence had not decreased since the last set of hearings.

Moreover, he presented evidence from a number of studies showing a causal link between aggressive behavior and watching violent television. In addition, Senator Kenneth B. Keating (D-NY) introduced a Federal Bureau of Investigation (FBI) report showing that, in the past seven years, crime in the United States had increased five times faster than the population. J. Edgar Hoover, Keating added, believed that the increase in the overall crime rate in the country could be attributed to crime and violence in the media (Cooper 1996).

Once again, the hearings indicated that little substantive research had been conducted, and the general conclusion was that the industry would not do any. The report issued by the Subcommittee on to Investigate Juvenile Delinquency, in addition, was very critical of the ineffectiveness of network self-regulation through the National Association of Broadcasters (NAB) Code (Liebert and Sprafkin 1988). This report concluded that there was a relationship between viewing crime and violence on television and engaging in antisocial behaviors (Rubinstein 1980).

The National Commission on the Causes and Prevention of Violence

In the mid- to late 1960s, the United States experienced considerable turmoil, civil disobedience, and urban unrest. There were four assassinations—President John F. Kennedy, Senator Robert Kennedy, the Reverend Dr. Martin Luther King, Jr., and Malcolm X, as well as mounting concern about the country's increasing involvement in Vietnam. Television again came under scrutiny; was television violence related to or responsible for the rise in violence around the country? The National Commission on the Causes and Prevention of Violence (Eisenhower Commission) was established in 1968 to examine and hold hearings on issues relating to violence, including the impact of the mass media. This commission asked a number of scholars to review the body of existing research and sponsored one new project (Gerbner 1969), a content analysis to isolate the amount of violence in prime-time and weekend-daytime network dramatic programming (Baker and Ball 1969).

The commission's hearings focused on several topics, including the networks' coverage of the chaotic 1968 Democratic National Convention in Chicago, violence in entertainment programming, and the effects of televised violence on viewers. Once again, the industry was asked to defend a seeming contradiction—how they could support and encourage the use of television commercials as an effective way to get messages to the public while, at the same time, saying that the messages of media violence were of no consequence to viewers, particularly children (Cooper 1996).

The final report was written by a group that sought to maintain the political status quo. It was carefully documented and discussed issues so as to avoid as much confrontation as possible (Rowland 1983). Nevertheless, the commission issued a rather strong statement essentially indicting violence on television. "We are deeply troubled by television's constant portrayal of violence, not in any genuine attempt to focus artistic expression on the human condition, but rather in pandering to a public preoccupation with violence that television itself has helped to generate" (NCCPV 1970, 160).

The report also suggested that the constant diet of violent behavior on television had a negative effect on people, especially children; encouraged violent behavior; and fostered unacceptable values about violence. Although the report did not say that violence on television was a principal cause of violence in society, it did suggest that television violence was an important contributing factor. Specifically, television's effects had to be assessed in relation to each person's degree of mental stability and particularly his or her predisposition to behaving violently. In short, there was ample reason for concern about television violence (Murray 1995).

The report of the National Commission on the Causes and Prevention of Violence never received the attention or public play it deserved. Even before it was issued, the Surgeon General's Program on Television and Social Behavior was organized and funded, and research began under the impetus of Senator John Pastore (D-RI), chair of the Senate Subcommittee on Communications. This program, a major undertaking, allocated $1 million for new research (Liebert and Sprafkin 1988).

The Program on Television and Social Behavior

The Television and Social Behavior Program framed television violence as a public health issue (Murray 1995). It was modeled after the surgeon general's 1964 report, *Smoking and Health,* and, like that program, had an advisory committee of twelve distinguished social scientists. Unfortunately, the credibility and impartiality of the committee came under scrutiny when it was revealed that five members had direct ties to the television industry and seven distinguished social scientists had been blackballed by broadcasters when the committee was established (Liebert and Sprafkin 1988).

The program was supervised by the National Institute of Mental Health's (NIMH's) Scientific Advisory Committee on Television and Social Behavior, appointed by the surgeon general. Senator Pastore and the Senate Subcommittee on Communications, however, maintained a close involvement with the project and charged them with an almost impossible task—to determine, scientifically, the effects of violent television programs on children (NIMH 1972).

The research consisted of twenty-three individual projects, selected from forty formal proposals. It included laboratory, field, and institutional/organizational studies as well as surveys of how people watch television. The research commissioned as part of the Eisenhower Commission—the content analysis focusing upon violent content—was refunded (Gerbner 1972). The studies provided a wealth of information, increasing the published research literature on television's effects on children by 20 percent (Rubinstein 1980). The results were summarized in the final report, *Television and Growing Up: The Impact of Televised Violence*. It incorporated and distilled thousands of pages of reports. Although it had to satisfy two extremely different viewpoints, it stated, in several places and in several ways, that there was some evidence of a causal relation between aggressive behavior and watching violence on television (see, for example, NIMH 1972, 10–11). Specifically, even though viewing violence increases the likelihood that children will become more aggressive, not all children are affected in the same way. Yet there was sufficient evidence to say that watching violent programs on television could be harmful to children.

Unfortunately, most people did not get this impression when reading conflicting newspaper accounts of the report. A number of reporters, including Jack Gould from the *New York Times*, received an advance or "leaked" copy of the summary chapter of the report (Cater and Strickland 1975). His story, particularly the headline, published before the official release of the report and the five volumes of technical reports, misinterpreted the findings of the committee. Gould did not quote the key conclusion that there was preliminary evidence of a causal relationship. Rather, he noted: "The office of the United States Surgeon General has found that violence in television programming does not have an adverse effect on the majority of the nation's youth, but may influence small groups of youngsters predisposed by many factors to aggressive behavior" (Gould 1972, 1).

Gould's article resulted in an enormous furor and accusations that the report was an industry "whitewash." Researchers were incensed that their findings had been misinterpreted. Moreover, a later analysis of press coverage, found that Gould's misinterpretation was never fully corrected (Tankard and Showalter 1977).

Hearings were held in March 1972 to try to dispel some of the confusion, to reassess the report, and to address the question of specific policy recommendations. These hearings gave government officials (FCC commissioners, the surgeon general), researchers, industry executives, and citizen advocacy groups a chance to talk about the report and its results. The researchers used these hearings to refute the conclusions stated in the final report because most believed that the report favored industry interests by misrepresenting the findings. Broadcasters, however, used the hearings to focus on those portions of the report they believed exonerated the industry (Cooper 1996).

At the end of the hearings, the surgeon general reiterated that the committee had come to a unanimous conclusion. The committee members, including the network executives, all agreed that there was too much violence on television and that specific remedial actions were needed (Rubinstein and Brown 1985). In addition, Senator Pastore requested the establishment of an annual Violence Index to map the degree of violence on television on a yearly basis as well as provide a mechanism by which to keep the issue of television violence in the public arena and on the public agenda (Cooper 1996).

Hearings during the 1970s

At the hearings held in 1974, Professor George Gerbner (Dean, The Annenberg School for Communication, University of Pennsylvania) reported the ongoing results of his annual analyses of television programming (Violence Index), and Dr. Eli Rubinstein, examining the actions of broadcasters, reported that little, if nothing, had been done to reduce violence on television since the release of the surgeon general's report. Moreover, as expected, network representatives presented conflicting testimony that, according to their measures, there was now less violence on television (see Chapter 2). Pastore concluded this hearing with a challenge to the broadcasters to show a real decrease in television violence at the next year's FCC oversight hearings (Cooper 1996).

During 1974 the FCC was pressured by Congress to make recommendations to protect children from television's plethora of violent programming. In 1975 the FCC reported that the number of complaints they had received about television violence had increased since 1972. Once again, the FCC publicly acknowledged the need for self-regulation by the industry. Chairman Richard Wiley's four-part proposal asked the industry to (1) reduce violent programming, (2) schedule programs that were unsuitable for children after 9 PM, (3) include both video and audio warnings at the start of programs deemed unacceptable for children, and (4) include these warnings in television listings and promotions. All but the second of these proposals were rejected by the networks. This proposal, subsequently called the Family Viewing Hour, was formally included in the NAB Television Code (Cooper 1996).

This small victory was, however, short-lived. A few months after the Family Viewing Hour was formally adopted, the courts ruled it violated the industry's First Amendment right to free speech. Public sentiment, however, was not with the broadcasters. A 1975 Gallup poll indicated that two-thirds of all television viewers found that television programming contained an unacceptable level of violence. The numbers of citizen advocacy groups increased, keeping this issue in the public eye. One of the most important of these groups, the National Citizens' Committee for Broadcasting (NCCB), began to publish a list of companies most likely to advertise during violent programs and urged viewers to boycott their products (Cooper 1996).

Hearings were held in 1976 and 1977. Once again, numerous sides of the issue were discussed. The American Medical Association (AMA), for example, testified that television violence was an environmental health risk. The NCCB presented its most recent list of advertisers who supported the most violent programs. At the same time, many witnesses supported the industry's contention that the body of available research on the effects of television violence was inconclusive. Most important, many spoke out against government intervention in regard to television. Overall, little was done to try to reconcile opposing views (Cooper 1996).

The Senate Subcommittee on Communications, with a vote of 8 to 7, issued its final report in September 1977, noting that television violence was a cause for concern and that it might harm viewers, especially children. Nevertheless, the report essentially blamed the American public for the amounts of excessive violence on television. Furthermore, the report concluded that parents could play an important role in curbing the negative effects of watching violent programming and that they should carefully monitor what and how much television their children watched.

The 1970s were also marked by an increase in public campaigns against television violence. One particularly important effort was undertaken by the AMA in 1976, when it issued a policy statement that (1) stated TV violence was a risk factor threatening the health and welfare of American children, (2) committed the AMA to finding ways to make television better, and (3) encouraged people to oppose TV violence and boycott companies who sponsored violent programs. Other campaigns were undertaken by the National Parent-Teacher Association (PTA), the American Psychological Association (APA), and the National Coalition on Television Violence (NCTV).

Hearings during the 1980s

In 1982 a comprehensive review updating the 1972 Report of the Surgeon General's Advisory Committee on Television and Social Behavior was published by the National Institute of Mental Health. This report, like that of the 1972 surgeon general's committee, was leaked to the press before its official release and made front-page headlines. This time, however, the newspaper articles were accurate, although they gave more coverage to violence-related issues than the report itself. The report stated that television violence is related to children's aggressive behavior and that television violence often taught children that violent or aggressive behavior was an appropriate way to resolve conflict. Finally, the report took the broadcast industry to task for maintaining its high levels of violent programming despite the concerns of both Congress and citizens (Murray 1995).

The television industry immediately claimed that the report was "inaccurate." In 1983 ABC issued a booklet (Wurtzel and Lometti 1983) that tried to refute the major conclusions about the relationship between television violence and aggressive behavior. The NIMH seven-member advisory committee, however, made a point-by-point response to the ABC booklet, comparing the television industry's stance to that taken by the tobacco industry in trying to refute evidence linking smoking with serious health problems (Rubinstein and Brown 1985).

The 1980s brought numerous changes to the television industry, including the rise of multinational media giants. The NAB code was eliminated because it violated antitrust laws. Deregulation, in particular, was responsible for the perception that television was just another business whose major concern was the marketplace—attracting the most viewers for the least amount of money. This environment is perhaps best summed up by FCC chair Mark Fowler's description of television in 1984 as a "toaster with pictures." Nevertheless, concern about television violence continued.

As the story goes, one evening in the mid-1980s, Senator Paul Simon (D-IL) turned on the television in his hotel room to see a scene of such extreme violence that he wondered how such programming would affect children. He saw it as an indication that the broadcast industry was not adequately serving the public interest. In June 1986 he sponsored a bill designed to extend limited antitrust immunity to the networks and cable companies so they could work together to find ways to reduce television violence. The idea was that if everyone had a common set of rules for reducing violence, there might be less violence on television (Cooper 1996).

Given the volatile nature of this topic, the bill met with considerable opposition, and it took numerous attempts to get it signed into law. The first version, although approved by the Senate, died in the House of Representatives. It was reintroduced (as the Television Violence Act of 1987) and approved by the Committee on the Judiciary and the Subcommittee on Antitrust, Monopolies, and Business Rights but once again died when the House failed to act. The Television Violence Act of 1989, now cosponsored by Representative Dan Glickman, was reviewed by the House Subcommittee on Economic and Commercial Law in May 1989. Despite a lack of support for this bill by the television networks and the American Civil Liberties Union (ACLU), the bill (the Television Improvement Act of 1990) was passed on October 28, 1989, to be in effect for three years. It was signed into law by President George H. W. Bush two months later (Cooper 1996).

As expected, broadcasters reacted negatively to the act and, over the course of the next two years, did little to comply with its stated expectations. Similarly, the public did not think that this act would make a difference in the amount of violence on television. Social scientists, however, believed that it would be the impetus the industry needed to finally reduce the amount of violence on television.

Hearings during the 1990s

In 1992, two congressional hearings examined youth violence. A hearing before the Senate Committee on Governmental Affairs discussed television violence as one of the factors that contributed to violence by juveniles. Leonard Eron testified that children's aggression could be linked to television violence, which often resulted in a cycle in which children who watched violence on television became more aggressive and then watched more violent programming in an attempt to justify their actions. A second hearing before the House Judiciary Committee Subcommittee on Crime and Criminal Justice also discussed the relationship between watching television violence and juvenile acts of violence. Testimony at this hearing indicated that although the amount of violence shown during the prime-time hours in 1990 and 1991 had decreased slightly, violence in children's weekend-daytime programming was at an all-time high (U.S. House Judiciary Committee 1992). Interestingly, cable television also came under investigation at this hearing.

Hearings continued during the spring and summer of 1993 as the Television Improvement Act of 1990 came close to its expiration date. These hearings, chaired by Representative Edward Markey (D-MA), attempted to put pressure on broadcasters to do more to control television violence. The hearings took place during May, one of the four months (sweeps) in which audience ratings are calculated for all television stations so the stations can establish new advertising rates. Typically, programming during the sweeps period is strategically selected, often using violence, to attract the largest audiences possible. The programs during the May 1993 sweeps period were particularly violent, leading Senator Markey in his opening statements to comment about the ongoing overabundance of mayhem and murder on television (U.S. House Committee on Energy and Commerce 1993). The tone of these hearings was decidedly in favor of enacting tougher government regulation of programming because the self-regulatory measures of the broadcast industry clearly were not working. Once again, expert witnesses testified that violence on television was plentiful and that there was a decided link between viewing televised violence and behaving aggressively. For example, L. Rowell Huesmann (professor of psychology at the University of Michigan) testified that television violence often served to desensitize children to the implications of real-life violence, and Terry

Rakolta (president of Americans for Responsible Television) suggested the need for a television ratings system. Testimony was also heard about technological innovations, such as the V-chip, that could be used to block programs (Cooper 1996).

Six weeks into the hearings, the television industry realized that it had to do something and announced that parental warnings would be displayed before programs deemed particularly violent. In addition, warnings would be shown during commercial breaks and included in all promotional materials. Cable operators also agreed to label their programming. Reaction was mixed. Some, such as Markey, thought it was an important step and that the ratings would be a real help for parents. Others, mostly journalists, felt that labeling was undertaken to prevent further government intervention and that the labeling did not go far enough (Cooper 1996).

Congressional hearings continued during 1993. Markey proposed a ratings system similar to that used by the motion picture industry, as well as a bill requiring that all new television sets be equipped with a V-chip that would enable parents to block specific types of programs. Although none of the bills passed, the Television Improvement Act of 1990 was extended at the end of 1993. Simon also called upon the industry to begin to monitor its programming. Consequently, the industry undertook two projects during 1994. The networks commissioned the Center for Communication Research at the University of California at Los Angeles (Cole, 1995, 1996) to monitor their programming, and the cable industry contracted with a consortium of researchers from four universities (NTVS 1997, 1998a, 1998b) to monitor cable and broadcast programming.

The passage of the Telecommunications Act of 1996, a major overhaul of the Communications Act of 1934, dealt primarily with issues relating to station ownership and access to new communications technology and was to provide for increased media competition. (In actuality it reduced competition by allowing corporations like Clear Channel to buy hundreds of radio stations and create a domineering influence on the industry.) The act also called for two provisions to deal with television violence. First, it mandated that a program ratings system be implemented by the industry, and second, it called for the installation of the V-chip in all 13-inch or larger television sets manufactured after July 1, 1999. The ratings system was designed by broadcasters under the leadership of Jack Valenti, president of the Motion Picture Association, and put into effect in January 1997 (see Chapters 2 and 3).

Why Media Violence Matters: Theoretical Perspectives

Numerous theories have been posited to explain and predict the effects of violent media content, whether the content is seen on television, in the movies, in video games, or elsewhere. The most important theories offer explanations and predictions as to how violent content may influence people, including its behavioral and physiological effects as well as cognitive/affective effects (Perse 2001). Theories of the behavioral and physiological effects of media violence are concerned with the relationship between aggressive behaviors and exposure to media violence—that is, they ask the question, does watching result in aggressive behavior? Some of these theories (social learning theory, cognitive cueing/priming) are based on cognitive models; others (arousal, desensitization) examine physiological reactions to media violence. Theories of the cognitive/affective effects of media violence (fear, cultivation), however, are concerned with the relationship between violence and people's thoughts, feelings, and ideas about the world (social reality).

Social Learning Theory

Observational or social learning theory, first proposed by Albert Bandura and Richard Walters in 1963, focuses upon the role of modeling in learning. The theory posits that people learn social and cognitive skills through imitation; children, for example, learn by imitating parents, siblings, and peers. When this perspective is expanded to include the media, the theory postulates that viewers, especially children, use or model the behavior of television or film characters and/or other video representations (Lefkowitz and Huesmann 1980). For example, interpersonal conflicts on television are often solved through physical aggression. Watching television may then provide successful models of aggressive behaviors that television characters have used to solve interpersonal conflicts. Viewers, particularly children, may then imitate and hence learn to use aggression to solve problems.

Observational or social learning theory has evolved from a purely behavioral theory into a cognitive (thought-related) theory, stressing that the media provide the rules and strategies (schemas, scripts) as well as the traditional why, what, and when of behavior change (Bandura 2002). Social learning theory says, in short, that people learn both by direct experience and by observing others. The media, particularly television, provide almost limitless opportunities for viewers to observe and consequently learn scripts or schemas (rules and strategies) for many different kinds of behaviors. Viewers can incorporate from television and other media not only specific responses but also ways to copy what they observe. Briefly, observational learning involves four subprocesses that operate on both cognitive and behavioral levels: (1) paying attention to the behavior, (2) retention of the behavior by rehearsing and integrating it into existing behavioral patterns, (3) replicating or reproducing the behavior, and (4) having the motivation to remember the behavior as well as its subsequent reinforcements (positive or negative) that contribute to maintaining the behavior.

Social learning theory suggests that modeling may take place at an abstract as well as behavioral level, through the use of schemas and scripts that may evolve into more innovative behavior. Bandura (2002) notes that abstract modeling typically denotes a higher level of learning. For example, viewers pick up the specific rules underlying the actions and/or judgments of others, including television characters, and these rules can then be used to extrapolate behaviors to other situations. Viewers may learn scripts that they can apply when in similar situations. Of course, because real life does not always proceed according to the scripts one has acquired through the media, abstract modeling is critical.

Priming, Schemas, and Scripts

Cue theory was an early refinement of social learning theory and the forerunner of later theories of priming effects and schemas. Leonard Berkowitz (1965) postulated that when angry people watched violent television they learned both the aggressive behaviors and the signals that could trigger aggressive behavior. Similarly, elements in the programs (e.g., guns, "bad" or evil characters) could serve as cues or signals that, when later encountered, might stimulate aggressive behavior. Violence, for example, is a particularly potent cue or prime. In an experimental setting, Berkowitz and Joseph Alioto (1973) found that participants who thought they had seen violent documentaries displayed more aggressive behaviors than participants who thought they had seen violent fictional stories. Similarly, identification may increase priming effects. Subjects in an experiment who were told to imagine that they were boxers behaved more aggressively after watching a prize fight (Turner and Berkowitz 1972). A number of experiments have shown that names can also be powerful cues; aggressors and/or victims with names similar to a confederate in an experiment typically evoked more aggressive reactions (Berkowitz and Geen 1966). Moreover, when subjects were asked to write down the things they thought after watching a violent scene in a movie, the more violent the scene, the more angry feelings/thoughts they expressed (Bushman and Geen 1990).

This theory was later expanded to incorporate a cognitive component (cognitive neo-associationism) in the form of schemas or scripts (Berkowitz 1993)—mental structures that organize knowledge about concepts, people, issues, or events. In this refinement, media content activates or primes schemas, moving the schema to the forefront of awareness. L. Rowell Huesmann (1988) notes that scripts learned in childhood are potentially the most influential. Children develop and learn scripts by observing behaviors (either mediated or actual) and encoding/interpreting them in specific scenarios. If these scripts are then rehearsed (either when the child thinks about them or behaves according to them), they are more likely to become fixed in the child's repertoire of possible behaviors. Moreover, as is discussed in Chapter 2, television's store of violent and antisocial messages provides a wealth of aggressive behaviors that viewers can observe and, hence, learn and form scripts that may influence their later reactions or behaviors.

Elizabeth Perse (2001) notes that social learning is more likely to occur if the observed behaviors are relevant and/or adaptive, thus increasing their importance as primes. Relevant behaviors are those that have some connection to people's lives. In addition, W. James Potter (1999) posits that content that is perceived as more realistic enhances social learning. A series of experiments examining the similarity of the subjects, both victims and aggressors, found increased aggression when subjects encountered a victim with similar characteristics (e.g., the same name) as someone they disliked (Berkowitz and Geen 1966). Similarly, children become more fearful when the characters who commit violence are seen as very similar to real people (Cantor 2002).

Disinhibition or Habituation

Disinhibition theory postulates that television viewing may lower inhibitions about behaving aggressively as well as supply signals that indicate whether a specific behavior is appropriate (Severin and Tankard 1992). This theory has had considerable empirical support. For example, Richard Walters and Edward Thomas (1963), using three different samples of subjects, found that those subjects who saw a knife-fight scene (compared to those who saw a more constructive film) gave stronger shocks to other participants who made mistakes in a learning task after they saw the film than before they saw the film. In another experiment, children who saw a violent and aggressive movie were less likely than children in the control condition to try to stop what sounded like a serious fight in an adjoining room (Thomas, Horton, Lippincott, and Drabman 1977). Disinhibition theory has also incorporated cognitive processing into its more recent formulations. A critical end product of desensitization is that the availability of high levels of media violence may contribute to increased desensitization to violence in society.

Cultivation Theory

The cultivation hypothesis (Gerbner et al. 2002) is one of a number of theories concerned with people's views about the world (the construction of social reality). In its simplest form, cultivation tries to ascertain if those who spend more time watching television are more likely to perceive the world in ways that reflect the most common and repetitive messages and lessons of the television world. The cultivation hypothesis is perhaps best known for its research on violence and fear, postulating that the lessons of television violence and especially the patterns of victimization, are fear, intimidation, and a sense of vulnerability. Studies support the hypothesis that those who watch more television will express greater interpersonal mistrust, perceive the world as a "mean" place, and endorse statements that reflect alienation and gloom (Signorielli 1990). Although much of the research relies on data from surveys, one test of cultivation theory in an experimental setting (Bryant, Carveth, and Brown 1981) found that undergraduates asked to focus their television viewing on action-adventure programs for a six-week period said that they thought the world was a more dangerous place and that they had a higher chance of being personally involved in violence than undergraduates who did not see as many action-adventure programs.

This theoretical formulation has been subjected to numerous criticisms. One of the criticisms is that the data analyses rely on correlational (relational) statistical techniques (Doob and Macdonald 1979; Hirsch 1980). Another criticism is that the size of the findings are typically modest, that control variables, such as education, may reduce the absolute size of the effect (see, for example, Potter 1999), and that survey respondents typically say things happen with greater frequency than they actually do (see Perse 1986). Yet it is plausible that cultivation effects are real because of the high degree of consistency in the findings from a very large number of studies, conducted both in the United States and abroad (Shanahan and Morgan 1999). In addition, although cultivation effects are typically small, in reality small effects may be extremely potent. A shift of a few degrees in the average temperature can lead to global warming, a single percentage point change in ratings can lead to the loss or gain of millions of dollars in advertising revenue, and, as Americans saw in the 2000 presidential election, an extremely small percentage of votes generated considerable havoc in determining the outcome of the election. More support for cultivation theory comes from the work of L. J. Shrum (2002), who found that those who watch more television tend to reply to questions more quickly and give answers that are consistent with those cultivation theory would predict. These findings are important because responses that are given quickly are more readily accessible to the respondents (i.e., they do not have to think very much about their answer). In short, Shrum's work is both supportive of cultivation theory and "also suggests that television does not necessarily *change* attitudes, but that it makes them *stronger*" (Gerbner et al. 2002, 58).

Catharsis

There is, however, one theory that has no real support in the literature but yet continues to surface as a way to explain the effects of television and/or media violence—the catharsis hypothesis. Catharsis has had a long and colorful history. It was first suggested by Aristotle, who postulated that drama provided members of the audience with opportunities to purge their feelings of fear, grief, pity, and so on. Catharsis is related to psychoanalytic and drive theories and makes the assumption that when a drive (such as aggression) is increased (for example, through frustration), the individual must find a way to reduce it. This hypothesis posits that watching television violence vicariously reduces viewers' aggressive drive (Severin and Tankard 1988). There are, however, only one or two studies that show support for the catharsis hypothesis (Feshbach and Singer 1971), and they are technically flawed (Liebert, Sobol, and Davidson 1972; Huesmann et al. 1991). Moreover, the original finding has never been replicated. Today, the catharsis hypothesis has little, if any, support in the academic community. Indeed, Bushman and Huesmann (2001) note that *"there is not a shred of convincing scientific data to support this theory"* (236, emphasis added). Berkowitz makes a particularly effective case in dismissing the credibility of this theory when he notes that "motorists will not become less aggressively inclined as a result of shooting a toy machine gun at another driver, and children won't become friendlier and nicer by playing with toy weapons" (1993, 342).

Conclusion

Television has been part of the American landscape for more than half a century. Practically every American home has television, and today it is almost impossible to find someone who did not grow up with television. From the beginning, violence has been a part of the fabric of television programming, as has the resultant concern about its effects.

Since 1952 there have been more than thirty separate sets of hearings about television violence—roughly one hearing every one and a half years. These hearings were often held in response to real-life violence, including the assassinations of Martin Luther King, Jr., Robert Kennedy, the gang rape of a jogger in New York's Central Park, and a death attributed to a young boy watching *Beavis and Butthead* (Cooper 1996). Aside from network executives, witnesses at these hearings included people from all walks of life and with numerous concerns—academics, industry officials, members of Congress, teachers, and children's activists. Unfortunately, the hearings rarely tried to reconcile divergent testimony. Typically, contradictory points of view were expressed, but those holding the hearings made no attempt to ascertain validity or come to a conclusion.

Television violence is a topic that has provided considerable visibility for members of Congress without necessitating specific action. Keisha Hoerrner notes the fact that Congress has spent almost fifty years examining this issue while passing only two pieces of legislation shows that "Congress has succeeded in symbolically framing television violence as a social concern that resonates with its constituents" (1999, 694). Moreover, although 183 members of Congress have shown interest in television violence during the past fifty years, only seven have persistently worked toward providing solutions, even if the end result was to enhance their reputations and visibility on a national level.

There are several theories that explain why television violence is such an important area to study. Theories such as social cognitive/learning theory and cue/priming theory, for example, illustrate how watching violent images may provide viewers with potential scenarios for their own behaviors. Similarly, disinhibition theories explain how a steady diet of violent messages may result in people becoming immune to violence and violent behaviors in their own lives. Finally, cultivation theory explains that one of the long-term consequences of living with violent images is a heightened sense of fear and risk and how steady diets of violence may lead viewers to be more willing to give up personal freedom, if that will provide more peace of mind.

Most important, in today's world multinational media giants play a major role in determining media content. It is important to remember that today's content is often determined on the basis of its profitability. Although violence is not necessarily the most popular programming (see Chapter 2), it has the unique position of "traveling well" (Gerbner 2003, 298) in that it transcends language (needs little translation) and, consequently, is very profitable.

Notes

1. Of course, the easy accessibility of guns, as well as family and emotional factors, cannot and should not be discounted when trying to understand the level of violence in society and particularly violent actions committed by teens. Television and other media are just other possible factors.

References

American Medical Association. 1997. RE: CS docket no. 97-55. Industry Proposal for Rating Video Programming. FCC submission, April 8.

American Psychological Association. 1993. *Violence and Youth: Psychology's Response. Vol. 1, Summary Report of the American Psychological Association Commission on Violence and Youth.* Washington, DC: American Psychological Association.

Baker, R. K., and S. J. Ball. 1969. *Mass Media and Violence: Staff Report to the National Commission on the Causes and Prevention of Violence.* Vol. 9. Washington, DC: U.S. Government Printing Office.

Bandura, A. 2002. "Social Cognitive Theory of Mass Communication." In J. Bryant and D. Zillmann, eds., *Media Effects: Advances in Theory and Research,* pp. 121–154. 2d ed. Hillsdale, NJ: Lawrence Erlbaum Associates.

Bandura, A., and R. H. Walters. 1963. *Social Learning and Personality Development.* New York: Holt, Rinehart, and Winston.

Berkowitz, L. 1965. "Some Aspects of Observed Aggression." *Journal of Personality and Social Psychology* 2: 359–336.

———. 1993. *Aggression: Its Causes, Consequences, and Control.* Philadelphia: Temple University Press.

Berkowitz, L., and J. T. Alioto. 1973. "The Meaning of an Observed Event as a Determinant of Its Aggressive Consequences." *Journal of Personality and Social Psychology* 28: 206–217.

Berkowitz, L., and R. G. Geen. 1966. "Film Violence and the Cue Properties of Available Targets." *Journal of Personality and Social Psychology* 3: 525–530.

Blumer, H. and P. M. Hauser. 1933. *Movies, Delinquency, and Crime.* New York: Macmillan.

Bryant, J., R. A. Carveth, and D. Brown. 1981. "Television Viewing and Anxiety: An Experimental Examination." *Journal of Communication* 31, no. 1: 106–119.

Bushman, B. J., and R. G. Geen. 1990. "Role of Cognitive-Emotional Mediators and Individual Differences in the Effects of Media Violence on Aggression." *Journal of Personality and Social Psychology* 58: 156–163.

Bushman, B. J., and L. R. Huesmann. 2001. "Effects of Televised Violence on Aggression." In D. G. Singer and J. L. Singer, eds., *Handbook of Children and the Media,* pp. 223–254. Thousand Oaks, CA: Sage.

Cantor, J. 2002. "Fright Reactions to Mass Media." In J. Bryant and D. Zillmann, eds., *Media Effects: Advances in Theory and Research,* pp. 287–306. Mahwah, NJ: Lawrence Erlbaum Associates.

Cater, D., and S. Strickland. 1975. *TV Violence and the Child: The Evolution and Fate of the Surgeon General's Report.* New York: Russell Sage.

Charters, W. W. 1933. *Motion Pictures and Youth: A Summary.* New York: Macmillan.

Cole, J. 1995. *The UCLA Television Violence Monitoring Report.* Los Angeles: UCLA Center for Communication Policy.

Cole, J. 1996. The UCLA Television Violence Monitoring Report. Los Angeles: UCLA Center for Communication Policy.

Cooper, C. A. 1996. *Violence on Television: Congressional Inquiry, Public Criticism, and Industry Response: A Policy Analysis.* Lanham, MD: University Press of America.

Dale, E. 1935. *The Content of Motion Pictures.* New York: Macmillan.

Doob, A. N., and G. E. Macdonald. 1977. "Television Viewing and Fear of Victimization: Is the Relationship Causal?" *Journal of Personality and Social Psychology* 37, no. 2: 170–179.

Feshbach, S., and R. Singer. 1971. *Television and Aggression.* San Francisco: Jossey-Bass.

Gerbner, G. 1969. "Dimensions of Violence in Television Drama." In R. K. Baker and S. J. Ball, eds., *Violence in the Media,* pp. 311–340. Staff Report to the National Commission on the Causes and Prevention of Violence. Washington, DC: U.S. Government Printing Office.

———. 1972. "Violence in Television Drama: Trends in Symbolic Functions." In G. A. Comstock and E. A. Rubinstein, eds., *Television and Social Behavior.* Vol. 1, *Media Content and Control,* pp. 28–187. Washington, DC: U.S. Government Printing Office.

———. 2003. "Television Violence." In M. Morgan, ed., *Against the Mainstream: The Selected Works of George Gerbner,* pp. 290–302. New York: Peter Lang.

Gerbner, G., L. Gross, M. Morgan, N. Signorielli, and J. Shanahan. 2002. "Growing Up with Television: The Cultivation Perspective." In J. Bryant and D. Zillmann, eds., *Media Effects: Advances in Theory and Research.* 2nd ed. Hillsdale, NJ: Lawrence Erlbaum Associates.

Gould, J. 1972. "TV Violence Held Unharmful to Youth." *New York Times,* January 11.

Hirsch, P. 1980. "The Scary World of the Nonviewer and Other Anomalies: A Reanalysis of Gerbner et al.'s Findings on Cultivation Analysis." *Communication Research* 7: 403–456.

Hoerrner, K. L. 1999. "Symbolic Politics: Congressional Interest in Television Violence." *Journalism and Mass Communication Quarterly* 76, no. 4: 684–698.

Huesmann, L. R. 1988. "An Information Processing Model for the Development of Aggression." *Aggressive Behavior* 14: 13–24.

Huesmann, L. R., L. D. Eron, L. Berkowitz, and S. Chaffee. 1992. "The Effects of Television Violence on Aggression: A Reply to a Skeptic." In P. Suedfeld and P. Tetlock, eds., *Psychology and Social Policy,* pp. 191–200. New York: Hemisphere.

Lazarsfeld, P. F. 1955. "Why Is So Little Known about the Effects of Television and What Can Be Done?" *Public Opinion Quarterly* 19: 243–251.

Lefkowitz, M. M., and L. R. Huesmann. 1980. "Concomitants of Television

Violence Viewing in Children." In E. L. Palmer and A. Dorr, eds., *Children and the Faces of Television: Teaching, Violence, Selling,* pp. 163–181. New York: Academic.

Liebert, R. M., M. P. Sobol, and E. S. Davidson. 1972. "Catharsis or Aggression among Institutionalized Boys: Fact or Artifact?" In G. A. Comstock, E. A. Rubinstein, and J. P. Murray, eds., *Television and Social Behavior.* Vol. 5, *Television's Effects: Further Explorations,* pp. 351–358. Washington, DC: U.S. Government Printing Office.

Liebert, R. M., and J. Sprafkin. 1988. *The Early Window: Effects of Television on Children and Youth,* 3rd ed. New York: Pergamon.

Maccoby, E. E. 1954. "Why Do Children Watch Television?" *Public Opinion Quarterly* 18: 239–244.

Murray, J. P. 1995. "Children and Television Violence." *Kansas Journal of Law and Public Policy* 4, no. 3: 7–14.

National Association of Radio and Television Broadcasters (NARTB). 1956. "The Television Code." Washington, DC: NARTB, July.

National Commission on the Causes and Prevention of Violence. 1970. *Final Report.* Washington, DC: U.S. Government Printing Office.

National Institute of Mental Health (NIMH). 1972. *Television and Behavior.* Vol. 1. Washington, DC: U.S. Government Printing Office.

National Institute of Mental Health. 1972. *Television and Growing Up: The Impact of Televised Violence.* Report to the Surgeon General. Washington, DC: Government Printing Office.

National Television Violence Study. 1997. Vol 1. Thousand Oaks, CA: Sage.

National Television Violence Study. 1998a. Vol 2. Thousand Oaks, CA: Sage.

National Television Violence Study. 1998b. Vol. 3. Thousand Oaks, CA: Sage.

Perse, E. 1986. "Soap Opera Viewing Patterns of College Students and Cultivation." *Journal of Broadcasting and Electronic Media* 30: 175–193.

Perse, E. 2001. *Media Effects and Society.* Mahwah, NJ: Lawrence Erlbaum Associates.

Peterson, R. C., and L. L. Thurstone. 1933. *Motion Pictures and the Social Attitudes of Children.* New York: Macmillan.

Potter, W. J. 1999. *On Media Violence.* Thousand Oaks, CA: Sage.

Rowland, W. 1983. *The Politics of TV Violence.* Beverly Hills, CA: Sage.

Rubinstein, E. A. 1980. "Television Violence: An Historical Perspective." In E. L. Palmer and A. Dorr, eds., *Children and the Faces of Television: Teaching, Violence, Selling,* pp. 113–127. New York: Academic.

Rubinstein, E. A., and J. D. Brown. 1985. "Television and Children: A Public Policy Dilemma." In E. A. Rubinstein and J. D. Brown, eds., *The Media, Social Science, and Social Policy for Children*, pp. 93–117. Norwood, NJ. Ablex Publishing.

Severin, W. J., and T. W. Tankard, Jr. 1992. *Communication Theories: Origins, Methods, and Uses in the Mass Media.* New York: Longman.

Shanahan, J., and M. Morgan. 1999. *Television and Its Viewers: Cultivation Theory and Research.* Cambridge: Cambridge University Press.

Shrum, L. J. 2002. "Media Consumption and Perceptions of Social Reality: Effects and Underlying Processes." In J. Bryant and D. Zillmann, eds., *Media Effects: Advances in Theory and Research*, pp. 69–96. 2nd ed. Mahwah, NJ: Erlbaum.

Signorielli, N. 1990. "Television's Mean and Dangerous World: A Continuation of the Cultural Indicators Perspective." In N. Signorielli and M. Morgan, eds.,. *Cultivation Analysis: New Directions in Media Effects Research,* pp. 85–106. Newbury Park, CA: Sage.

Tankard, J. W., and S. W. Showalter. 1977. "Press Coverage of the 1972 Report on Television and Social Behavior." *Journalism Quarterly* 54: 293–298.

Thomas, M. H., R. W. Horton, E. C. Lippincott, and R. S. Drabman 1977. "Desensitization to Portrayals of Real-Life Aggression as a Function of Exposure to Television Violence." *Journal of Personality and Social Psychology* 35: 450–458.

Turner, C. W., and L. Berkowitz. 1972. "Identification with Film Aggressor (Covert Role Taking) and Reactions to Film Violence." *Journal of Personality and Social Psychology* 21: 256–264.

U.S. House Committee on Energy and Commerce. 1993. *Violence on Television.* Hearings before the Subcommittee on Telecommunications and Finance, 103rd Congress, 2nd Session.

U.S. House Committee on Interstate and Foreign Commerce. 1952. *Investigation of Radio and Television Programs, Hearings and Report.* 82nd Congress, 2nd session, June 3–December 5, 1952. Washington, DC: U.S. Government Printing Office.

U.S. House Judiciary Committee. 1992. *Violence on Television.* Testimony before the Subcommittee on Crime and Criminal Justice, 102nd Congress, 2nd session.

U.S. Senate Committee on the Judiciary, Subcommittee to Investigate Juvenile Delinquency. 1954a. *Juvenile Delinquency (Part 1-B: Television Programs).* Hearings, 83rd Congress, Washington, DC: U.S. Government Printing Office.

U.S. Senate Committee on the Judiciary, Subcommittee to Investigate Juvenile Delinquency. 1955b. *Juvenile Delinquency (Television Programs).* Hearings, 84th Congress, 1st session, April 6–7, 1955. Washington, DC: U.S. Government Printing Office.

Walters, R. H. and E. L Thomas. 1963. "Enhancement of Punitiveness by Visual and Audiovisual Displays." *Canadian Journal of Psychology* 17(2): 244–255.

Wertham, F. 1954. *Seduction of the Innocent.* New York: Rinehart.

Wurtzel, A., and G. Lometti. 1983. *A Research Perspective on Television and Violence.* New York: American Broadcasting Company.

2

What We Know
about Media Violence

A paradigm or model for understanding a phenomenon of mass communication, such as television violence, involves three areas. First, a study must be made of the institutions of mass communication, including the people and companies that create, produce, and distribute media messages, as well as those government agencies involved in regulating the media. This area of study provides information about the policies, practices, rules, and regulations regarding media. For example, as Chapter 1 discussed, congressional hearings, the passage of the Telecommunications Act of 1996, lobbying by the National Association of Broadcasters, and the growth of a few large, multinational communication companies have all contributed, in some way, to today's climate of media violence. Second, the study of media content, especially what is on television, tells us about the messages of violence that are seen by most adults and children. And, third, we must understand the effects of these mediated images of violence on both adults and children. This chapter looks at parts two and three of this model and focuses on what we currently know about the content and effects of mediated violence, particularly in relation to television. The primary focus is on mediated violence in the United States, but where relevant, comparisons are made on an international level.

Media Content

Violence on Television

Although some studies of television violence were conducted during the 1950s and 1960s, most of the information about the amount of violence on television in the United States comes from the long-term analysis of prime-time network programs (1967 to 2002) conducted as part of the Cultural Indicators project (CI) and the short-term analysis (1994–1995 to 1996–1997) of a more extensive sample of network and cable channels by the National Television Violence Study (NTVS). In the United Kingdom (U.K.), the understanding of television violence comes from an analysis of samples of programs from 1994–1995 and 1995–1996 (Gunter, Harrison, and Wykes 2003). Knowledge about television violence in other countries (Japan or the Netherlands, for example) comes from a number of studies looking at violence in samples of programs taken at one point in time. Most of these studies, whether conducted in the United States or another country, focus specifically on physical violence because emotional violence is extremely difficult to define and isolate in a consistent and reliable way.

The CI research team of George Gerbner, Larry Gross, Michael Morgan and Nancy Signorielli has worked together for more than thirty years, conducting studies both individually and collectively. Their studies examine and measure the amount of physical violence on television by monitoring prime-time and weekend daytime network broadcast television programming. This information is then used to examine how people's viewing is related to their conceptions of social reality. The most recent study using this perspective examined samples of network, prime-time programs broadcast between the spring of 1993 and the fall of 2002 (Signorielli 2003). These CI studies show that the levels of violence on television are quite high and have been relatively stable for the past thirty years. Gerbner, Morgan, and Signorielli (1994) found, for samples of prime-time programs broadcast between 1973 and the fall of 1992 (N=1,306), that violence appeared in seven out of ten programs at the rate of 4.6 incidents per program and that half of the major characters in these programs were involved in violence. Signorielli (2003) found that between 1993 and 2002 (N=1,127), violence appeared in six out of ten programs at an average rate of 4.5 acts of violence per program. Thus, although the overall percentage of programs with violence in the most recent samples is lower, the overall prevalence of violence, in terms of the numbers of violent actions per program, has remained very stable.

Researchers at four universities, including W. James Potter, Ed Donnerstein, Barbara Wilson, and Dale Kunkel collaborated to conduct The National Television Violence Study (1998). This team examined physical violence in three yearly samples (1994–1995, 1995–1996, and 1996–1997) of composite weeks of programming across twenty-three channels operating between 6:00 AM and 11:00 PM each day (sampled by a modified equal probability method of programs aired between October and June). The sample (N=8,200) included broadcast (commercial networks, independent stations, and public television) and cable channels (basic and premium, HBO). All genres except game shows, religious programs, "infomercials" or home shopping channels, sports, instructional programs, and news were included. This sample presents a broader picture of violence on television than the CI perspective. Nevertheless, Signorielli's (2003) analysis should not be discounted because in today's competitive media environment and proliferation of channels, sources of original dramatic programming are declining and media outlets are increasingly dependent upon syndication packages (Gerbner, Gross, Morgan, Signorielli, and Shanahan 2002). In all of the programming sampled, the NTVS found no change in the prevalence of violence from the 1994–1995 to the 1996–1997 television seasons. Moreover, roughly 60 percent of the programs in each sample contained violence, findings very similar to those of the CI researchers.

There were two other major studies of television violence in the United States in the 1990s. An industry-funded study (Cole 1995, 1998) monitored at least four episodes of every prime-time and Saturday morning (7:00 AM to noon) network program in each of three seasons (1994–1995, 1995–1996, and 1996–1997) and two weeks of programs on independent stations, public television, and pay cable. Although this analysis did not provide overall measures of the level of violence, there was a drop from 1994–1995 to 1996–1997 in the number of television series that raised frequent concerns about the way violence was presented. The only programs that raised more concerns at the end of this three-year period were reality shows (e.g., *World's Most Dangerous Animals* and *World's Scariest Police Chases*).

The Center for Media and Public Affairs (Lichter and Amundson 1992) isolated physical violence on ten channels (network, independent, and cable) during one day. Violence appeared most frequently during the afternoon (2 to 5 PM), with 191 acts per hour; early morning (6 to 9 AM), with 158 acts per hour; and prime time, with 102 acts per hour. An update of programming in the 1998–1999 season (Lichter, Lichter, and Amundson 1999) showed isolated acts of violence in two randomly selected, composite weeks of prime-time network and cable fictional programs (N=284) and fifty movies on cable and broadcast television. They found twelve acts of violence per episode in broadcast programs and ten per episode in cable programs.

The U.K. study (Gunter, Harrison, and Wykes 2003) sampled programming for twenty days in both 1994–1995 and 1995–1996. In the first sample, four weeks of programs from eight channels were sampled between October 1994 and February 1995 (N=5,607); the second sample used composite weeks of programs from ten channels constructed over seven-week periods between July 1995 and June 1996 (N=7,237). In both samples, the percentage of programs with violence was considerably smaller than in the U.S. studies, although there was an increase in the percent of programs with violence in the second year. In the 1994–1995 sample, 37 percent of the programs were violent, whereas in the 1995–1996, sample 45 percent of the programs were violent. The increase was due to inclusion of programs on the satellite channels as well as the addition of two additional satellite channels (TNT/Cartoon network and Sky Sports) in the second year of the study. Both the NTVS and the U.K. study found that the premium movie channels had the most violence—more than eight out of ten of the programs in these samples contained violence.

There have been several studies of television violence in other countries. Japanese television programs, for example, are considerably more violent than programs in most other countries but quite similar to U.S. programming (Iwao, deSola Pool, and Hagiwara 1981). Japanese television violence, however, tends to be more graphic than violence seen in other countries. Interestingly, many recent cartoon programs now seen in the United States (Pokémon, Dragon Ball Z, Digimon, etc.) are Japanese animation (anime) that are specifically translated for the U.S. market (Rutenburg 2001). Violence in the programming seen in the Netherlands is similar in levels of violence to programs seen in the United States (Bouwman and Signorielli 1985). Canadian television, particularly that broadcast on the public stations, is considerably less violent than U.S. programming. Nevertheless, because most Canadians can easily see a considerable amount of U.S. television, audiences would see less violence only if they watched primarily Canadian-produced programs (Gosselin, deGuisse, and Paquette 1997). Finnish programming is also less violent than U.S. television, although again, imported programs tend to be more violent (Mustonen and Pulkkien 1993). Likewise, Korean television is less violent than U.S. programming (Kapoor, Kang, Kim, and Kim 1994).

Overall, the U.S. studies, particularly those conducted in the 1990s, show stability in the amount of violence on television—violence appears in roughly six out of ten programs in the United States. Consequently, whether viewers watch network broadcast channels or cable channels, it is relatively difficult to avoid violence. From an international perspective, countries that import considerable amounts of programming from the United States have levels of violence on television similar to those seen in the United States, whereas those who do not import many programs have lower levels of violence. Interestingly, except in Japan, domestic programs tend to be less violent than the imports. One of the reasons for the high level of violence in imported (typically U.S.) programs is that violence is a program staple that transcends language barriers—it is relatively easy to translate because the pictures are rather self-explanatory. Comedy, however, does not translate (travel) very easily because it is so dependent upon language.

The Context of Violence

The way violence is presented on television (i.e., the context in which it appears) is an important focus in this research. Many things are related to the context of violence. CI examined humor and program genre in relation to violence. During the 1970s, slightly more than a quarter of prime-time programs were comic in nature, and less than half included violence at a rate of 2.0 incidents per program. In addition, close to half of the network prime-time programs had action-adventure themes, with 94.5 percent containing some violence at a rate of 7.8 incidents per program (Gerbner, Gross, Morgan, and Signorielli 1980). In an analysis of programs aired through the fall of 1985, Signorielli (1990) found that only one in five prime-time programs had humorous violence.

The NTVS advanced the understanding of the way violence is presented on television, particularly its contextual elements. It examined the consequences of violence, whether humor was involved, the graphic nature of the violence, whether weapons were used, and the degree of realism in the violence. The analysis of data from 1994 to 1995 found that the context in which violence is presented poses risks for viewers (NTVS 1994–1995). In particular, three-quarters of the violent scenes were committed by characters who were not punished, negative consequences of violence were rarely presented, one-quarter of the violence incidents involved the use of a handgun, and less than one in twenty programs emphasized antiviolence themes. Yet television violence was not particularly graphic (bloody or gory). Although the analysis found that broadcast network programs had less violence than cable channels, the context of violence on both broadcast and cable was similar (Smith, Nathanson, and Wilson 2002). Similarly, S. Robert Lichter, Linda Lichter, and Daniel Amundson (1999) found that most television violence did not have either psychological or physical consequences and occurred in a moral vacuum because heroes were seen as committing violence that was justified (in self-defense, in a law enforcement context, etc.).

Stacy Smith, Amy Nathanson, and Barbara Wilson (2002) found that prime-time broadcast network programming and basic cable programming were less likely than premium cable programming to include violent interactions that depicted pain or harm. Consequently, prime-time network broadcast programs are relatively devoid of pain and suffering. Similarly, Signorielli (2003b) found that violence tends to lack context and that most programs do not show any long-term consequences of violence, such as remorse, regret, or sanctions. The lack of contextual elements is not limited to U.S. programming. Barrie Gunter, Jackie Harrison, and Maggie Wykes (2003) found that programming in the United Kingdom also does not show violence that is particularly harmful and that there was little evidence of blood, gore, and pain. Most of the motives for violence in U.K. television were related to evil and destruction. The major situations in which violence occurred were interpersonal disputes and crime, followed by scenes focusing on power and self-preservation.

Who Is Involved?
Any discussion of the amount of violence on television must examine the characters who are involved in violence—those who do the hurting and killing or are hurt and killed. CI has shown that television violence illustrates and provides lessons about power. Violence shows who's on top and who's on the bottom, who gets hurt and who does the hurting, and who wins and who loses. These studies consistently find a power structure related to character

demographics, with earlier studies showing women and minorities more likely to be hurt than to hurt others.

Research in the CI tradition consistently shows that during prime time, men are more likely than women to be hurt (victimized) or hurt others (commit violence) (Signorielli 1990). There have been some changes in these patterns, however, in the past thirty-five years. In the programs of the 1980s, men were slightly less likely to be involved in violence than in the programs of the 1970s. Fewer characters still were involved in violence between 1993 and 2002 (Signorielli 2003). Only one-third of the major and supporting characters were involved in violence during that period, and although more men than women were involved (38 percent of the men, compared to 27 percent of the women), whites and minorities were equal likely to be victimized or commit violence (about a quarter of both whites and minorities). During the 1990s, the ratios of hurting to being hurt changed from the patterns seen in the 1970s and 1980s for women but not for men. Today, for every ten male characters who hurt or kill, eleven are victimized, the same ratio found in the earlier analysis. For women, however, instead of sixteen women being victimized for each woman who hurts or kills, the odds are even—women are equally likely to hurt or kill as to be hurt or killed. Moreover, although whites are a little more likely to be victimized than hurt others, the odds for minority characters are even.

Although the NTVS did not generate a profile of all characters on television, it did examine the demographic characteristics of perpetrators (those who commit) and targets (victims) of violence. Most of the perpetrators (close to three-quarters) were men; only one in ten was a woman. Few perpetrators were categorized as heroes, and most were white. Similarly, most of the targets were men (71 percent)—only 10 percent were women—and most were white (Smith, et al. 1998). W. James Potter and colleagues (1995), in looking at a composite week of evening programming (6 PM to midnight) on four networks, also found that television typically presents an unrealistic picture of serious aggression in regard to the race of those who commit the acts as well as those who are victimized. In short, television overrepresents both white perpetrators and white victims of aggression. Although the study by Potter and colleagues, the NTVS, and the CI reports differ in how they isolate characters' involvement in violence, the patterns are similar—more men than women and more whites than minorities. Similarly, studies conducted in the United Kingdom found that women were much less likely to be involved in violence and that the onscreen time devoted to female violence was considerably less than that devoted to male violence (Gunter et al. 2003).

Overall, it appears that the consensus of findings from studies of media content indicated that contemporary television programs may not adequately support or reinforce the lesson that "crime does not pay." The lack of adequate contexts for violent behaviors may transmit the lesson that violence is "sanitary," that it is not necessarily immoral, and that those characters who commit violence are not sorry for their actions and may not be punished for their transgressions—in short, there are few, if any, consequences for committing violence. From a social learning perspective, these messages could lead viewers, particularly children, to learn and even accept aggressive behaviors. Thus, the environment of violent entertainment in which many people, including children, spend most of their free time may be potentially harmful. Moreover, television's lack of realistic contexts for violence may signal that aggression and violence are acceptable modes of behavior.

Violence in Video Games

During the past thirty years, video games have increased in popularity. The Kaiser Family Foundation reports that most homes with children now have a video game system (1999). Children start playing video games as early as age three and continue playing through high school, college, and beyond.[1] At all ages, boys play more than girls, and older children play more than younger children. There are particular concerns about the violence in video games and how it may influence players.

Video games have changed enormously from the 1970s, when *Pong* (an arcade, tennis-like, visual-motor activity) became a hit with young adults. Today, most children play real-time, first-person shooter (FPS) games in which the "players view the world through the eyes of the video game character that they control" (Espejo 2003, 6). Moreover, recent technology permits players to personalize game playing by scanning pictures of peers, teachers, or other people they know onto the images of the potential victims in the games (Funk 2002).

The potential effects (and theoretical perspectives) of video games on aggression are similar to those of television violence. Although a recent meta-analysis (Sherry 2001) found that the overall effect of video game playing on aggression is considerably smaller than the effects of television violence, there is cause for concern because children are the primary users of this medium and those who play video games become intentionally and actively involved in the action. Joseph Dominick (1984), for example, notes that playing video games is quite different from watching television because of the higher level of concentration and attention needed to play, which may give greater credibility to the images on the screen. Moreover, parents are even less likely to actively participate in video game playing and may be relatively unaware of the kinds of images seen in these games.

Although Derek Scott (1995) found that video game playing had no appreciable effect on aggression among university students, other studies have found that video game playing is associated with increased aggression and hostility (Bushman and Anderson 2002). A. Roland Irwin and Alan Gross (1995) found that second-grade children who played a martial arts game were more aggressive than children who played a motorcycle racing game. Game playing may also increase desensitization. Jeanne Funk (2002) found that game playing is related to exhibiting less empathy and more proviolence attitudes. For example, Mark Barnett and colleagues (1997), using a sample of fifteen- to nineteen-year-olds, found a negative relationship between preferences for violent video games and empathy. Nevertheless, the research also shows that children's preexisting traits, such as being empathic or aggressive, may have more influence on their behavior than short-term game playing. Funk (2002) also found that nine- to eleven-year-old children who played either violent or nonviolent games did not differ in aggressive and empathic responses, but those children who said their favorite game was aggressive were more aggressive than those who preferred nonviolent games and those who initially were more empathetic had higher empathy scores after playing. Funk concludes that although there may be some short-term negative effects of game playing, youngsters' preexisting characteristics (e.g., empathy) may be equally important in determining how they respond to game playing.

The long-term effects of video games cannot be studied in a laboratory setting because of the research model that looks at what happens over years of playing in many different types of situations—individually, with friends, with different types of games. Typically, studies rely on surveys that generate relational findings. Craig Anderson and Karen Dill (2000) found a relationship between measures of aggressiveness and preference for violent video games among a sample of college students and that those who spent more time playing had lower grade point averages than those who spent less time playing. Other studies have found relationships between stated preferences for violent games and psychopathology as measured by the Youth Self-Report, a measure of adolescent psychopathology (Funk 2002).

Aside from the possibility that game playing is related to increased aggressive behavior, video game playing raises several other specific concerns, including addiction and health risks such as temporary musculoskeletal injury (Greene and Asher 1982), seizures, and hypertension (Panee and Ballard 2002), particularly for black children (Murphy et al. 1995) and boys (Musante, Turner, Treiber, Davis, and Strong 1996). Other risks such as obesity may be due to the sedentary behavior of game playing. There is some evidence that some children may become addicted to game playing, playing every day for longer than they originally intend and neglecting homework (Phillips, Rolls, Rouse, and Griffiths 1995). Similarly, a small percentage of adults may become addicted and/or dependent on chatrooms and/or online games because these activities enhance their self-esteem and enable them to ignore real-life problems (Tevlin 2003). There is also solid evidence that those who are photosensitive, even those without a prior history of seizures, may suffer from video-game-related seizures due to screen flicker, brightness, and/or image patterns (Ricci and Vigevano 1999). Seizures typically disappear if those afflicted stop playing.

There is considerable concern that video game skills (motor and cognitive) generalize to other venues. Lieutenant Colonel David Grossman believes that violent games, particularly first-person shooter games, are effective teachers of antisocial behavior (Grossman and DeGaetano 1999). Grossman believes that the game-playing practices of the young man responsible for killing three students and injuring five others at Heath High School in Paducah, Kentucky, on December 1, 1997, taught him to be an effective marksman (Espejo 2003). Similar concerns were raised in the wake of the 1999 Columbine High School tragedy in Littleton, Colorado, during which twelve students and a teacher were killed and an additional twenty-three students injured by two seniors, allegedly players of *Doom* and *Duke Nukem,* two extremely violent first-person shooter games. Moreover, Elisa Song and Jane Anderson (2003), note that Grossman has said that the techniques needed to be a successful first-person shooter game player are those used by the U.S. military to train soldiers to kill.

Greg Costikyan (2003) believes, however, that video game violence is exaggerated and that most games are about puzzle solving and feature monsters. He notes that multiplayer first-person shooter games in which players go after other players, not monsters, are not much different from paintball and the old-fashioned game of tag. Others feel that video games may help people improve their health. Beyond Online Limited (2003), an Australian-based television series about technological and scientific advances, shows how video games may facilitate biofeedback regimens, distract people from their ongoing pain, and/or help people overcome stress or phobic disorders. In addition, video game playing may help people process information faster and become more aware of their surroundings. These skills may, in turn, help people become better drivers because they can more easily see cars or pedestrians entering or leaving the road (RDHealth 2003).

Reviews of this literature indicate that video games are most problematic for young children. Lillian Bensley and Juliet Van Eenwyk (2001) and Mark Griffiths (1999) show that studies of young children (four to eight years old) consistently found increases in aggression after video game playing but that results were mixed for adolescents and college students. In addition, Griffiths (1997) believes that the empirical evidence supports social learning theory rather than catharsis theory. Overall, however, Sherry's (2001) meta-analysis shows that violent video games have an effect on aggressive play, although these effects are less significant than those related to television violence. In particular, there is a sense that the results of all these studies should be examined from a developmental perspective because age is a critical factor in assessing the overall effects of video game playing.

How Media Violence Affects Us

There are numerous ways media violence affects us. Potter (2003) differentiates effects that are immediate or short-term from those that are long-term. Researchers, including John Murray (2003) and Potter (2003), further delineate three ways in which media violence may affect viewers: fostering aggression, becoming desensitized to violence, and becoming fearful. Each of these effects, in turn, may have both short- and long-term consequences.

Aggression and Aggressive Behavior

One of the biggest concerns about media violence is that exposure to violent images will result in aggression and aggressive behavior. There is a sizable body of research that supports this position. Although the discussion in Chapter 3 shows that there is some disagreement with this statement, the number of researchers in this camp is rather small, and some have ties to the broadcast industry. The strength of the evidence led the American Psychological Association (1985) to conclude that one factor in the development of aggressive and/or antisocial behavior in children is a steady diet of real and/or mediated violence. Similarly, the 1982 report by the National Institute of Mental Health concluded that children and teens who watch violence on television tend to exhibit more aggressive behavior. The research evidence on which these conclusions were based comes from experimental studies, longitudinal studies, and meta-analyses (a particular type of analysis that simultaneously compares the statistical results from a large number of existing studies on the same topic).

Some of the earliest research on mediated violence was experimental in nature and found that filmed or televised (mediated) images affected behavior. Glenn Ellis and Francis Sekyra (1972) and O. Ivar Lovaas (1961) found that children exposed to media violence behaved aggressively shortly after seeing violence. Another study comparing violent and prosocial (positive messages) programs (Stein and Friedrich 1972) found that children who saw positive or prosocial programs (e.g., *Mister Roger's Neighborhood*) increased their helping behaviors, whereas those who saw violent images behaved more aggressively. Overall, numerous studies have found a causal relation between seeing violent portrayals and later aggressive behavior. L. Rowell Huesmann and Laurie Miller conclude: "In these well-controlled laboratory studies there can be no doubt that it is the children's observation of the scenes of violence that is *causing* the changes in behavior" (1994, 163).

Another strong line of evidence of long-term effects comes from studies conducted over several years (longitudinal studies), specifically the research of Leonard Eron and L. Rowell Huesmann. One study of young boys begun in the 1970s in New York state that was able to control for intelligence quotient (IQ), initial levels of aggressiveness, and social class found that the amount of violence seen on television at age eight was related to aggressiveness at age eighteen, as well as involvement in antisocial behavior (fights and spouse abuse) and criminal acts at age thirty (Hues-mann and Miller 1994). Similar results were found in samples of youngsters in Chicago as well as children from other countries, including Finland, Poland, and Israel. These studies found that more aggressive children, compared to less aggressive children, watched more television, preferred programs that were more vio-lent, and perceived mediated violence as closer to real life. The most recent study in this tradition (Huesmann, Moise-Titus, Podol-ski, and Eron 2003) found that watching violence, identification with same-sex aggressive characters, and a perception that televi-sion violence is realistic were related to adult aggression, regard-less of how much aggression was exhibited as a child.

A particularly interesting and important longitudinal study (Joy, Kimball, and Zabrack, 1986) was conducted in the late 1970s in three communities in Canada as part of a larger study by Tan-nis MacBeth (formerly Williams). While vacationing in Canada, MacBeth visited an area in which a new and more powerful trans-mission tower was being built that would have a major impact on television reception in the area. One town located in the valley, Notel, would receive television for the first time. Unitel, a town about 50 miles away that had been receiving one television chan-nel, would increase its reception by a second channel with the new transmitter. The third community, Multitel, was located close to the U.S. border and received numerous television channels originating both in Canada and the United States. The researchers gathered data relating to aggression, gender roles, and academic achieve-ment both before and two years after the installation of the more powerful transmitter. The results showed that the children in Notel exhibited more aggressive behavior (both verbal and physical) after the introduction of television. Aggressive behavior increased for both boys and girls, for children of different ages, and for those who had different initial levels of aggressiveness. Interestingly, this comprehensive study also found that after the introduction of tel-evision, that children's gender role stereotyping increased and measures of academic success (e.g., reading levels) decreased (Williams 1986).

A recent cross-cultural study of twelve-year-old children (2,788 boys and 2,353 girls) from twenty-three different countries (funded by the United Nations Education, Scientific, and Cultural Organization, or UNESCO) found an interactive relationship between media violence and real violence such that "media can contribute to an aggressive culture" (Groebel 2001, 265). In short, these studies found that aggressive people, particularly those who live in more aggressive environments, use the media to confirm their attitudes and beliefs, which are then reinforced by media content. For example, the study found that one of the messages of aggressive content is that aggression is a good way to solve conflicts and that it is fun and provides status. Moreover, the study found that successful media figures, such as the Terminator (Arnold Schwarzenegger) and Rambo (Sylvester Stallone), had become cross-cultural heroes.

Another line of naturalistic research is the work of Brian Centerwall, MD (1989a; 1989b). Using an epidemiological approach, Centerwall examines relationships between the introduction of television in a society (e.g., the United States, Canada, and South Africa) and changes in homicide rates among the white population in these countries. In comparison with South Africa, where television was banned until 1975, Centerwall found that the white homicide rates in both the United States and Canada increased 90 percent between 1945 and 1975, whereas homicide rates for the white population in South Africa remained stable. These increases held despite the implementation of statistical controls for economic growth, urbanization, alcoholism, gun ownership, and so on. Moreover, in South Africa homicide rates in South Africa's white population increased by 56 percent between 1975, when television was introduced in the country, and 1983. Although most social scientists find Centerwall's research compelling, Elizabeth Perse (2001) notes that South Africa may not have been a good choice for comparison because it was a highly controlled and repressed society and had a higher homicide rate before the introduction of television. Moreover, Perse notes that Centerwall's method, a simple bivariate graphical analysis, does not dispel the possibility that the relationships may be due to a third, unmeasured, variable. Nevertheless, many find that these data are very compelling in that they show convincing, statistically significant increases in homicide rates of the white population over time.

Another solid base of evidence about the detrimental effects of media violence comes from a number of meta-analyses, a statistical technique that analyzes findings from a large number of studies about a particular topic. The first meta-analysis (Andison 1977) examined sixty-seven separate studies (experiments, surveys, longitudinal) conducted between 1956 and 1996 that examined over 30,000 participants. This analysis found strong support for a relationship between watching media violence and subsequent aggression. An analysis of samples of children, teens, and adults in 230 separate studies found a positive relationship between antisocial behavior (behaving aggressively, rule breaking, etc.) and exposure to violent media in most of the studies (Hearold 1986). Similarly, Haejung Paik and George Comstock's (1994) meta-analysis of 217 studies found statistically significant and positive correlations between viewing and subsequent aggression in samples of adults, children, and teens. Meta-analyses thus show a solid and consistent base of evidence supporting the relationship between watching media violence and behaving aggressively.

Desensitization

A second major concern is that media violence may be related to increased desensitization; that is, viewers may become less sensitive to the violence they see and thus become willing to tolerate a more violent society (Murray 2003). Laboratory studies have shown that adults and children become callous and even punitive after watching violent images. Children in the third grade, for example, who either did not see mediated violence or were shown a short clip from a violent western, were then asked to monitor two younger children by listening to the noise of them playing through an intercom. As they listened to the children, it became apparent that their play had become physically aggressive (Drabman and Thomas 1974). The children who saw the violent episode took considerably longer to get adult help than those who did not see violence. Similarly, Daniel Linz, Edward Donnerstein, and Steven Penrod (1984) found that a group of college men who viewed violent "slasher" films for five consecutive days rated the films as less violent and degrading to women at the end of the week. Moreover, after watching these films and then watching a documentary about a trial for sexual assault, these young men were less sympathetic toward the rape victim than the group of young men who had not seen the slasher films. Similarly, Stacy Smith and Edward Donnerstein (1998) note that the more viewers see graphic media violence, the more they rate material they originally perceived as offensive or degrading as less offensive or degrading.

Desensitization is particularly a concern as the amount of viewing increases. Several studies have shown that those who watch more violent programming may become more desensitized. Victor Cline, Roger Croft, and Steven Courrier (1973) found that those who saw more graphic violent portrayals were more likely to become physiologically desensitized—in short, the images stopped having an impact. In some situations, however, desensitization may have positive outcomes. Repeated exposure to an initially frightening or threatening image or character (e.g., the Incredible Hulk, the Wizard of Oz) can reduce children's fears (Cantor and Wilson 1984). Humor also contributes to desensitization (Potter 1999). Emotional disturbed children (e.g., those with attention deficit hyperactivity disorder) are especially vulnerable to media violence and desensitization. Tom Grimes, Eric Vernberg, and Teresa Cathers (1997) found that after watching television violence, children with emotional problems (compared to a matched group of children without these disorders) showed less concern for the victims of violence and believed that the media violence they saw characters commit was justified.

Fear

Media violence may be related to fear, in both the short and long terms. Joanne Cantor (2002) has studied fright as both a physiological and emotional reaction and found that children may become fearful after seeing violent media images. These reactions typically do not last very long, but it is possible for some to last for several days, months, or even longer. For example, Kristen Harrison and Cantor (1999) found that nine out of ten college students said that they had an intense fear reaction to a media depiction that lasted for a long time. Some of the things that evoke fear responses include injuries and dangers as well as deformities and/or distortions, such as monsters or ghosts. Several factors are likely to induce fear or fright reactions. Viewers who identify and/or empathize with the target of violence are likely to feel more fearful. Similarly, viewers who think the violence could happen to them often become more fearful. Although these reactions may be immediate and short-lived, there may be some long-term consequences. For example, children may become scared while watching a movie or program and perhaps hide their eyes or scream and have nightmares. Fear, however, differs by age. Young children typically are more fearful of images that are fantastic, threatening, and just look scary; older, children, however, are more fearful of more realistic dangers, things that could possibly happen to them.

There is also evidence of a generalized fear effect—the result of long-term exposure to violent media. Cultivation theory posits a positive relationship between watching more television and being fearful and exhibiting the "mean world syndrome." Studies testing this theory show that those who watch more television believe that there are more people employed in law enforcement, exaggerate the numbers of people involved in violence in a given week, overestimate their own chances of being a victim of violence, are more likely to believe they need more protection, and believe that, in general, the world is a mean and scary place in that most people "cannot be trusted" and are "just looking out for themselves" (Gerbner et al. 2002, 52). Although there is some criticism of this approach (see Chapter 3), it is a position that takes into consideration the fact that the media are an ongoing facet of day-to-day life and that the influence of the media (cultivation) is "a continual, dynamic, ongoing process of interaction among messages, audiences, and contexts" (Gerbner et al. 2002, 49).

Cultivation, however, may be culturally determined. There is less evidence of fear-related cultivation effects in the United Kingdom. Mallory Wober (1978) reports no relationship between television viewing and notions of fear and violence. There are, however, several cultural differences that may explain the lack of relationship. First, as noted above, U.K. television is considerably less violent and U.S. imports make up only a small portion of available programming. Second, programming in the United Kingdom must follow the government's family viewing policy requirements. This policy ensures that programs with potentially objectionable content are scheduled later in the evening and that programs unsuitable for children cannot be shown before 9 PM. Moreover, in the United Kingdom televised films are given age-based ratings (Gunter, Harrison, and Wykes 2003). Similarly, in the Netherlands, Harry Bouwman (1984) found only weak associations between viewing and perceptions of violence, mistrust, and victimization. Even though the Netherlands imports a considerable amount of U.S. programming and Dutch and U.S. programming provides similar messages about violence, many viewers choose to watch programs that are more "informational" in nature.

Nevertheless, some cultures have shown cultivation effects. For example, students in Australia who watched more U.S. crime/adventure programs had higher scores on the "mean world" and "violence in society" indices (Pingree and Hawkins 1981). Other analyses have found evidence of the cultivation of conceptions of sex roles and political orientations as well as violence. For example, in South Korea, watching U.S. television was related, for women, to more liberal perspectives about gender roles and family values. Among the male students, however, seeing more U.S. programming was related to exhibiting greater protectiveness of Korean culture and more hostility toward the United States (Kang and Morgan 1988). Overall, the findings from numerous studies conducted in the cultivation tradition show that if televised images are less homogeneous and repetitive than those seen in the United States, the results of cultivation analyses are less consistent and predictable (Gerbner et al. 2002).

Who Will Be Influenced?

The research discussed in this section can be interpreted in three different ways: (1) that media violence is inconsequential and people, including children, are not affected by these images, particularly what they see on television (e.g., Fowles 1999); (2) that media violence will affect some people some of the time (Potter 2003); and (3) media violence will always have a very negative impact (as believed, for example, by grassroots groups such as the National Coalition on Television Violence).

The evidence from numerous research studies indicates that the first and third interpretations are too extreme. The position that media violence is inconsequential has only a few supporters. For example, during the 1970s, when NBC was actively involved in a research program, Ronald Milavsky and others (1982) conducted a three-year longitudinal study (1970–1973) of 2,400 elementary school children and 800 teenage boys and reported no evidence of a relationship between television violence and aggressive behavior. A re-analysis of this data set, however, found a relationship between television violence and aggression (Turner, Hesse, and Peterson-Lewis 1986). Huesmann and Miller (1994) also interpret the NBC data as consistent with other research findings that support a relationship.

Similarly, the position that television violence always has a negative impact on people, particularly impressionable children, is also too extreme and again has very few supporters. The one group that has supported this outcome, the National Coalition on Television Violence (http://www.nctvv.org) was founded in 1980 and has been active in both rating television programs for violence and assessing which companies advertise on the most violent programs. Although the lion's share of the research shows a relationship between viewing and behaving aggressively, media violence is only one of many potential causes of aggression and/or violence in people. For example, child abuse or living in an excessively violent neighborhood may also play a critical role in subsequent aggressive behavior. Consequently, it is unreasonable to say that television violence will always have negative effects on viewers.

The most reasonable argument to make in understanding the effects of violent media content is to say that not everyone is affected in the same way; indeed, the same person may respond to violence differently on different occasions. Violent media content may have large effects on a small number of adults and/or children or small effects on large numbers of viewers. The large, consistent body of literature points to a positive relationship between television violence and aggressive behavior. Moreover, even though findings may be modest in size, the relationship must be taken seriously because of the large numbers of children who watch television each day, largely unsupervised. Even though their aggressive behavior may not put society at risk, it still may have negative social and cognitive consequences, such as the alienation of their peers and teachers (Singer and Singer 1988).

There is, however, another potentially important consequence. Although many people are reluctant to admit that they or their children could be affected by media violence, they believe that others are affected. This perspective, called "third-person effects" (Davison 1983), is particularly illusionary because it allows people to believe that they (and their children) are immune from the effects of media, but their neighbors (and their children) are not. People tend to overestimate the media's effects on others while underestimating its effects on themselves. An example might be the person who claims not to pay attention to advertising and states that advertising does not influence his or her purchasing decisions, yet won't buy anything but brand-name products and typically wears brand-name clothing such as T-shirts from the Gap or Abercrombie and Fitch.

Potter (2003) believes that third-person effects constitutes one of the "myths of television violence" mentioned in the title of his book. This myth is troublesome because people do not understand how they may be affected by media violence. Although most people do not copy violent behavior they see in the media (and if they did with any regularity, the world would be extremely chaotic), that violence has numerous long-term effects, including physiological and/or emotional habituation and the cultivation of fear and the belief that the world is mean. Another of Potter's myths is that "children are especially vulnerable to the risks of negative exposure to media violence" (2003, 67). Classifying this statement as a myth does not mean that children are not vulnerable, for indeed they may be particularly influenced by media violence. Rather, this myth underscores the third-person effects because it diminishes the fact that people of all age groups may be negatively influenced by media violence.

Finally, as cultivation theory postulates, the ultimate long-term effects of watching television violence may post threats for civil liberties and freedom. Cultivation studies have found that those who watch more television, compared to those who watch less, are more likely to overestimate their chances of being involved in violence, believe that fear of crime is an important personal problem, and assume that crime is rising. Those who spend more time watching television tend to believe that they are living in a mean and dangerous world and express feelings of alienation and gloom (Gerbner et al. 2002). Because violent images are almost impossible to avoid, those who watch more television may express sentiments of dependency and be willing to accept deceptively simple, strong, and hard-line political and religious postures, if these beliefs seem to promise to relieve existing insecurities and anxieties. From the perspective of cultivation theory, the overall long-term effects of television violence may be the ready acceptance of repressive political and social environments that could translate into a loss of personal liberties.

Conclusion

This large and solid body of research about media violence shows generally stable levels of violence on television and interesting relationships between media use and violence, particularly aggression. As in any field of research, throughout the years there have been numerous controversies about different findings and ways of conducting research. Chapter 3 addresses some of the major controversies relating to media violence and offers some possible solutions to the problem of media violence.

Notes

1. Although recent surveys (Kaiser Family Foundation 1999; Annenberg Policy Research Center 2000) focused only on children ages eighteen and

under, my personal experience (my college-age children, their friends, and students in my classes at the University of Delaware) indicates that video game playing does not end with graduation from high school and that earlier gender differences still prevail.

References

American Psychological Association. 1985. *Violence on Television.* Washington, DC: APA Board of Social and Ethical Responsibility for Psychology.

Anderson, C. A., and K. E. Dill. 2000. "Video Games and Aggressive Thoughts, Feelings, and Behavior in the Laboratory and in Life." *Journal of Personality and Social Psychology* 78: 772–790.

Andison, F. S. 1977. "TV Violence and Viewer Aggression: A Cumulation of Study Results, 1956–1976." *Public Opinion Quarterly* 41: 314–331.

Barnett, M. A., G. D. Vitaglione, K. K. G. Harper, S. W. Quackenbush, L. A. Steadman, and B. S. Valdez. 1997. "Late Adolescents' Experiences with and Attitudes towards Videogames." *Journal of Applied Social Psychology* 27: 1316–1334.

Bensley, L., and J. Van Eenwyk. 2001. "Video Games and Real-Life Aggression: Review of the Literature." *Journal of Adolescent Health* 29, no. 4: 244–257.

Beyond Online Limited. 2003. "Video Games Can Be Used for Therapeutic Purposes." In R. Espejo. ed., *Video Games,* pp. 65–68. San Diego: Greenhaven.

Bouwman, H., and N. Signorielli. 1985. "A Comparison of American and Dutch Programming." *Gazette* 35: 93–108.

Bushman, B. J, and C. A. Anderson. 2002. "Violent Video Games and Hostile Expectations: A Test of the General Aggression Model." *Personality and Social Psychology Bulletin* 28: 1679–1686.

Cantor, J. 2002. "Fright Reactions to Mass Media." In J. Bryant and D. Zillmann, eds., *Media Effects: Advances in Theory and Research,* pp. 287–306. Mahwah, NJ: Lawrence Erlbaum Associates.

Cantor, J., and B. J. Wilson. 1984. "Modifying Fear Responses to Mass Media in Preschool and Elementary School Children." *Journal of Broadcasting* 28: 431–443.

Center for Communication and Social Policy, University of California, Santa Barbara. *National Television Violence Study.* 1998. Vol. 3. Thousand Oaks, CA: Sage.

Centerwall, B. S. 1989a. "Exposure to Television as a Cause of Violence." In G. Comstock, ed., *Public Communication and Behavior,* pp. 1–58. Vol. 2, Orlando, FL: Academic.

————. 1989b. "Exposure to Television as a Risk Factor for Violence." *American Journal of Epidemiology* 129: 643–652.

Cline, V. B., R. G. Croft, and S. Courrier. 1973. "Desensitization of Children to Television Violence." *Journal of Personality and Social Psychology* 27: 260–265.

Cole, J. 1995. *The UCLA Television Violence Monitoring Report.* Los Angeles: UCLA Center for Communication Policy.

————. 1998. *The UCLA Television Violence Monitoring Report, Year 3.* Los Angeles: UCLA Center for Communication Policy.

Costikyan, G. 2003. "The Problem of Video Game Violence Is Exaggerated." In R. Espejo, ed., *Video Games,* pp. 27–34. San Diego: Greenhaven.

Davison, W. P. 1983. "The Third-Person Effect in Communication." *Public Opinion Quarterly* 47: 1–15.

Dominick, J. R. 1984. "Videogames, Television Violence, and Aggression in Teenagers." *Journal of Communication* 34: 136–147.

Drabman, R. S., and M. H. Thomas. 1974. "Does Media Violence Increase Children's Toleration of Real-Life Aggression?" *Developmental Psychology* 10: 418–421.

Ellis, G. T., and F. Sekyra III. 1972. "The Effect of Aggressive Cartoons on the Behavior of First Grade Children." *Journal of Psychology* 81: 7–43.

Espejo, R., ed. 2003. *Video Games.* San Diego: Greenhaven.

Fowles, J. 1999. *The Case for Television Violence.* Thousand Oaks, CA: Sage.

Funk, J. B. 2002. "Electronic Games." In V. C. Strausburger and B. J. Wilson, *Children, Adolescents, and the Media,* pp. 117–144. Thousand Oaks, CA: Sage.

Gerbner, G., L. Gross, M. Morgan, and N. Signorielli. 1980. *Violence Profile No. 11: Trends in Network Television Drama and Viewer Conceptions of Social Reality, 1967–1979.* Philadelphia: Annenberg School for Communication.

Gerbner, G., L. Gross, M. Morgan, N. Signorielli, and J. Shanahan. 2002. "Growing Up with Television: The Cultivation Perspective." In J. Bryant and D. Zillmann, eds., *Media Effects: Advances in Theory and Research.* 2nd ed. Hillsdale, NJ: Lawrence Erlbaum Associates.

Gerbner, G., M. Morgan, and N. Signorielli. 1994. "Television Violence Profile No. 14: The Turning Point." Philadelphia: Annenberg School for Communication.

Gosselin, A., J. deGuise, and G. Paquette. 1997. "Violence on Canadian Television and Some of Its Cognitive Effects." *Canadian Journal of Communications* 77, no. 2, http://www.wlu.ca/~wwwpress/jrls/cjc/BackIssues/22.2/gosselin.html.

Greene, J. A., and I. Asher. 1982. "Electronic Games." *Journal of the American Medical Association* 248: 1308.

Griffiths, M. 1997. "Video Games and Aggression." *Psychologist* 10, no. 9: 397–401.

———. 1999. "Violent Video Games and Aggression: A Review of the Literature." *Aggression and Violent Behavior* 4, no. 2: 203–212.

Grimes, T., E. Vernberg, and T. Cathers. 1997. "Emotionally Disturbed Children's Reactions to Violent Media Segments." *Journal of Health Communication* 2, no. 3: 157–168.

Groebel, J. 2001. Media Violence in Cross-Cultural Perspective." In D. G. Singer and J. L. Singer, eds., *Handbook of Children and the Media*, pp. 25–268. Thousand Oaks, CA: Sage.

Grossman, D., and G. DeGaetano. 1999. *Stop Teaching Our Kids to Kill: A Call to Action against TV, Movie and Video Game Violence*. New York: Crown.

Gunter, G., J. Harrison, and M. Wykes. 2003. *Violence on Television: Distribution, Form, Context, and Themes*. Mahwah, NJ: Lawrence Erlbaum Associates.

Harrison, K. and J. Cantor. 1999. "Tales from the Screen: Enduring Fright Reactions to Scary Media." *Media Psychology* 1, no. 2: 97–116.

Hearold, S. 1986. "A Synthesis of 1043 Effects of Television on Social Behavior." In G. Comstock, ed., *Public Communications and Behavior*, pp. 65–133. *Vol. 1*. New York: Academic.

Huesmann, L. R., and L. S. Miller. 1994. "Long-Term Effects of Repeated Exposure to Media Violence in Childhood." In L. R. Huesmann, ed., *Aggressive Behavior: Current Perspectives*, pp. 153–186. New York: Plenum.

Huesmann, L. R., J. Moise-Titus, C. Podolski, and L. D. Eron. 2003. "Longitudinal Relations between Children's Exposure to TV Violence and Their Aggressive and Violent Behavior in Young Adulthood, 1977–1992." *Developmental Psychology* 39, no. 2: 201–221.

Irwin, A. R., and A. M. Gross. 1995. "Cognitive Tempo, Violent Video Games, and Aggressive Behavior in Young Boys." *Journal of Family Violence* 10: 337–350.

Iwao, S., I. deSola Pool, and S. Hagiwara. 1981. "Japanese and U.S. Media: Some Cross-Cultural Insights into TV Violence." *Journal of Communication* 31, no. 2: 28–36.

Joy, L. A., M. M. Kimball, and M. L. Zabrack. 1986. "Television and Children's Aggressive Behavior." In T. M. Williams. ed., *The Impact of Television: A Natural Experiment in Three Communities*, pp. 303–360. Orlando, FL: Academic.

Kaiser Family Foundation. 1999. *Kids and Media @ the New Millennium: A Comprehensive National Analysis of Children's Media Use*. Menlo Park, CA: Kaiser Family Foundation.

Kang, J. G., and M. Morgan. 1988. "Culture Clash: U.S. Television Programs in Korea." *Journalism Quarterly* 65, no. 2: 431–438.

Kapoor, S., J. G. Kang, W. Y. Kim, and S. K. Kim. 1994. "Televised Violence and Viewers' Perceptions of Social Reality: The Korean Case." *Communication Research* 11: 189–200.

Lichter, S. R., and D. Amundson. 1992. *A Day of Television Violence.* Washington, DC: Center for Media and Public Affairs.

Lichter, S. R., L. S. Lichter, and D. R. Amundson. 1999. *Merchandizing Mayhem: Violence in Popular Entertainment, 1998–99.* Washington, DC: Center for Media and Public Affairs.

Linz, D., E. Donnerstein, and S. Penrod. 1984. "The Effects of Multiple Exposures to Filmed Violence against Women." *Journal of Communication* 34, no. 3: 130–147.

Lovaas, O. I. 1961. "Effects of Exposure to Symbolic Aggression on Aggressive Behavior." *Child Development* 32: 37–44.

Milavsky, J. R., R. Kessler, H. Stipp, and W. S. Rubens. 1982. "Television and Aggression: Results of a Panel Study." In D. Pearl, L. Bouthilet, and J. Lazar, eds., *Television and Behavior: Ten Years of Scientific Progress and Implications for the 80s,* pp. 138–157. Vol. 2. Washington, DC: U.S. Government Printing Office.

Murphy, J., C. M. Stoney, B. S. Alpert, and S. S. Walker. 1995. "Gender and Ethnicity in Children's Cardiovascular Reactivity: Seven Years of Study." *Health Psychology* 14: 48–55.

Murray, J. P. 2003. "The Violent Face of Television: Research and Discussion." In E. L. Palmer and B. M. Young, eds., *The Faces of Televisual Media: Teaching, Violence, Selling to Children.* Mahwah, NJ: Lawrence Erlbaum Associates.

Musante, L., R. Turner, F. A. Trieber, H. Davis, and W. B. Strong. 1996. "Moderators of Ethnic Differences in Vasoconstrictive Reactivity in Youth." *Ethnicity and Disease* 6: 224–234.

Mustonen, A., and L. Pulkkinen. 1993. "Aggression in Television Programs in Finland." *Aggressive Behavior* 19: 175–183.

National Coalition of Television Violence (NCTV). No date. "Ten Common Myths about the V-Chip and the Facts." http://www.nctvv.org.

National Institute for Mental Health. 1982. *Television and Behavior: Ten years of Scientific Progress and Implications for the Eighties.* Vol. 1, *Summary Report.* Washington, DC: U. S. Government Printing Office.

National Television Violence Study, Executive Summary. 1994–1995. Studio City, CA: Media Scope.

Paik, H., and G. Comstock. 1994. "The Effects of Television Violence on Antisocial Behavior: A Meta-Analysis." *Communication Research* 21: 516–546.

Panee, C. D., and M. E. Ballard. 2002. "High Versus Low Aggressive Priming during Video-Game Training: Effects on Violent Action during Game Play, Hostility, Heart Rate, and Blood Pressure." *Journal of Applied Social Psychology* 32, no. 12: 2458–2474.

Perse, E. 2001. *Media Effects and Society.* Mahwah, NJ: Lawrence Erlbaum Associates.

Phillips, C. A., S. Rolls, A. Rouse, and M. D. Griffiths. 1995. "Home Video Game Playing in Schoolchildren: A Study of Incidence and Patterns of Play." *Journal of Adolescence* 18: 687–691.

Pingree, S., and R. P. Hawkins. 1981. "U.S. Programs on Australian Television: The Cultivation Effect." *Journal of Communication* 31, no. 1: 97–105.

Potter, W. J. 1999. *On Media Violence.* Thousand Oaks, CA: Sage.

———. 2003. *The Eleven Myths of Media Violence.* Thousand Oaks, CA: Sage.

Potter, W. J., M. Vaughan, R. Warren, K. Howley, A. Land, and J. Hagemeyer. 1995. "How Real is the Portrayal of Aggression in Television Entertainment Programming?" *Journal of Broadcasting & Electronic Media* 39, 496–516.

RDHealth. 2003 "Video Games and Your Vision." *Reader's Digest* (September): 190.

Ricci, S., and A. Vigevano. 1999. "The Effect of Video-Game Software in Video-Game Epilepsy." *Epilepsia* 40: 31–37.

Rutenberg, J. 2001. "Violence Finds a Niche in Children's Cartoons." *New York Times,* Jan. 28.

Scott, D. 1995. "The Effect of Video Games on Feelings of Aggression." *Journal of Psychology* 129: 121–132.

Sherry, J. L. 2001. "The Effects of Violent Video Games on Aggression: A Meta-Analysis." *Human Communication Research* 27: 409–431.

Signorielli, N. 1990. "Television's Mean and Dangerous World: A Continuation of the Cultural Indicators Perspective. In N. Signorielli and M. Morgan, eds., *Cultivation Analysis: New Directions in Media Effects Research,* pp. 85–106. Newbury Park, CA: Sage.

———. 2003. "Prime-Time Violence, 1993–2001: Has the Picture Really Changed?" *Journal of Broadcasting and Electronic Media* 47, no. 1: 36–57.

Singer, J. L, and D. G. Singer. 1988. "Some Hazards of Growing Up in a Television Environment: Children's Aggression and Restlessness." In S. Oskamp, ed., *Television as a Social Issue,* pp. 171–188. Newbury Park, CA: Sage.

Smith, S. L., and E. Donnerstein. 1998. "Harmful Effects of Exposure to Media Violence: Learning of Aggression, Emotional Desensitization, and Fear." In R. G. Geen and E. Donnerstein, eds., *Human Aggression: Theories, Research, and Implications for Social Policy.* San Diego: Academic.

Smith, S. L., A. I. Nathanson, and B. J. Wilson. 2002. "Prime-Time Television: Assessing Violence during the Most Popular Viewing Hours." *Journal of Communication* 52, no. 1: 84–111.

Smith, S. L., B. J. Wilson, D. Kunkel, D. Linz, J. Potter, C. Colvin, and E. Donnerstein. 1998. "Violence in Television Programming Overall: University of California, Santa Barbara Study." In Center for Communication and Social Policy, University of California, Santa Barbara, ed. *National Television Violence Study, Vol. 3*. Thousand Oaks, CA: Sage.

Song, E., and J. E. Anderson. 2003. "Violence in Video Games May Harm Children." In R. Espejo, ed., *Video Games*, 9–17. San Diego, CA: Greenhaven.

Stein, A. H., and L. K. Friedrich, with F. Vondracek. 1972. "Television Content and Young Children's Behavior. In J. P. Murray, E. A. Rubinstein, and G. A. Comstock, eds., *Television and Social Behavior*. Vol. 2, *Television and Social Learning*, pp. 202–317. Washington, DC: U.S. Government Printing Office.

Tevlin, J. 2003. "Joy Sick: Games Can Be an Addiction." In R. Espejo, ed., *Video Games*, pp. 50–60. San Diego: Greenhaven.

Thomas, M. H., R. W. Horton, E. C. Lippincott, and R. S. Drabman. 1977. "Desensitization to Portrayals of Real-Life Aggression as a Function of Exposure to Television Violence." *Journal of Personality and Social Psychology* 35: 450–458.

Turner, C. W., B. W. Hesse, and S. Peterson-Lewis. 1986. "Naturalistic Studies of the Long-Term Effects of Television Violence." *Journal of Social Issues* 42: 51–73.

Williams, T. M., ed. 1986. *The Impact of Television: A Natural Experiment in Three Communities*. Orlando, FL: Academic.

Wober, M. 1978. "Televised Violence and Paranoid Perceptions: The View from Great Britain." *Public Opinion Quarterly* 42, no. 3: 315–321.

3

Problems, Controversies, and Solutions

This chapter focuses on existing problems and controversies and potential solutions relating to media violence. The problems and controversies refer to some of the research discussed earlier and provide a way for readers to see media violence in another perspective. Solutions are presented in terms of possible options that viewers and parents can use to mitigate the effects of pervasive violence in the media.

Media Content

As different media have become part of everyday life, their content, especially that related to violence, has sparked interest, concern, and intense debate. In the late 1800s, concern focused on the possibly unsavory and violent content of the "dime" novels. In the early 1900s, the focus shifted to the movies, again with concern focusing on violent content. When television became part of daily life, once again concerns were raised about its content, particularly that related to violence. As Chapter 1 showed, many of these concerns were voiced in the numerous congressional hearings held since the 1950s, but there have been few long-term, effective solutions.

In regard to television, there is general agreement that programs do contain violence, but because of differences in the way violence is defined and measured, there is little agreement and considerable controversy about the degree or amount of violence (Signorielli, Gerbner, and Morgan 1995; Lometti 1995).

Measuring Violence

Images on television, including the amount of violence on television, are typically isolated by a research procedure known as content analysis. This is a systematic research design that defines what is being isolated, how to quantify it (e.g., violence), and measures the reliability or dependability of the measures and variables. Content analyses define violence as well as the way it is isolated and counted. Of course, the way a thematic element, such as violence, is defined influences what is categorized as violence and how much violence is found (Signorielli, Gross, and Morgan 1982).

Violence is something that most people believe they can recognize when they see, yet it is difficult to define unambiguously. Most definitions focus on physical hurting and/or killing. During the 1970s and 1980s (and up to the present), one of the major controversies surrounding the definition of violence was whether comic violence, accidents, or "acts of nature" should be included. Researchers at CBS (Blank 1977) and NBC (Coffin and Tuchman 1972) argued against their inclusion, whereas the research of the Cultural Indicators (CI) project (Eleey, Gerbner, and Tedesco 1972; Gerbner et al. 1977) argued for their inclusion, provided that the images deal with human or humanlike characters. In the CI perspective, comic violence was counted if it included a credible indication or infliction of overt physical pain, hurting, or killing. Interestingly, while denying children could learn harmful messages from comic violence, CBS researchers, in a public relations booklet "Learning While They Laugh" (see Signorielli, Gross, and Morgan 1982), said children would learn prosocial (good or positive) messages set in a comic context. Similarly, network researchers did not include accidental violence or violence that was the result of an "act of nature," except if it occurred in a violent context (e.g., trying to escape from the scene of a crime). The CI researchers, however, included these types of violence because, in fiction, there are no real accidents or acts of nature. Writers invent accidents, disasters, and acts of nature as part of the storytelling process, and such acts serve to eliminate and/or incapacitate characters. This is particularly important in today's "reality" programs because producers and/or writers, in a process called gatekeeping, specifically select those incidents that are included in programs and thus seen by viewers. Gatekeepers make specific decisions whether to show scenes of violence or other thematic elements.

The National Television Violence Study's (NTVS's) definition of violence also focused on credible threats or the use of physical force and included all types of violence, provided there was an intention to harm (NTVS 1998). Acts of violence were included that were seen as well as inferred through harmful consequences (e.g., a character with a bloody nose). The analytic framework of the NTVS was designed to be sensitive to the context in which violence was presented (violence committed by heroes or villains, punished or rewarded, etc.). It also used a conservative definition of violence to guard against the artificial inflation of estimates of violence on television. Similarly, a study of UK programming focused on physical violence that showed an intention to harm or intimidate. This study also included accidental violence and violence caused by a catastrophe, if it was caused by humans (Gunter, Harrison, and Wykes 2003).

A criticism of these definitions of violence is that they focus only on physical violence. Anu Mustonen and Lea Pulkkinen (1997) believe that psychological violence (aggressive humor, verbal abuse) should also be included. Their definition of violence includes physical and/or psychological actions (threats, nonverbal behavior, anger) that are designed to or actually cause harm. Their coding schemes are sensitive to contextual elements of televised violence as well as the frequency, intensity, and attractiveness of violence. The primary difference between their approach and other approaches is the inclusion of psychological violence. The major concern, however, with including psychological violence is that it is very difficult to isolate consistently or reliably. Indeed, in their study of Finnish television, Mustonen and Pulkkinen admit that their measures of psychological violence are less reliable than measures of physical violence.

Unitization and Sampling

Two other critical elements in designing a solid content analysis of media violence are how to isolate (unitize) the phenomenon and how to sample the resultant units used in the analysis. Units of analysis define the body of content that will be analyzed. The unit must be easy to isolate and work with. In most studies, the two simplest units are the program as a whole and the characters who appear in the programs. Most of the studies discussed in Chapter 2 use the program as a basic unit of analysis. The process of isolating characters, however, differs from study to study. The CI group (Gerbner, Morgan, and Signorielli 1994) isolated all talking characters, paying special attention to those who were cast in roles central to the plot (the major characters). Signorielli (2003b) analyzed major and supporting characters, again focusing on those roles that were central to the story. The NTVS (1998) focused on characters only in terms of the perpetrators (P) and targets (T) who were part of the violent interaction (PAT). The studies typically isolate violence on both the program level and as specific actions. CI isolated the "violent action," a scene of violence confined to the same agents, whereas the NTVS isolated both scenes of violence and the specific violent actions (PAT). Similarly, the UK research (Gunter, Harrison, and Wykes 2003) focused on programs, violent actions, and perpetrators and victims.

Studies also differ in how they choose to sample the units of analysis. The sampling procedure typically involves selecting the most basic of the units of analysis, the program, which then provides the basis for isolating other units (characters, violent actions/scenes). Some studies, such as CI, focused only on broadcast (over-the-air) network prime-time programs.[1] Prime time was selected because it is the body of programming watched by most people. CI research sampled a full week of programming, typically drawn around the same time each year; the fall samples in late September and early October and the winter and early spring samples in January and March (sweeps months were omitted).[2] This sample thus provides a snapshot of all broadcast network programming available at one period of time. The CI team conducted numerous tests to assess the validity of week-long samples and found that a week of programming gives a fairly accurate description while being cost- and time-effective (Signorielli, Gross, and Morgan 1982). Moreover, a recent examination of seven weeks of prime-time programs broadcast in September and October 2003 found that the basic distributions of programs by genre (situation comedies, action programs, reality programs, etc.) was remarkably similar from week to week. Thus, one week is as indicative of the kinds of network programs broadcast as any other week (Signorielli 2003a).

Other studies, including the NTVS (1998) and research in the U.K. (Gunter, Harrison, and Wykes 2003), sampled programming available throughout the day on broadcast, satellite, and/or cable channels. These studies have typically used versions of composite weeks of programming; that is, they draw one day a week over a period of seven weeks. The NTVS, for example, used composite weeks to collected three yearly samples (1994–1995, 1995–1996, and

1996–1997) of programming across twenty-three channels operating between 6:00 AM and 11:00 PM each day. The sample included broadcast (commercial networks, independent stations, and public television) and cable channels (basic and premium offerings). All genres except game shows, religious programs, "infomercials" or home shopping channels, sports, instructional programs, and news were included. Some studies, however, may be concerned with just one genre of programming. Mary Beth Oliver (1994), for example, sampled only reality-based programs.

Media Effects

Is media violence, particularly that found on television and in video games, harmful? There is a large body of research whose numbers range from estimates of around 3,000 studies and/or articles (Wartella, Olivarez, and Jennings 1998) to a count of 300 specific empirical studies (Potter 2003). As seen in Chapter 2, most of the research supports the contention that media violence may have a negative influence on viewers, but there are some who discount this evidence.

Experimental Studies

Although the major body of research shows support for the relationship between violence and aggressive behavior, there are criticisms of this conclusion. One of the major criticisms is that experimental studies conducted in laboratories cannot be used to postulate what will actually happen because laboratory manipulations are artificial. Watching television in a laboratory does not mirror the way people view at home, and responses may be limited to a narrowly defined set of behaviors. There are, however, relatively few proponents of this position. For example, Jonathan Freedman notes that the laboratory does not measure "actual aggression" and that reactions allowed and perhaps encouraged in the laboratory would be discouraged in other environments (1992, 180). Similarly, he believes that even though aggressive responses are found in the laboratory, that finding does not prove that they would occur in other situations, such as at home or at school. Similarly, Jib Fowles (1999) notes that research conducted in the laboratory may be so far from reality that it should be discredited. Freedman also believes that experiments are open to a phenomenon called experimenter demand or influence (subjects do what they think is expected of them). Freedman and Fowles note that when watching at home, children select what they want to watch, and parents do not tell their children to imitate the characters in the program. In addition, they argue that experiments show subjects a short, often violent, segment of a program that may be taken out of context. This procedure bears little resemblance to home viewing, where commercials permit breaks in the action and the set is turned on and off at will. Freedman believes that it is critical to take program content into account. In particular, he notes that social learning theory posits that children might learn aggressive behaviors because a considerable portion of television violence is rewarded—those who commit violence are the "good guys" (police) and are legally allowed to use violence in order to catch the "bad guys" whose use of violence is then punished. Finally, Freedman and Fowles argue that the results of the hundreds of field or nonexperimental studies are inclusive, inconsistent, and too dependent upon correlational statistical techniques. Because correlations only say whether or not two things are related to each other, they do not permit causal interpretations. Consequently, interpretations may resemble a "Which came first, the chicken or the egg?" scenario. Do those who watch aggressive programs behave more aggressively? Or, are those who are more aggressive attracted to violent programming? Do they prefer it?

Even though there is some concern that laboratory experiments should not be used to predict real-world occurrences, the bulk of the evidence (see Chapter 2) shows that viewing and real-world violence (aggression, desensitization, fear) are related. W. James Potter (1999), who has conducted an extremely extensive examination of this body of research, concludes that as little as one exposure to media violence may result in aggressive behavior. At the same time, he believes there is some evidence of a reciprocal process because those who are more aggressive may be more attracted to media violence. Finally, the most solid base of evidence showing the implications of media violence comes from the longitudinal research of Leonard Eron and L. Rowell Huesmann (see Chapter 2). Longitudinal studies are particularly compelling because they are time-ordered and hence permit comparisons from time 1 to time 2 or time 3. Moreover, these designs tend to be more realistic and lack the artificiality of experiments. Overall, despite the critiques of Freedman and

Fowles, the evidence, particularly the meta-analyses, clearly shows some degree of relationship between media violence and aggressive behavior.

Cultivation Analysis

Another major area of research that has been criticized is cultivation theory. These critiques by a number of different investigators were published primarily during the early 1980s and centered around questions of control variables and spuriousness (that results may be due to factors not originally included in the research design) (Morgan and Signorielli 1990). Around the same time, Michael Hughes (1980), Paul Hirsch (1980, 1981) and George Gerbner et al. (1980a, b) found that many of the relationships between watching television and conceptions about the world (such as the mean world syndrome, a composite measure that shows whether people think the world is an inherently mean or violent place) that were tested using data from the General Social Survey (fielded by the National Opinion Research Center) changed when the analysis simultaneously controlled for multiple demographic variables. The early analyses of these data used separate controls for gender, age, and education and found that the relationships remained stable. When these controls were applied simultaneously, however, the relationships became much smaller, and some disappeared entirely. Yet, looking at the data more closely, the CI group found that meaningful associations remained when the analyses were conducted separately for different subgroups (e.g., men and women) and simultaneously controlled for other relevant demographic variables. This discovery led to the refinement and enhancement of cultivation theory through the concept of mainstreaming (See Gerbner et al. 1980b, 1982). Mainstreaming, in essence, means that differences that would ordinarily be attributed to people's different perspectives (e.g., age, political orientation) are diminished or totally reduced once television viewing is taken into account. Mainstreaming thus shows that television has become the true melting pot for recent generations of Americans. Although these exchanges made for considerable controversy in the academic community, the end result was that cultivation theory evolved conceptually and helped generate significant new issues and questions of importance in understanding the role the media, particularly violent media, play in society.

Solutions

Is media violence harmful? Although there is evidence to support both a "yes" and a "no" answer to this question, the evidence that media violence can be harmful is considerably stronger than the evidence it is benign. In regard to television violence, scores and scores of researchers have shown connections between violent images and people's specific aggressive behaviors and/or their perceptions of fear, whereas those who debunk the negative effects of television violence are relatively few in number and, as we've seen above, primarily rely upon methodological shortcomings to bolster their position. As Potter (2003) and others have noted, methodological shortcomings exist because it is almost impossible to design a perfect experiment or study. Moreover, a major limitation in this research is that it is extremely difficult to find people who do not use media. Nonviewers are almost nonexistent, and earlier research found that those who say they do not watch television are an extremely diverse and eclectic group (Jackson-Beeck 1977). In addition, watching television is an activity many people are reluctant to admit they do. Rather, when asked if they watch, they give "socially desirable" responses (they say they only watch PBS, sports, the news, A&E, or other seemingly "higher quality" programs). Most people, however, watch what is best termed "entertainment" and tend to watch a great deal.

There are three areas, in particular, that provide possible solutions to the problem of media violence: having an awareness of media content, using the V-Chip and rating systems, and becoming a media-literate viewer.

Content

In the current market-driven media environment, television programs exist as the "bait" to lure viewers to see, not the programs, but the commercials. Similarly, when people read a magazine or the newspaper, the industry hopes that they will also pay attention to the advertisements. The television industry must attract the most viewers (for the least cost), particularly viewers who have the most money to spend. Interestingly, those in the industry who are quick to invoke their First Amendment freedoms when faced with opposition and/or concerns about programming or discussions that television violence is a public health risk (AMA 1999) rarely say a word about the influence of advertising (Strasburger and Wilson 2002).

The public typically agrees that television content is problematic—it is too violent, too graphic, and too suggestive. For example, a survey by the Annenberg Public Policy Center (2000) found that parents are more concerned about media content than the amount of time their children spend with media. Similarly, a survey by Common Sense Media (Penn, Schoen, and Berland 2003) found that parents were most concerned that media today contributed to children (both their own and other children) behaving in antisocial or violent ways, using coarse language, being more materialistic, and losing their innocence too soon.

But the public, compared to those who rigorously study this phenomenon, generally underestimates the amount and degree of violence on television. In discussing myths of television violence, Potter (2003) notes that when the public calls for a decrease in the overall amounts of violence, the only violence called into question is that which is perceived as extremely graphic or offensive. Moreover, some types of violence (comic or verbal) are not noticed and hence not perceived as a problem. What is missing from this scenario is the fact that all types of violence influence viewers and that it is the steady diet of homogenized, entertainment violence—what George Gerbner (1990) refers to as "happy" violence—that has the most far-reaching impact on the public.

The industry defends its programming practices by stating that the programs on the air are the types of programs people want to see, that violence (and sex) sell. James Hamilton (1998) notes that this may be true for one particular segment of the population, those, particularly males, between eighteen and thirty-four, an exceptionally attractive group for advertisers. Violence is thus seen as a function of how much income the particular program will generate for its sponsors. In addition, violence is an attractive component of programming because it transcends language or "travels well" (Gerbner 2003, 298) and reaps higher profits from foreign sales (Hamilton 1998). At the same time, there is evidence that does not support the contention that violence attracts more viewers. Television programs with less or no violence have overall higher audience (Nielsen) ratings than those with more violence (Signorielli 2001). Similarly, PG-13 and PG movies often have higher box office revenues than R-rated films (Funk 2002). Another concern is that the media target youngsters. A Federal Trade Commission study (FTC 2002) found that the industry markets movies, video games, and music that have parental warnings or age-restricted ratings and the advertises these products in outlets most popular with children under seventeen. Moreover, promotions for television programs are often filled with excessive violence and sex, which are used to attract viewers (Soley and Reid 1985).

One solution to video violence is to take content into consideration. Victor Strasberger and Barbara Wilson, based on their work with the National Television Violence Study, for example, offered several suggestions. Specifically, the television and movie industry should "accept responsibility for and discontinue the deceptive marketing practices documented in the FTC report of September 2000" (2002, 386–387). The industry should also reduce the amount of violence in programs, and when violence is included, it should be punished; its consequences should be clearly delineated and not justified. In addition, more prosocial (positive) programming, especially for children, should be developed. Policymakers can also play a role in helping reduce violence by understanding the connection between media violence and public health and that "there is a cohesive body of research that documents certain risks associated with beaming media violence at young people" (Strasburger and Wilson 2002, 386). Last, but certainly not least, policymakers should continue to pay attention to the levels of and types of violence on television and in the movies. Parents, too, are key to solving this dilemma. In particular, parents need to take responsibility for their children's viewing; they need to set rules and abide by them. Parents also must become media-literate, critical consumers of the media and take advantage of those tools (rating systems and the V-chip) that are currently available (Strasburger and Wilson 2002).

Other countries, such as the United Kingdom, have more stringent rules about program scheduling. Restrictive scheduling has been used for many years to protect children, and both the Independent Television Commission (ITC) and the British Broadcasting Corporation (BBC) have explicit and comprehensive codes regarding the portrayal of sex, bad language, and violence. Barrie Gunter, Jackie Harrison, and Maggie Wykes (2003) note that programs aired before 9 PM must be suitable for children and that there is a sliding scale of what is considered suitable programming for the rest of the evening. For example, an "adult" program may air at 10 PM or later but would not be suitable for showing at 9 PM. Premium cable and satellite channels have more flexibility because the higher subscription costs tend to limit children's accessibility to this programming. Likewise, British broadcasters have also adapted movie and video age-based ratings to use with televised films. There are also some standards in place in Europe, although it is difficult to fully implement them due to differences from country to country. Nevertheless, the V-chip is not used in Europe, again because the technology of television sets and broadcasting differs from country to country (Gunter, Harrison, and Wykes 2003). However, it is highly unlikely that the United States could institute similar time-based restrictions. An attempt in the late 1970s to specify a "family viewing hour" was dismissed by the courts (see Chapter 1).

Rating Systems and the V-Chip
The V-chip is the longest-lasting, industry-wide and cooperative attempt at self-regulation. The V-chip, mandated as part of the Telecommunications Act of 1996, is found in all 13-inch and larger TV sets manufactured after 1999 and can be activated by parents or other caregivers. It works with a six-category age-based rating system that is accompanied by designations for program content. The ratings are similar to those used in the motion picture industry and are displayed in the upper left-hand corner of the television screen during the first fifteen seconds of the program. In addition, ratings are sometimes included in newspaper television listings. The six age-based ratings are

TV-Y: suitable for children of all ages

TV-Y7: suitable for children age seven and older

TV-G: suitable for all audiences

TV-14: may be inappropriate for children under fourteen

TV-PG: parental guidance suggested

TV-MA: mature audiences; material may be unsuitable for children under seventeen

The content-based advisories include

V for violence

S for sexual situations

D for suggestive dialogue

L for course language

FV for fantasy violence (for children's program ratings)

One of the major concerns with implementing the V-chip technology and its accompanying rating system is whether or not it violates the First Amendment. The American Civil Liberties Union (ACLU) believes that the V-chip and rating system is a violation of the First Amendment as a form of censorship because it is not a "voluntary" system. They argue that rather than giving parents control over their children's viewing, the government through the V-chip will usurp parental control over their children's viewing (ACLU 1996). Moreover, the ACLU feels that the V-chip is not needed because there are products that give parents/caregivers the capability to block and/or choose what their children watch. The ACLU, in short, is opposed to the V-chip because they fear it will undermine American democracy and freedom.

There are, however, numerous arguments against the ACLU's position. Some argue that it is still the parents/caregivers and not the government who actually decide when and how to activate the V-chip. The V-chip has an on-off switch and thus its use is voluntary and is no more unconstitutional than those who physically turn the set on or off (NCTV, no date). In addition, organizations such as the National Parent-Teacher Association (PTA) have indicated that the V-chip is needed and is not a violation of First Amendment rights because parents/caregivers want help from the industry to ascertain what is good programming (Liebowitz 1997). In short, because the V-chip can be programmed individually by each family and because it has an on-off switch, the technology does not promote censorship. Moreover, the argument that other blocking products are available does not acknowledge that some families may not be able to afford blocking technology or may not have the technical skill to implement such a device.

Do Ratings Help?
Does the TV rating system do what it is supposed to do? Do the ratings accurately reflect program content? Do parents pay attention to the ratings and use them to monitor and/or limit what their children watch? Do parents use the V-chip technology? Do the ratings influence children's viewing by increasing rather than decreasing viewing?

Ratings can be used with and without the V-chip because they are listed in the newspaper and/or *TV Guide* and displayed for the first fifteen seconds a program is on the air. Although the newspaper or *TV Guide* listings only give age-based ratings, the onscreen ratings give both the age- and content-based ratings.

Consequently, parents and caregivers can easily select what is appropriate material for their children to watch. However, as Gerbner (2002) notes, the decision to watch television is often made by the clock rather than selecting a particular program. Those who publish the ratings, however, may confuse this choice with the one made when going to the movies. In short, the first few minutes of a program are not the optimum time to make viewing choices. And if one tunes in a few minutes late, the rating information is no longer available.

There is also some evidence that the ratings may not accurately reflect television content and that the newspaper listings may not include them. In an analysis of a sample of programs seen on eight major broadcast and cable networks, the Kaiser Family Foundation found that age-based ratings provided useful and accurate information but that content-based advisories are often incorrect because many programs with violence, sex, or adult language do not list the appropriate advisory (Kunkel et al. 1998). Moreover, because cartoons are typically not rated, some of the most violent programs on television are rating-free. Finally, there is evidence that the ratings, which are applied by individual producers, are inconsistent (Gerbner 2002).

Nancy Signorielli (2003a) found that more than eight out of ten programs in samples of prime-time network programs broadcast between the fall of 1997 and the fall of 2003 were labeled with an age-based rating, with more than half labeled TV-PG (parental guidance suggested). Relatively few programs, however, had content-based (V, S, L, D) ratings—less than four in ten. The age-based ratings reflect program genre and provide a good barometer of sexual and violent themes in the programs. All of the TV-MA programs had either sex or violence, and most included both ratings. Yet many programs that were not rated also contained sex and violence. Consequently, ratings are not a fail-safe way to protect children because many programs with sex and violence are not labeled. Thus viewers, particularly parents with young children, may find it difficult to avoid programs with content they feel is undesirable or unsuitable for their children.

Signorielli (2003a) also found that age-based ratings do not pull viewers toward the more mature programs. Although programs without ratings (mostly, news-magazine-award) had the highest audience (Nielsen) ratings, those labeled TV-MA (mature audiences only) had the lowest. The TV-14 programs and TV-PG programs had the next highest audience ratings, and TV-G programs had fairly low audience ratings. Programs without content-based ratings had higher audience (Nielsen) ratings than the programs with the content-based ratings. Thus, it appears that content-based ratings do not attract more viewers. A limitation of this analysis, however, is that the audience ratings used in this analysis (from *Broadcasting and Cable*) reflect only the general audience. Ratings for specific demographic subgroups, such as children, young men, or boys, may show very different results.

There have been a number of studies, however, showing that ratings may be superfluous. In a study of parents in 752 households, Robert Ableman found that the ratings "preach to the choir" (1999, 544). Those parents who use ratings also have viewing rules in place. Moreover, the children in these households tend to be low to moderate viewers and good students (high achievers), and more often than not are female. At the same time, those households and children who are more likely to need the information in the ratings are those least likely to pay attention to them. Another concern is that parents may not be well informed about their existence (Cantor 2002) and that the industry has been uncooperative in getting this information to the public.

Video Game Ratings

There are some things that can be done to make game playing a positive rather than negative experience for children. Elisa Song and Jane Anderson (2003) note that parents can lessen the potential problems that may arise from video game playing. First, because younger children may be more at risk than older children, parents should limit their game playing, particularly of the violent, first-person shooter games. Second, children who have problems in school (academic and/or behavior), should be limited in their video game (and television) use. Third, parents should become advocates in their community, making sure that outlets for video games (stores, tape rental facilities, etc.) do not rent or sell games that require parental approval to underage children.

Video games are also rated, and parents should avail themselves of the ratings when choosing games for their children. Entertainment Software Board Ratings (ESRB) consist of age-based rating symbols that give general information about game content (http://www.esrb.org/esrbratings_guide.asp). The ratings are on the front of the game boxes with content descriptors (e.g., blood, blood and gore, alcohol references, mature humor) on the back. The age-related symbols are:

EC: Early Childhood (content suitable for ages three and older). These games do not contain material that parents would find inappropriate.

T: Teen (ages thirteen and older). May contain violent content, mild or strong language, and/or suggestive themes.

AO: Adults Only (content suitable only for adults). May include graphic depictions of sex and/or violence. Not intended for persons under the age of 18.

E: Everyone (content may be suitable for persons ages six and older). May contain minimal violence and some comic mischief or crude language.

M: Mature (content may be suitable for persons ages seventeen and older). May contain mature sexual themes or more intensive violence or language.

RP: Rating Pending (product has been submitted to the ESRB and is awaiting final rating).

Media Literacy

Media literacy is one of the most important solutions to the problems of media violence and other potentially unsuitable elements of program content. Media literacy involves numerous components, including learning to analyze, understand, and evaluate contemporary media images (Potter 2001). For example, people should be aware of the way the media may shape their views about people of different races, men and women, political candidates, products, violence, and problem solving. Media literacy also involves an understanding of how media are produced, of who owns and controls the media, and how profits (providing audiences for advertisers) guide and influence the way the industry operates. Last, but certainly not least, media literacy skills enable viewers to be critical of what they see, hear, and/or read.

A media log is a particularly useful tool for parents to use to keep track of the family's media use. It is typically maintained for a week and keeps track not only of what and when media are used, but why they are used and what family members "got out of" watching, playing, listening, or reading. A first step in keeping a log is to define what constitutes media (books, magazines, newspapers, music, television, movies, the World Wide Web, video games). Along with noting what media is used, parents or care-givers might ask their children to keep track of all the advertise-ments they see during the course of the day. Another good exer-cise is to have children assess their clothes (and that of their friends and acquaintances) to see how many different brand names and/or logos they can find. A similar exercise can be accomplished in looking at their everyday surroundings—what logos and/or brand names are easily seen and/or difficult to avoid?

Parents and caregivers should also work with their children to help them become aware of the models the media, particularly television, provide about problem solving. It is in this area that an understanding of the way violence is used as a thematic element becomes important. By watching as a family, children can be alert-ed to some of the destructive, as well as constructive, problem-solving techniques that are employed in the programs they watch. For example, the family could develop a definition of violence and spend an evening watching television to count the number of times violence appears, who does the hurting or killing, who gets hurt or killed, and how often violent behavior seems to be glamorized. Indeed, watching with their children, particularly those under the age of seven, is one of the most effective strategies parents can use to help their children become critical and selective media con-sumers (Parents and Media 2003, http://www.kff.org/entmedia/3353-index.cfm).

One way in which parents can try to counteract the role of the media is to set limits and develop workable rules for media use. However, in today's multiset environment, in which many chil-dren's rooms are equipped with "entertainment systems" (TV, computer, video games), this is often easier to say than actually do. Research has shown that an optimum level of viewing is about two hours a day and that those who watch for more than two hours a day typically do less well in school (Strasberger and Wilson 2002). Above all, parents should watch with their children and talk about what they see. Indeed, this practice has the added benefit of giv-ing parents "real-world" opportunities to talk with their children about difficult topics (drinking, drug use, sex, and violent behav-ior). The NTVS, in particular, had several suggestions for parents. Specifically, parents should take the child's developmental matu-rity into account—older children can watch and understand differ-ent types of media than younger children. Yet parents need to be aware that media violence (movies, video games, on TV) may be risky for their children and that despite the benign appearance of some violent cartoons, they are not good for children, especially younger children, to watch. As noted above, parents should use and teach their children to use and respect program advisories and ratings. Moreover, if their TV set has the V-chip, it should be implemented. Last, but certainly not least, parents should know what their children are watching and take the time to watch with them. It is highly unlikely that media violence will disappear from the media environment, but with these tools and suggestions, its impact on children can be lessened.

Notes

1. The early work of CI, conducted prior to the 1990s, included children's weekend-daytime programs.

2. Sweeps periods are the time that all the viewership of all stations is assessed in the form of Nielsen ratings (the percent of all households with television that are watching a particular program). Stations use these figures to determine the rates they will charge for commercials.

References

Ableman, R. 1999. "Preaching to the Choir: Profiling TV Advisory Ratings Users." *Journal of Broadcasting and Electronic Media* 43: 529–550.

American Civil Liberties Union (ACLU). 1996. "Violence Chip: Why Does the ACLU Oppose the V-Chip Legislation Currently Pending in Congress?" http://www.aclu.org/library/aavchip.html.

American Medical Association. 1999. "Media Violence Should Be Treated as a Public Health Problem." In W. Dudley, ed., *Media Violence: Opposing Viewpoints*, pp. 119–124. San Diego: Greenhaven Pres.

Annenberg Public Policy Center. 2000. "The Fifth Annual Survey of Parents and Children." Philadelphia: Annenberg Public Policy Center.

Blank, D. M. 1977. "The Gerbner Violence Profile and Final Comments on the Violence Profile." *Journal of Broadcasting* 21: 273–279, 287–296.

Cantor, J. 2002). "The Unappreciated V-Chip." In J. D. Torr, ed., *Violence in Film and Television*, pp. 171–178. San Diego: Greenhaven.

Coffin, T. E., and S. Tuchman. 1972. "Rating Programs for Violence: A Comparison of Five Surveys and a Question of Validity: Some Comments on "Apples, Oranges, and the Kitchen Sink." *Journal of Broadcasting* 17: 3–20, 31–33.

Eleey, M. F., G. Gerbner, and N. Tedesco (Signorielli). 1972a. "Apples, Oranges and the Kitchen Sink: An Analysis and Guide to the Comparison of 'Violence Ratings and Validity, Indeed!'" *Journal of Broadcasting* 17: 21–31; 34–35.

Federal Trade Commission (FTC). 2002. "Marketing Violence to Children." In J. D. Torr, ed., *Violence in Film and Television,* pp. 148–155. San Diego: Greenhaven.

Fowles, J. 1999. *The Case for Television Violence.* Thousand Oaks, CA: Sage.

Freedman, J. L. 1992. "Television Violence and Aggression: What Psychologists Should Tell the Public." In P. Suedfeld and P. I. Tetlock, eds., *Psychology and Social Policy,* pp. 179–200. New York: Hemisphere.

Funk, J. B. 2002. "Electronic Games." In V. C. Strausburger and B. J. Wilson, eds., *Children, Adolescents, and the Media,* pp. 117–144. Thousand Oaks, CA: Sage.

Gerbner, G. 1990. "Epilogue: Advancing on the Path of Righteousness (Maybe)." In N. Signorielli and M. Morgan, eds., *Cultivation Analysis: New Directions in Media Effects Research,* pp. 249–262. Newbury Park, CA: Sage.

———. 2002. "TV Ratings' Deadly Choice: Violence or Alcohol." In M. Morgan, ed., *Against the Mainstream: The Selected Works of George Gerbner,* pp. 474–478. New York: Peter Lang.

———. 2003. "Television Violence." In M. Morgan, ed., *Against the Mainstream: The Selected Works of George Gerbner,* pp. 290–302. New York: Peter Lang.

Gerbner, G., L. Gross, M. F. Eleey, M. Jackson-Beeck, S. Jeffries-Fox, and N. Signorielli. 1977. "'The Gerbner Violence Profile'—An Analysis of the CBS Report and 'One More Time': An Analysis of the CBS 'Final Report.'" *Journal of Broadcasting* 21: 280–286, 297–303.

Gerbner, G., L. Gross, M. Morgan, and N. Signorielli. 1981. "A Curious Journey into the Scary World of Paul Hirsch." *Communication Research* 8, no. 1: 39–72.

———. 1982. "Charting the Mainstream: Television's Contribution to Political Orientations." *Journal of Communication* 48: 283–300.

———. 1980a. "Some Additional Comments on Cultivation Analysis." *Public Opinion Research* 44, no. 3: 408–410.

———. 1980b. "The "Mainstreaming" of America: Violence Profile no. 11." *Journal of Communication* 30, no. 3: 10–29.

Gerbner, G., M. Morgan, and N. Signorielli. 1994. "Television Violence Profile no. 14: The Turning Point." Philadelphia: Annenberg School for Communication.

Gunter, G., J. Harrison, and M. Wykes. 2003. *Violence on Television: Distribution, Form, Context, and Themes.* Mahwah, NJ: Lawrence Erlbaum Associates.

Hamilton, J. T. 1998. *Channeling Violence: The Economic Market for Violent Television Programming.* Princeton, NJ: Princeton University Press.

Hirsch, P. M. 1980. "The 'Scary World' of the Nonviewer and Other Anomalies: A Reanalysis of Gerbner et al.'s Findings of Cultivation Analysis, Part I." *Communication Research* 7, no. 4: 403–456.

———. 1981. "On Not Learning from One's Own Mistakes: A Reanalysis of Gerbner et al.'s Findings on Cultivation Analysis, Part II." *Communication Research* 8, no. 1: 3–37.

Hughes, M. 1980. "The Fruits of Cultivation Analysis: A Re-examination of the Effects of Television Watching on Fear of Victimization, Alienation, and the Approval of Violence." *Public Opinion Research* 44, no. 3: 287–302.

Jackson-Beck, M. 1977. "The Non-viewers: Who Are They?" *Journal of Communication* 27: 65–72.

Kunkel, D., W. J. M. Farinola, K. Cope, E. Donnerstein, E. Biely, and L. Zwarun. 1998. *Rating the TV Ratings: An Assessment of the Television Industry's Use of V-Chip Ratings.* Menlo Park, CA: Kaiser Family Foundation.

Liebowitz, H. K. 1997. "Government Regulations Restricting Media Violence May Be Necessary." Reprinted in D. L. Bender and B. Leone, eds. 1999. *Media Violence: Opposing Viewpoints,* pp. 70–76. San Diego: Greenhaven.

Lometti, G. E. 1995. "The Measurement of Televised Violence." *Journal of Broadcasting and Electronic Media* 39: 292–295.

Morgan, M., and N. Signorielli. 1990. "Cultivation Analysis: Conceptualization and Methodology." In N. Signorielli and M. Morgan, eds., *Cultivation Analysis: New Directions in Media Effects Research,* pp. 13–34. Newbury Park, CA: Sage.

Mustonen, A., and L. Pulkkinen. 1997. "Television Violence: Development of a Coding Scheme." *Journal of Broadcasting and Electronic Media* 41: 168–189.

National Coalition of Television Violence (NCTV). No date. "Ten Common Myths about the V-Chip and the Facts." http://oak.cats.ohiou.edu/~kr257699/vfacts.htm#top.

National Television Violence Study. 1998. Vol. 3. , Center for Communication and Social Policy, University of California, Santa Barbara, ed. Thousand Oaks, CA: Sage.

Oliver, M. B. 1994. "Portrayals of Crime, Race, and Aggression in "Reality Based" Police Shows: A Content Analysis." *Journal of Broadcasting and Electronic Media* 38: 179–192.

Penn, Schoen, and Berland Associates and American Viewpoint. 2003. "The 2003 Common Sense Media Poll of American Parents. May. http://www.commonsensemedia.org/resources/polls.php#poll2.

Potter, W. J. 1999. *On Media Violence.* Thousand Oaks, CA: Sage.

———. 2001. *Media Literacy.* 2nd ed. Thousand Oaks, CA: Sage.

———. 2003. *The 11 Myths of Media Violence.* Thousand Oaks, CA: Sage.

Signorielli, N. 2001. "Prime-Time Violence in the 90s: Has the Picture Really Changed?" Paper presented at the Annual Conference of the National Communication Association, Chicago, IL, November.

———. 2003a. "Age-Based Ratings, Content Designations and Television Content: Is There a Problem?" Paper presented at the Annual Conference of the National Communication Association, Miami, FL.

———. 2003b. "Prime-Time Violence, 1993–2001: Has the Picture Really Changed?" *Journal of Broadcasting and Electronic Media* 47, no. 1: 36–57.

Signorielli, N., G. Gerbner, and M. Morgan. 1995. "Violence on Television: The Cultural Indicators Project." *Journal of Broadcasting and Electronic Media* 39, no. 2: 278–283.

Signorielli, N., L. Gross, and M. Morgan. 1982. "Violence in Television Programs: Ten Years Later." In D. Pearl, L. Bouthilet, and J. Lazar, eds., *Television and Social Behavior: Ten Years of Scientific Progress and Implications for the Eighties,* pp. 158–173. Rockville, MD: National Institute of Mental Health.

Soley, L.C., and L. N. Reid. 1985. "Baiting Viewers: Violence and Sex in Television Program Advertisements." *Journalism Quarterly* 62, no. 1: 105–110, 131.

Song, E. H., and J. E. Anderson. 2003. "Violence in Video Games May Harm Children." In R. Espejo, ed., *Video Games,* pp. 9–17. San Diego: Greenhaven.

Strasburger, V. C., and B. J. Wilson. 2002. *Children, Adolescents, and the Media.* Thousand Oaks, CA: Sage.

Wartella, E., A. Olivarez, and N. Jennings. 1998. "Children and Television Violence in the United States." In U. Carlsson and C. von Feilitzen, eds., *Children and Media Violence,* pp. 55–62. Goteborg, Sweden: UNESCO International Clearinghouse on Children and Violence on the Screen.

4

Chronology

late Concern expressed about violent content in "dime"
1800s novels.

1927 Passage of the Radio Act of 1927, which establishes the
Federal Radio Commission, forerunner of the Federal
Communications Commission (FCC). The Federal Radio
Commission oversees licensing of radio stations and
reduces station chaos.

1930s Payne Fund Studies on Movies isolate considerable violent content and claim that the content had an adverse
effect upon adolescents (Charters 1933).

1933 The Legion of Decency is created by members of the
Roman Catholic Church. Films are rated; those films
deemed immoral are condemned. Roman Catholics are
strongly advised to follow the legion's ratings when
going to the movies and to avoid any condemned film.

1934 Passage of the Communications Act of 1934, which
establishes the Federal Communications Commission
(FCC). The FCC regulates radio, telephones, and the tele-
graph and oversees station licensing but is prohibited
from censoring. It determines if stations operate in the
public interest, convenience, and necessity.

Hearing, U.S. House of Representatives, Committee on
Interstate and Foreign Commerce. *Federal Motion Picture
Commission*. 73rd Congress, 2nd Session.

1934 Film producers officially adopt the Hollywood Produc-
cont. tion Code.

1936 Hearing, U.S. House of Representatives, subcommittee of
the Committee on Interstate and Foreign Commerce.
Motion-Picture Films. 74th Congress, 2nd session.

1949 The Fairness Doctrine is introduced by the FCC, requiring broadcasters to provide reasonable discussion of controversial topics.

1952 Hearing, U.S. House of Representatives, Committee on
Interstate and Foreign Commerce, Federal Communications Commission Subcommittee. *Investigation of Radio
and Television Programming.* Chair, Oren Harris, D-AR
(June, September, December). 82nd Congress, 2nd Session. The hearings focus on whether television programs
contain offensive or immoral content or emphasize violence, crime, and/or corruption.

First television code is announced by the National Association of Broadcasters (NAB).

1954 Hearing, U.S. Senate, Committee on the Judiciary. Subcommittee to Investigate Juvenile Delinquency. *Juvenile
Delinquency (Television Programs).* Chair, Robert Hendrickson, R-NJ (June, October). 83rd Congress, 2nd Session The hearings focus on whether crime and horror on
television are related to the rise in juvenile delinquency
and on the negative effects of movies and comics; TV
executives indicate that they would consider any attempt
to regulate program content as censorship.

1955 Hearings, U.S. Senate Committee on the Judiciary. *Television and Juvenile Delinquency.* Chair, Estes Kefauver, D-TN
(April). 84th Congress, 1st Session. These hearings continued those started in 1954 to explore the long-term
effects of television violence. Eleanor Maccoby and Paul
Lazarsfeld, two prominent social scientists, testify. Testimony is mixed on long-term effects. The hearings indicate the need for continued research.

1955
cont.   Interim Report, U.S. Senate. *Comic Books and Juvenile Delinquency.*

Interim Report, U.S. Senate. *Television and Juvenile Delinquency.*

1961–
1962   Hearings, U.S. Senate Committee on the Judiciary. *Investigation of Juvenile Delinquency in the United States, Part 10, Effects on Young People of Violence and Crime Portrayed on Television* (June, July; January, May). 87th Congress, Sessions 1 and 2. Chair, Thomas Dodd, D-CT. Subcommittee staff finds increases in the number of programs with violence, and some writers testify they had been asked to increase violence in programming. Again, the need for more definitive research is detailed and requested.

1961   FCC chair Newton Minow refers to television as a "vast wasteland" in a speech before the National Association of Broadcasters.

1963   *The People Look at Television,* a report of research conducted by Gary Stiner and sponsored by CBS, is released. The first report to focus on television from a uses and gratifications perspective, it discusses what people like about and how they use television. It does not offer any new information about television's effects.

1964   Hearings, U.S. Senate, Judiciary Committee, Subcommittee to Investigate Juvenile Delinquency (July). *Juvenile Deliquency: Part 16. Effects on Young People of Violence and Crime Portrayed on Television.* 88th Congress, 2nd Session. Chair, Thomas Dodd, D-CT. Testimony notes a relationship, for youngsters, between watching crime and violence on television and exhibiting antisocial behavior and attitudes. Television, however, is not seen as the sole determinant of juvenile delinquency. The testimony of Senator Keating indicates that J. Edgar Hoover, head of the Federal Bureau of Investigation (FBI), believes the increase in crime in the country could be attributed to crime and violence in the media.

1964
cont.

Interim Report, U.S. Senate. *Television and Juvenile Delinquency.*

1968

President Lyndon Johnson sets up the National Commission on the Causes and Prevention of Violence (Chair, Milton Eisenhower) after the assassinations of Dr. Martin Luther King, Jr. (April 4, 1968) and Senator Robert Kennedy (D-MA) (June 5, 1968). The commission examines existing research and commissions a study of television content led by George Gerbner, Dean of the Annenberg School of Communications at the University of Pennsylvania (beginning of Cultural Indicators Project).

1969

Hearings, U.S. Senate, Committee on Commerce, Subcommittee on Communications. *Federal Communications Commission Policy Matters and Television Programming.* 91st Congress, 1st Session. Chair, John Pastore, D-RI (March).

Publication of the National Commission on the Causes and Prevention of Violence, Report of the Task Force on Mass Media and Violence, *Violence and the Media: Mass Media and Violence,* Vol. 9, by Robert K. Baker and Sandra J. Ball. The report indicates a relationship between viewing violence and aggressive behavior, yet in regard to the general problem of societal violence, the report indicates that there is "no single explanation of its causes, and no single prescription for its control" (Baker and Ball 1969, 160).

The Surgeon General's Scientific Advisory Committee on Television and Social Behavior and the Television and Social Behavior Program are created. One million dollars is appropriated to fund twenty-three research projects. Seven social scientists are "blackballed" from the advisory committee, and five members have direct ties to the broadcasting industry.

1970

The Prime Time Access Rule is implemented.

1971

First Notice of Inquiry, Federal Communications Commission. *In the matter of Petition of Action for Children's Television (ACT) for Rulemaking Looking Toward the Elimi-*

1971 *nation of Sponsorship and Commercial Content in Children's*
cont. *Programming and the Establishment of a Weekly 14 Hour*
Quota of Children's Television Programs (January).

Hearings, U.S. Senate. *Scientific Advisory Committee on TV and Social Behavior.* Chair, Senator John Pastore, D-RI (September). 92nd Congress, 1st Session. The committee seeks to check leakage of research findings that may reduce the importance of the final report as well as enhance the image that the subcommittee would take necessary actions, if needed (Rowland 1981).

1972 Publication of reports by the Surgeon General's Scientific Advisory Committee entitled *Television and Social Behavior.* Includes summary report and five volumes. George Comstock, John P. Murray, and Eli A. Rubinstein, editors. Research studies indicate that violence is an integral part of television programming and that for some children, there are relationships between viewing violence and behaving aggressively. The conclusions are heavily qualified and presented cautiously and conservatively.

Hearings, U.S. Senate, Committee on Commerce, Subcommittee on Communications. *Surgeon General's Report by the Scientific Advisory Committee on Television and Social Behavior.* Chair, Senator John Pastore, D-RI (March). 92nd Congress, 2nd Session. The hearings note the relationships between viewing violent programming and aggressive behavior but do not suggest possible appropriate remedies. The role of parents in safeguarding their children is discussed, as is the notion of reducing the amount of violence on television.

1974 Hearings, U.S. Senate, Committee on Commerce, Subcommittee on Communications. *Violence on Television* (April). 93rd Congress, 2nd Session. Chair, John Pastore, D-RI. George Gerbner and Eli Rubinstein report little change in the amount of violence on television. Network researchers counter that there have been decreases in television violence since the 1972 hearings. Pastore challenges broadcasters to show real decreases at next year's FCC oversight hearings.

1974
cont.
Report, Federal Communications Commission. *Children's Television Report and Policy Statement* (October).

1975 Report, Federal Communications Commission. *Report on the Broadcast of Violent, Indecent, and Obscene Material* (February).

The family viewing hour is implemented by the networks and NAB. Programming between 8 PM and 9 PM must be appropriate for general family viewing.

The Writers Guild files a lawsuit against the networks and the FCC, charging that the family viewing hour violated their First Amendment rights.

A resolution adopted by the national Parent-Teacher Association (PTA) demands the reduction of violence in television programs and commercials. The resolution is reaffirmed in 1989.

1976 Hearings, U.S. House of Representatives, House Committee on Interstate and Foreign Commerce, Subcommittee on Communications. *Sex and Violence on Television.* Chair, Lionel Van Deerlin. 94th Congress, 2nd Session. (D-CA) (July, August). Members of the American Medical Association provide testimony that defines violence as an environmental and public health risk.

Judge Warren J. Ferguson (U.S. District Court, Los Angeles) rules that the family viewing hour is unconstitutional and must be rescinded.

An $11 million negligence lawsuit is filed against NBC in California (Niemi case). The mother of a nine-year-old girl claims that her daughter's assailants were inspired by an attack seen in the NBC movie *Born Innocent*.

1977 Hearings, U.S. House of Representatives, House Committee on Interstate and Foreign Commerce, Subcommittee on Communications. *Sex and Violence on Television.* Chair, Lionel Van Deerlin (D-CA) (March). 95th Congress, 1st Session. Hearings conclude that the amount of

1977
cont.

violence on television is a serious concern and that viewing excessive violence may be harmful. Hearings, U.S.
Senate, Committee on Commerce, Science and Transportation, Subcommittee on Communications. *Television
Broadcast Policies.* 95th Congress, 2nd Session. The hearings examine charges of excessive sex, violence, and
obscenity on television as well as a lack of attention to
programming for children.

Report, U.S. House of Representatives, House Committee on Interstate and Foreign Commerce, Subcommittee
on Communications. *Violence on Television* (September).
Places blame for excessive television violence on viewers. Parental supervision is critical to limiting the potential negative effects of media violence on children. Self-
regulation by the industry can limit television violence.

Fifteen-year-old Ronny Zamora, accused of murdering
his eighty-two-year-old neighbor, enters a plea of not
guilty by reason of insanity that allegedly was caused by
excessive television viewing of crime programs. Zamora
is found guilty of first degree murder; the insanity plea
is dismissed.

1978
Report, Federal Trade Commission. *FTC Staff Report on
Television Advertising to Children* (February).

Notice of Proposed Rulemaking, Federal Trade Commission. *Children's Advertising* (April).

The Supreme Court rules that the FCC may take action
against stations that air indecent programming when
children might be listening.

1979
Report, Federal Communications Commission, Office of
Plans and Policy. *Television Programming for Children: A
Report of the Children's Television Task Force* (October).

Notice of Proposed Rulemaking. Federal Communications Commission. *Children's Television Programming and
Advertising Practices* (December).

1979   Justice Department files an antitrust suit against adver-
cont.   tising provisions in the NAB Code of Good Practice.

1981   Hearings, U.S. House of Representatives, Committee on
Energy and Commerce, Subcommittee on Telecommunications, Consumer Protection, and Finance. *Social/Behav-
ioral Effects of Violence on Television* (October). 97th Congress, 1st Session.

The Deer Hunter is shown on television; nineteen deaths
are reported due to reenactments of the Russian roulette
scene.

National Coalition on Television Violence begins to publish lists of the most violent programs and movies, using
a system that rates violence by severity (continued until
1992).

FCC chair Mark Fowler, finds television needs little regulation and is rich in programming and opportunity.
Using a marketplace focus, he describes television as a
"toaster with pictures."

MTV, the first station devoted to music videos, is established by Warner Cable Corporation and begins opera-
tions. It becomes an instant success.

1982   The National Institute of Mental Health publishes the
report *Television and Behavior: Ten Years of Scientific
Progress and Implications for the Eighties.* Includes summary and technical reports. Synthesizes and updates many
of the studies originally conducted for the Surgeon General's Television and Social Behavior Program
(1969–1972). Studies indicate a consensus on the link
between television violence and aggressive behavior

Federal district court rules that NAB Code of Good Practice violates antitrust laws.

The Niemi case is dismissed when, during opening statements, Niemi's attorney says he could not prove incite-
ment by NBC.

1983   The NAB television code is eliminated for violating antitrust laws.

Stations are no longer required to keep station logs or do ascertainment studies.

Hearing, U.S. House of Representatives, Committee on Energy and Commerce, Subcommittee on Telecommunications, Consumer Protection and Finance. *Children and Television* (March). 98th Congress, 1st Session.

Hearing, U.S. House of Representatives. House Judiciary Committee, Subcommittee on Crime. *Crime and Violence in the Media.* Chair, William Hughes (D-NJ) (April). 98th Congress, 1st Session.

1984   Task Force on Family Violence (chair, Attorney General) finds considerable evidence exists to show that television violence contributes to real-life violence (September).

American Academy of Pediatrics Task Force on Children and Television cautions physicians and parents that television may promote aggression.

Hearings, U.S. Senate, Senate Judiciary Committee, Subcommittee on Juvenile Justice. *Media Violence.* Chair, Arlen Specter (R-PA) (October). 98th Congress, 2nd Session.

Cable Communications Policy Act removes remaining cable TV regulations.

1985   A report by the American Psychological Association Commission on Youth and Violence indicates that research shows a link between television violence and real-life violence.

The American Psychological Association passes a resolution about the potential dangers that viewing violence on television can have for children.

1985
cont.
The Recording Industry Association of America begins to develop a rating system to alert consumers about offensive lyrics.

1986 Hearing, U.S. Senate. Committee on the Judiciary. *TV Violence Antitrust Exemption.* Chair, Strom Thurmond (R-SC) (June). 99th Congress, 2nd Session.

1988 Hearing, U.S. House of Representatives, Judiciary Committee, Subcommittee on Monopolies and Commercial Law. *Television Violence Act* (October). 100th Congress, 2nd Session.

Congress passes legislation prohibiting indecent programming being broadcast at any time.

1989 Hearing, U.S. House of Representatives, Judiciary Committee, Subcommittee on Economic and Commercial Law. *Television Violence Act of 1989.* Chair, Jack Brooks (D-TX) (May). 101st Congress, 1st Session.

Congress passes the Television Improvement Act (Simon-Glickman Television Violence Act). The television industry is granted a three-year antitrust exemption that will permit them to formulate a joint policy on television violence. The bill is signed into law in 1990. Networks do little.

1990 Passage of the Children's Television Act of 1990. Limits time that can be devoted to commercials (10.5 minutes/hour on weekends and 12.5 minutes/hour on weekdays). Stations are required to broadcast at least an hour of educational programming a week and must file a list of children's educational programs with the FCC each year.

1991 Newton Minow's book revisits the "vast wasteland." He notes that while in 1961 he was worried that his children would not benefit from television, today he worries that his grandchildren may actually be harmed (Minow 1991).

1992   An American Psychological Association study finds that research on the link between mediated and real violence is ignored. It calls for a federal policy to protect society from the harmful effects of televised violence.

Four days before Senate hearings, three major networks release a joint violence policy and agree to hold an industry-wide conference on televised violence.

Hearings, U.S. Senate, Committee on Governmental Affairs. *Youth Violence Prevention* (March). 102nd Congress, 2nd Session. As part of a series of hearings on youth violence, the hearings focus on the relationship between television viewing in childhood and subsequent aggressive behavior.

Hearings, U.S. House of Representatives, Judiciary Committee, Subcommittee on Crime and Criminal Justice. *Violence on TV.* Chair, Charles Schumer, (D-NY) (December). 102nd Congress, 2nd Session.

Cable Television Consumer Protection and Competition Act is approved by Congress (over President George H. W. Bush's veto). The act will regulate the cable industry and limit basic cable rates.

A report by the American Psychological Association Task Force on Television and Social Behavior concluded that thirty years of research confirms the harmful effects of television violence.

Courts reverse attempts by Congress to set aside a "safe harbor" (midnight to 6 AM) for indecent programming.

1993   Hearings, House of Representatives, Committee on Energy and Commerce, Subcommittee on Telecommunications and Finance. *Violence on Television.* Chair, Edward Markey, D-MA (May, June, September). 103rd Congress, 1st Session. Testimony stresses levels of violence on television and its effects. The V-chip is presented as way for parents to control children's viewing.

1993
cont.
Hearing, U.S. Senate. Judiciary Committee, Subcommittee on the Constitution, Subcommittee on Juvenile Justice. Chairs, Paul Simon, D-IL, and Herbert Kohl, D-WI (May, June).

High levels of violence on network programs broadcast during the May sweeps period coinciding with House and Senate hearings; feeds congressional concern about television violence.

A report by the American Psychological Association's Commission on Violence and Youth affirms the conclusions of the 1992 Task Force report. Media violence is related to aggression.

Attorney General Janet Reno supports regulation of violence on television. She believes that "TV violence legislation will pass constitutional muster" (McAvoy and Coe 1993, 6).

The House of Representatives and the Senate pass resolutions denouncing television violence.

Bills are introduced in the House of Representatives (Rep,. John Bryant, D-TX) and the Senate (Dave Durenberger, R-MN) requiring the FCC to establish standards to reduce violence on television (broadcast and cable) as well as radio. Violators will be subject to fines; repeat violations can lead to license revocation.

Legislation to establish a Presidential Commission on Television Violence is introduced in the House of Representatives by Charles Schumer (D-NY).

The Parents Television Empowerment Act is introduced in the House of Representatives by Joseph Kennedy (D-MA). The bill would require the FCC to set up toll-free phone lines for complaints about violence on both broadcast and cable channels and to publish, quarterly, the top fifty most violent programs.

The Children's Protection from Violent Programming

1993   Act is introduced in the Senate by Ernest Hollings (D-
cont. SC) and Daniel Inouye (D-HI). It would prohibit violence
        on television during those hours when children make up
        a substantial portion of the audience. Stations would be
        required to show advisories about violent content.

        Rep. Richard Durbin (D-IL) and Senator Byron Dorgan
        (D-ND) introduce the Television Violence Report Card
        Act in Congress. The bill requires the FCC to rate pro-
        grams by violence, identify companies that sponsor the
        most violent programs, and issue a quarterly report with
        this information.

1994 FCC Chair Reed Hundt says he does not want the FCC
        to become a censor; falls back on self-regulation by the
        industry.

        The UCLA Center for Communication Research is fund-
        ed by the networks to monitor network television pro-
        gramming.

        The National Television Violence Study (NTVS) is fund-
        ed by the cable industry to monitor cable and broadcast
        programming.

        Hearings, the House Subcommittee on Telecommunica-
        tions and Finance, Committee on Energy and Commerce.
        Violence in Video Games. 103rd Congress, 2nd Session.1995
        A ruling by the U.S. Court of Appeals upholds section
        16(a) of the Telecommunications Act of 1992. Indecent
        broadcasts may be limited to a "safe harbor" between
        midnight and 6 AM.

        Television Violence Report Card legislation is reintro-
        duced in the senate by Byron Dorgan (D-ND) and Kay
        Bailey Hutchinson (R-TX).

        FCC promulgated a rule-making procedure to enhance
        the implementation of the Children's Television Act of
        1990 requiring broadcasters to air three hours of educa-
        tional programming for children each week.

1994
cont.
Sen. Hollings (D-SC) reintroduces the Children's Protection from Violent Programming Act as S. 470. It is approved by the Senate Commerce Committee without amendment, on August 10, 1995.

The American Academy of Pediatrics notes the relationship between media violence and aggressive behavior, that media violence desensitizes children to real-life violence, and that media violence is related to children believing they live in a mean and dangerous world.

1996
Congress passes the Telecommunications Act of 1996. The V-chip must be part of every television set, 13 inches or larger, manufactured after 1999. The act includes the implementation of a ratings system by the networks within one year.

Jack Valenti, president of the Motion Picture Association of America (MPAA), announces the formation of a group to develop ratings for television programs.

Broadcasters agree to increase children's educational programming to three hours a week.

The American Medical Association affirms its stand that there is a strong relationship between media violence and aggression as well as other behavioral or psychological problems.

1997
TV parental guidelines (an age-based rating system) are put into place in February; content-based ratings are added in July.

NBC refuses to adopt content-based indicators (July).

Senator Hollings reintroduces the Children's Protection from Violent Programming Act.

1999
Senator Hollings reintroduces the Children's Protection from Violent Programming Act.

In the Columbine school shooting in Littleton, Colorado

1999   (April 20), two heavily armed young men, Dylan Klebold
cont.   and Eric Harris, open fire at the high school, killing twelve
        and injuring thirty-four. They then commit suicide.

        Presidential Summit on Youth Violence (White House)
        (May).

        Hearings, U.S. Senate Committee on Commerce, Science,
        and Transportation, *Television Violence*. Chair, Senator
        John McCain (R-AZ). 106th Congress, 1st Session (May).
        Hearing to consider the Children's Protection from Vio-
        lent Programming Act.

2000   Charles "Andy" Williams shoots and kills two students
        and wounds several others, then commits suicide at San-
        tana High School in Santee, California (March 5).

        The V-chip, a program blocking device, is required in all
        newly manufactured television sets 13 inches and larger.

        FCC commissioner Gloria Tristani raises questions of lax
        enforcement of indecency restrictions.

        At the Congressional Public Health Summit, the Ameri-
        can Medical Association, the American Academy of
        Pediatrics, the American Psychological Association, the
        American Academy of Child and Adolescent Psychiatry,
        the American Psychiatric Association, and the American
        Academy of Family Physicians issue a joint statement:
        watching violence is related to increased aggressive atti-
        tudes, behaviors, and values.

        A report by the Federal Trade Commission, "Marketing
        Violent Entertainment to Children: A Review of Self-Reg-
        ulation and Industry Practices in the Motion Picture,
        Music Recording and Electronic Game Industries," says
        violent entertainment is marketed aggressively to chil-
        dren by the entertainment industry.

2001   Sen. Hollings reintroduces the Children's Protection
        from Violent Programming Act as S. 341 (February).

2001 Former U.S. surgeon general David Satcher releases a
cont. report on youth violence, part of which addresses the
issue of media violence as a follow-up to the Columbine
incident. He, too, cites reasons to be concerned about
violence in television and on film and its effect on youth.

The FCC issues guidelines to help stations with indecency restrictions.

Michael Copps (Democrat) joins the FCC and works on
Tristani's anti-indecency cause.

September 11 terrorist attacks on the World Trade Center
(New York City) and the Pentagon (Washington, D.C.).
Beginning of the War on Terror.

The Patriot Act is passed by Congress (October), allowing the FBI to gather information about public speech.
Informers are required not to say that the FBI asked for
and received information.

2002 Washington-area snipers John Allen Muhammad and
Lee Boyd Malvo kill ten people in four states in the
Washington, D.C., area.

Opie and Anthony, DJs on an Infinity station, encourage
a couple to have sex in St. Patrick's Cathedral, sparking
national outrage.

The Homeland Security Act is passed by Congress.

2003 Senator Hollings reintroduces the Children's Protection
from Violent Programming Act as S. 161 (January).

Hearings, U.S. Senate, Commerce Committee, Subcommittee on Science, Technology, and Space. (April). 108th
Congress, 1st Session.

The FCC threatens to revoke licenses of broadcasters
who repeatedly violate restrictions on raunchy broadcasts.

2003
cont.
The FCC changes television ownership caps from 35 percent to 45 percent of television households. Congress opposes this move and seeks to set the cap at 39 percent.

2004
In a "costume malfunction," Janet Jackson's breast is exposed on national television during the Superbowl half-time show. Lawmakers express concern about commercials for a violent film during the Superbowl.

Hearing, U.S. Senate, Committee on Commerce, Science, and Transportation. *Protecting Children from Violent and Indecent Programming.* Chair, John McCain (R-AZ) (February). 108th Congress, 2nd Session. Representative McCain urges cable and satellite companies to give parents the ability to select channels in order to protect children from violence, sex, and profanity. The suggestion resonates with other lawmakers and regulators.

FCC commissioners call for a return of a family hour on prime-time television as well as implementation of tape and audio delay systems to eliminate indecent behavior from live events.

The Federal Trade Commission makes it easier for consumers to lodge complaints about excessive violence in advertisements and for the agency to track them.

The House Commerce Committee passes (49 to 1) an indecency bill that raises fines for indecent broadcasts and raises the threat of license revocation; a similar bill is passed by the House Telecommunications Subcommittee.

Michael Powell, FCC Chairman, requests that agency staff complete a study of broadcast television violence and its impact on children at the request of Joe Barton, Chair of the House Commerce Committee.

Activist groups, including the Parents Television Council (PTC) and the United Church of Christ, petition the FCC to revoke the licenses of six television stations in the Virginia, Maryland, and District of Columbia area (McConnell 2004, Sept. 20).

2004 Veteran's Day: Many ABC affiliates refuse to air the
cont. movie, *Saving Private Ryan* (which includes considerable
graphic violence and indecent language), in light of the
FCC's more stringent indecency policies.

References

Baker, R. K., and S. J. Ball. 1969. *Violence and the Media*. Washington, DC:
Government Printing Office.

Charters, W. W. 1933. *Motion Pictures and Youth: A Summary*. New York:
Macmillan.

Cooper, C. A. 1996. *Violence on Television: Congressional Inquiry, Public Criticism, and Industry Response: A Policy Analysis*. Lanham, MD: University
Press of America.

Eggerton, J. 2004. "D.C.'s Indecency Frenzy." *Broadcasting & Cable* 134, no.
7 (February): 8.

———. 2004. "Pols Push Raw Law for Potty Mouths." *Broadcasting & Cable*
133, no. 5 (February): 1.

———. 2004. "Caught in the Crosshairs." *Broadcasting & Cable* 134, no. 10
(March): 3.

———. 2004. "Freedom under Fire." *Broadcasting& Cable* 134, no. 27 (July): 3.

Hamilton, J. T. 1998. *Channeling Violence: The Economic Market for Violent
Television Programming*. Princeton, NJ: Princeton University Press.

McAvoy, K., and S. Coe. 1993. "TV Rocked by Reno Ultimatum." *Broadcasting & Cable* 123, no. 43: 6, 14.

McConnell, B. 2003. "FCC Says Cut Smut or Shut Down." *Broadcasting &
Cable* 133, no. 15 (April): 3.

———. 2003. "Passage of 39% Cap No Sure Thing." *Broadcasting & Cable*
133, no. 50 (December): 30.

McConnell, B. (2004). "Your Money or Your License." *Broadcasting & Cable*
134, no. 8 (September) 1, 48.

Minow, Newton N. 1961. "The "Vast Wasteland." Address to the National Association of Broadcasters, Washington, DC, May.

———. 1991. "How Vast the Wasteland Now?" New York: Gannett Foundation Media Center, Columbia University.

National Association of Broadcasters. 2004. "FCC to Probe TV Violence."
Broadcasting & Cable 134, no. 21 (May), 4.

Potter, W. J. 2003. *The Eleven Myths of Media Violence*. Thousand Oaks, CA: Sage.

Rowland, W. 1983. *The Politics of TV Violence*. Beverly Hills, CA: Sage.

U.S. Senate. 1955. *Comic Books and Juvenile Delinquency: Interim Report*. Washington, DC: Government Printing Office.

———. 1955. *Television and Juvenile Delinquency: Interim Report*. Washington, DC: Government Printing Office.

5

Biographical Sketches

Sandra Ball-Rokeach (1941–)

Sandra Ball-Rokeach was born in Ottawa, Canada, received her B.A. in sociology from the University of Washington in 1963, and continued her studies there for her M.A. and Ph.D. degrees. Dr. Ball-Rokeach has been on the faculty of several universities, including the University of Alberta (Canada), Michigan State University, the University of Western Ontario, and Washington State University. In 1986, Professor Ball-Rokeach joined the faculty of The Annenberg School for Communication at the University of Southern California and is currently professor and director of the Communication Technology and Community Program.

During her career, her research has focused on several issues, all with some relation to mass communication. She takes a sociological perspective in her work, studying media effects, mass media theory, values and belief systems, gender equality, community intercultural issues, and both interpersonal and collective violence. Her chapter on the legitimization of violence (1971) in Short and Wolfgang's *Collective Violence* is particularly relevant and important in her contribution to the study of media violence.

Dr. Ball-Rokeach began her career as an assistant professor at the University of Alberta in Edmonton, Canada, in the fall of 1967. A year later she became codirector of the Mass Media and Violence Task Force for the National Commission on the Causes and Prevention of Violence and remained on the task force from 1968 to 1969. Her work with the task force resulted in the report *Violence and the Media* (Baker and Ball 1969), which sparked considerable public interest and was instrumental in Senator John Pastore securing funding for the Surgeon General's Television and Social Behavior Project. This volume reported the results of the content analysis conducted by Dr. George Gerbner (Annenberg School for Communication, University of Pennsylvania) of prime-time broadcast programs as well as findings from a national survey of people's experience with and beliefs about violence. The convergence of these two sets of results indicated that although television in the late 1960s was considerably more violent than the real world, those survey respondents who preferred violent media content often had more personal experience with violence and endorsed norms that tolerated violence. The conclusion of Baker and Ball-Rokeach was that television can reinforce and legitimize violent beliefs and violent actions.

Dr. Ball-Rokeach made another significant contribution to the study of mass communication in her work with Milton Rokeach on values. An important part of the work was *The Great American Values Test* (Ball-Rokeach, Rokeach, and Grube 1984), a study set in a natural setting, that found television could shape and influence attitudes, values, and behaviors.

Professor Ball-Rokeach has been both a Rockefeller and a Fulbright Fellow. She was the coeditor of *Communication Research* and was on the editorial board of *Public Opinion Quarterly*. She has received numerous research grants from the National Highway Traffic Safety Administration, the California Office of Traffic Safety, the Centers for Disease Control, and the National Institute of Mental Health (NIMH). She has been a member of the board of the McCune Foundation and on the advisory board of the Southern California Injury Prevention Research Center, located at the University of California at Los Angeles.

Albert Bandura (1925–)

Albert Bandura was born in the small town of Mundare, located in northern Alberta, Canada. His early education was completed in an extremely small school that taught both elementary and high school and stressed individual learning. In 1949 he received his bachelor's degree in psychology from the University of British Columbia; he earned his M.A. (1951) and Ph.D. (1952) from the University of Iowa in clinical psychology. In 1953, he joined the faculty at Stanford University. His studies on the modeling of aggressive behavior using the "Bobo" doll paved the way for his book, *Social Learning and Personality Development,* written with Richard H. Walters and published in 1963. In 1977 he published *Social Learning Theory,* which set out his theory of observational learning. In the mid-1980s, he expanded his theory to include a cognitive component (social cognitive theory) and published *Social Foundations of Thought and Action: A Social Cognitive Theory.*

His research most pertinent to television violence includes his early laboratory studies, conducted with Dorothea Ross and Sheila Ross and published in the early 1960s, on the imitation of aggressive behavior from observing models in specifically constructed films. This research, often referred to as the "Bobo doll" studies, illustrated that aggressive behaviors would be imitated by children who observed both adult models and animated models presented on film. This group of studies set the stage for countless studies looking for the connection between watching violent television and or films and subsequent aggressive behavior. This and similar research was the basis for his being one of the seven social scientists who were secretly blackballed and consequently not invited to serve on the Surgeon General's Scientific Advisory Committee on Television and Social Behavior, established in 1969 (Liebert, Sprafkin, and Davidson 1982). His recent writings on his social cognitive theory of mass communication are also instrumental in understanding the relationship between mass-mediated images of violence and people's subsequent behaviors, particularly aggressive behaviors.

Professor Bandura was elected a fellow of the American Psychological Association (APA) in 1964 and was awarded an endowed chair, the David Starr Jordan Professor of Social Science in Psychology, at Stanford in 1974. That year he was also elected president of the American Psychological Association. He has received numerous awards, including the Distinguished Scientific Contributions Award of the American Psychological Association in 1980, and in 1989 he was elected a member of the Institute of Medicine of the National Academy of Sciences. He has been awarded fourteen honorary degrees from numerous universities, including Penn State University, the City University of New York, and the State University of New York at Stony Brook. He has published seven books and more than 100 articles in both academic journals and in the popular press. He has served on the editorial boards of more than thirty academic journals.

Professor Bandura is one of the most well known and respected people who have been involved in the study of media violence.

Leonard Berkowitz (1926–)

Leonard Berkowitz received his doctorate in social psychology in 1951 from the University of Michigan. After completing his doctorate, he joined the U.S. Air Force Human Resources Center in San Antonio, Texas, where his work in social psychology took an applied perspective. In 1955 he joined the faculty at the University of Wisconsin at Madison, where he taught and conducted research in numerous areas until his retirement in 1993. As Vilas Research Professor in Psychology, he has studied both aggression and helping behavior.

His work in aggression and his theoretical perspective, cognitive neoassociationism, has been particularly important in the study of television violence. Specifically, his work has shown that the images of violence seen on television can serve as cues or primes for aggressive behavior. His work has also examined how the media may contribute to prosocial behaviors, attitudes, and emotions. In addition, his work consistently showed concern with how to apply psychological knowledge to both practical matters and social concerns.

Professor Berkowitz, although currently retired, continues to research and write. As he notes on the University of Wisconsin's faculty web page (http://psych.wisc.edu/faculty/bio/berkowitz.html), "Although retired, I am still trying to develop my analysis of the formation, operation, and regulation of emotional states, particularly anger. This formulation holds that particular feelings, ideas, memories, and expressive-motor reactions are linked together associatively in an emotion-state network. The activation of any one of these components through focal attention presumably activates the other components in the same network. In the case of anger, it is presumed that any unpleasant feeling will tend to activate rudimentary anger feelings as well as aggression-related ideas, memories, and expressive-motor reactions, theoretically because of a biologically determined association connecting negative affect with these components."

Professor Berkowitz has been very active in the study of the relationship between media violence and aggressive behavior and served as a consultant to the 1969 National Comission on the Causes and Prevention of Violence, Task Force on Mass Media and Violence. His early research in the 1960s indicating that aggressive behaviors can be stimulated by watching mediated images of aggression, along with his book on aggression published in 1962, led him to be blackballed from the Surgeon General's Scientific Advisory Committee on Television and Social Behavior, which was formed in 1969 (Liebert, Sprafkin, and Davidson 1982).

Berkowitz has written several books, including *Aggression: A Social Psychological Analysis* (1962) and *Aggression: Its Causes, Consequences, and Control* (1993) and over 170 scholarly articles. He is the recipient of the Distinguished Scientist Award given by the American Psychological Association.

Jane D. Brown (1950–)

Jane Brown was born in West Chester, Pennsylvania. She completed her undergraduate education in journalism at the University of Kentucky at Lexington and her graduate work at the University of Wisconsin at Madison's School of Journalism and Mass Communication (M.A., 1974; Ph.D., 1978). After completing a postdoctoral fellowship at the University of Michigan in 1977, Dr. Brown accepted a faculty position in the School of Journalism and Mass Communication at the University of North Carolina at Chapel Hill (UNC-CH). She is still on UNC-CH's faculty and is currently the James L. Knight Professor of Journalism and Mass Communication.

Professor Brown's research has focused on adolescents and the mass media, particularly with regard to health and sexual behaviors. She has published two books related to this topic: *Media, Sex and the Adolescent*, published in 1992 with Bradley Greenberg and Nancy Buerkel-Rothfuss (Hampton Press); and *Sexual Teens, Sexual Media: Investigating Media's Influence on Adolescent Sexuality*, published in 2002 and edited with Jeanne R. Steele and Kim Walsh-Childers. Another key study by Dr. Brown looked at music videos: "The Effects of Race, Gender, and Fandom on Audience Interpretations of Madonna's Music Videos" was published in the *Journal of Communication* in 1990.

Dr. Brown was a member of the consortium that conducted the National Television Violence Study. Her research group at the University of North Carolina at Chapel Hill focused on the evaluation of antiviolence public service announcements (PSAs) and educational programs. Their studies focused on the effects of PSAs on youngsters between ages twelve and nineteen. The UNC-CH group also conducted a content analysis of 100 antiviolence PSAs seen on television during 1994–1995. This study found that many of the PSAs featured a violent act without negative consequences.

The last study completed by Dr. Brown and her colleagues (J. M. Bernhardt and J. R. Sorenson) and published in *Health Education and Behavior* (2001), was titled "When the Perpetrator Gets Killed: Effects of Observing the Death of a Handgun User in a Televised Public Service Announcement." This study, using a sample of adolescents, examined whether PSAs with negative physical consequences such as using handguns were more effective than PSAs that did not depict any physical consequences. They found that PSAs with a resultant death were more effective than those depicting resultant paralysis, which, in turn, were more effective than PSAs that did not show any consequences of violence related to handguns.

Professor Brown is a member of Phi Kappa Phi and the recipient of the Hillier Kriegbaum under-40 Award from the Association for Education in Journalism and Mass Communication (AEJMC) for early career excellence in research, teaching, and service. In 1992 she received the David Brinkley Excellence in Teaching Award and, in 2002, received the University of North Carolina at Chapel Hill Cornelia Spencer Bell Award for outstanding contributions to the university.

Joanne Cantor (1945–)

Joanne Cantor was born in Newport News, Virginia, and grew up in suburban Washington, D.C. She received her B.A. degree from Cornell University in French literature in 1967. She completed her M.A. degree in communication from The Annenberg School for Communication at the University of Pennsylvania in 1971 and her Ph.D. in communication from Indiana University in 1974. She became a member of the faculty at the University of Wisconsin at Madison in 1974 and was awarded tenure in 1978. She served in many administrative capacities at Wisconsin, including director of graduate studies (1979–1980), department chair (1989–1990), and associate dean of the College of Letters and Science (1990–1994). Professor Cantor is currently professor emerita at the University of Wisconsin. She has testified before Congress, appeared on *The Oprah Winfrey Show,* and was featured on ABC's *20/20.*

Professor Cantor has published more than seventy scholarly articles and chapters and several books. The primary focus of her research is the effects of television on children, particularly their emotional reactions to scenes involving violence and other disturbing images. In particular, she has examined the kinds of media images that frighten children of different ages and is now the expert on children's fright reactions to television and other media. Her parenting book, *"Mommy, I'm Scared": How TV and Movies Frighten Children and What We Can Do to Protect Them,* provides parents with information and tactics for dealing with this almost everyday facet of growing up. She has also written a children's picture book, *Teddy's TV Troubles,* that provides ways for parents and children to cope with frightening media messages.

Professor Cantor was a member of the National Television Violence Study (NTVS) research team. In particular, she focused her work on television ratings and advisories. In addition to her work with the NTVS on ratings, she worked, in 1996, with the national Parent-Teacher Association (PTA) to determine what parents wanted from a television rating system. Her finding that parents wanted a ratings system based on program content rather than just age recommendations was instrumental in the addition of the four content ratings (V, S, L, and D) to the age-based ratings that are used with the V-chip. In addition, her studies found that children often had a "forbidden fruit" response to both age-based and content ratings.

Her research has been funded by the National Science Foundation, the National Institute of Mental Health, and the H. F. Guggenheim Foundation. She has received numerous awards. In 1999 she was named a fellow of the International Communication Association, and the University of Wisconsin awarded her the Hilldale Award for distinguished professional accomplishments. She is a consultant to Wisconsin Public Television and worked with the American Medical Association (AMA) in their development of the *Physician's Guide to Media Violence.*

Brandon S. Centerwall (1954–)

Brandon Centerwall was born in Los Angeles, California, and completed his B.S. from Yale University in 1975, his M.D. from the University of California at San Diego in 1979, and a Masters of Public Health from Tulane University in 1980. He was involved in establishing the research program on violence at the Centers for Disease Control in Atlanta, Georgia. He joined the faculty of the University of Washington in the departments of psychiatry and behavioral sciences in 1987 and then moved to the department of epidemiology in 1992. He is currently involved in clinical work and on the staff of the West Seattle Psychiatric Hospital.

Dr. Centerwall made a major contribution to the study of media violence with his groundbreaking study that, taking an epidemiological approach, found a link between increases in white homicide rates and the rising penetration of television in the United States, Canada, and South Africa. His 1989 article in the *American Journal of Epidemiology*, "Exposure to Television as a Cause of Violence," presented this argument, indicating that in all three cultures, homicide rates were static until about ten to fifteen years after the availability of television and then increased considerably. This research was augmented by a 1992 article in the *Journal of the American Medical Association*, "TV and Violence: The Scale of the Problem and Where to Go from Here.

Dr. Centerwall has testified before Congress on numerous occasions, including the 1993 hearings that resulted in the current system of program ratings and the requirement that television sets be equipped with the V-chip. He was awarded the Sandoz Award for Superior Academic Achievement and Contribution to Health Care in 1987.

Peggy Charren (1928–)

Peggy Charren was born in New York City and in 1949 received her B.A. degree from Connecticut College. In the late 1960s she and some of her neighbors in Newtonville, Massachusetts, met several times to discuss their concerns about the lack of quality television programming, its increasing level of commercialism, and the role television was playing in their children's lives. In 1968 she and two neighbors founded Action for Children's Television (ACT), a nonprofit organization. Although they were initially concerned about both the amount of violence and the amount of commercialism in children's programming, the major thrust of their work focused on trying to eliminate or reduce the amount of advertising in children's programming and providing more programming choices. Ms. Charren was responsible for adding concerns about commercialism and programming choice to the late 1960s agenda about the amount of violence on television.

Peggy Charren is also very concerned about censorship. During her years with ACT, she continually supported broadening rather than narrowing television viewing options for children. ACT strongly believed that children and young adolescents would be best served by programming designed especially for them rather than cleaned-up adult TV fare. She did not envision television, including children's programs, censoring ideas and controversial topics but rather believed that television should keep the public informed about all sides of controversial issues, particularly if these ideas were presented in age-specific ways. One of Peggy Charren's most important contributions was to suggest that when television was viewed in moderation and selectively, it could "encourage children to discuss, wonder about, and even read about new things . . . and lead them to ask questions" (Charren and Kim 1982).

Peggy Charren became one of the best known and successful advocates for children and children's television. She has testified numerous times before the Federal Trade Commission (FTC), the Federal Communications Commission (FCC), and Congress. She lobbied ceaselessly to make television better for children. When in the 1980s, deregulation of the television industry and the elimination of the NAB Television Codes led to increases in amount of time and the number of commercials in children's programming, she worked for the passage of the Children's Television Viewing Act. Although the Act was first vetoed by Ronald Reagan, ACT continued its efforts to gain support for this act in Congress, and in 1990 it finally became law. This law placed limits on the time that could be given to commercials in children's programs to 10.5 minutes per hour on weekends and 12 minutes an hour on weekdays. The law also required stations to air a few hours of educational programming for children each week. In 1992, citing the success of this legislation, Peggy Charren disbanded Action for Children's Television.

Peggy Charren has received many awards and accolades. She has been awarded honorary doctorates from numerous universities, including Tufts University, Emerson College, and Wheelock College. She has been awarded the Distinguished Public Information Service Award from the American Academy of Pediatrics, the Helen Homans Gilbert Award from Radcliffe College, a Distinguished Service Award from the Massachusetts Radio and Television Association, the Trustees Award of the National Academy of Television Arts and Sciences, a Peabody Award, and in 1995 a Presidential Medal of Freedom.

George Comstock (1932–)

George Comstock received his B.A. in 1954 from the University of Washington, where he studied journalism and economics. Upon graduation from Washington, he spent three years in the U.S. Air

Force. In 1958 he completed an M.A. in communication at Stanford University, after which he worked as a reporter for the *San Francisco Examiner* and then was the director of a Peace Corps television research project in Bogotá, Colombia. He returned to the academic community and completed his doctorate in communication at Stanford in 1967.

Comstock was a member of the staff and adviser to the Surgeon General's Scientific Advisory Committee on Television and Social Behavior between 1969 and 1972 and helped prepare the summary volume, *Television and Growing Up: The Impact of Televised Violence* (1972). In 1972 he moved to the Rand Corporation (Santa Monica, CA), where he was a senior social psychologist and the senior author of four books summarizing the research generated by the Television and Social Behavior Project. In 1977 he joined the faculty of the S. I. Newhouse School of Public Communications at Syracuse University and was named an S. I. Newhouse Professor in 1979. He continues to teach, conduct research, and write about television.

Comstock has made many notable contributions to the study of media violence. In particular, his work at the Rand Corporation (*Television and Human Behavior: The Key Studies*, 1975) was important because it made the research on this complex topic available to a wide range of people, including activists (such as Peggy Charren with Action for Children's Television) working to petition the FCC and FTC, professors, and students. In addition, the handbook of television research, *Television and Human Behavior*, that Comstock wrote with Steven Chaffee, Natan Katzman, Maxwell McCombs, and Donald Roberts in 1978 was named one of the twentieth century's best books in communication by *Journalism and Mass Communication Quarterly*.

During his long career, Comstock has been particularly interested in the role of the media in the socialization of children. His publications in the 1990s include *Television: What's On, Who's Watching, and What It Means* (1999; coauthored with Erica Scharrer) and *Television and the American Child* (1991). His more recent work includes several chapters reexamining issues related to television violence and aggression, as well as two meta-analyses of this large body of research.

Cultural Indicators Research Team

The Cultural Indicators Project is the longest continuous study of television content and its effects. Cultural Indicators began with the theoretical writings of George Gerbner and his "institutional approach" to mass communication, which was incorporated in the Cultural Indicators paradigm that Gerbner first wrote about in the mid-1960s. This paradigm says that a full understanding of mass communication can only come with knowledge about three areas: the institutions of mass communication, mass communication content, and media effects. Each of these areas has its own framework for study: institutional process analysis, message system (content) analysis, and cultivation analysis. Two early writings of George Gerbner are especially relevant to this approach: "An Institutional Approach to Mass Communications Research," published in 1966 in *Communication: Theory and Research*, edited by Lee Thayer (Charles C. Thomas); and an article that first appeared in 1969 in *AV Communication Review*, "Toward 'Cultural Indicators': The Analysis of Mass Mediated Message Systems."

The Cultural Indicators Project team consisted of faculty, students, and professional/research staff at The Annenberg School for Communication at the University of Pennsylvania. The earliest members of this group, Michael F. Eleey (M.A., The Annenberg School of Communication, 1966; M.B.A., the Wharton School,) and Nancy Signorielli (Ph.D. the University of Pennsylvania, 1975) became involved in the project with the awarding of a contract to George Gerbner to analyze the content of television programs, with a focus on television violence, for the National Commission on the Causes and Prevention of Violence (1968). Their involvement continued through the period of funding provided by the Surgeon General's Television and Social Behavior Project (1969–1972), followed by funding provided by the National Institute of Mental Health. Eleey and Signorielli were then joined by Professor Larry Gross (B. A., Brandeis University, 1964; Ph.D. Columbia University, 1967; currently dean at The Annenberg School for Communication at the University of Southern California), Suzanne Jeffries-Fox (Ph.D., University of Pennsylvania, 1979); and Marilyn Jackson-Beeck (Ph.D., University of Pennsylvania, 1979). When Eleey, Jeffries-Fox, and Jackson-Beeck embarked on different endeavors, Michael Morgan (Ph.D., University of Pennsylvania, 1980) joined the team. The most recent addition to the CI research group is James Shanahan (Ph.D., University of Massachusetts, 1991).

Although the CI research team is no longer housed under the same roof, the research tradition continues in the research of Signorielli, Morgan, and Shanahan and their students. Nancy Signorielli (professor of communication, University of Delaware) continues the study of prime-time broadcast television content. The continuation of the CI approach, examining programming during the 1990s and at the beginning of the twenty-first century, can be seen in a 2003 publication in the *Journal of Broadcasting and Electronic Media*, "Prime-Time Violence, 1993–2001: Has the Picture Really Changed?" and a 2004 publication in the *Journal of Broadcasting and Electronic Media*, "Aging on Television: Messages Relating to Gender, Race, and Occupation in Prime-Time." The work of Jim Shanahan (professor of communication, Cornell University) and Michael Morgan (chair and professor of communication, the University of Massachusetts at Amherst) is best seen in their book, *Television and Its Viewers: Cultivation Theory and Research* (1999, Cambridge University Press). In addition, Shanahan has applied cultivation theory to health-related issues, as seen in an article (written with Dietram Scheufele, Fang Yang, and Sonia Hizi), "Cultivation and Spiral of Silence Effects: The Case of Smoking," *Mass Communication and Society* (2004, 7: 413–428). The most recent description of cultivation theory by the team appears in the chapter by George Gerbner, Larry Gross, Michael Morgan, Nancy Signorielli, and James Shanahan (2002), "Growing Up with Television: Cultivation Processes," in *Media Effects: Advances in Theory and Research*, edited by Jennings Bryant and Dolf Zillmann (Lawrence Erlbaum Associates).

Leonard Eron (1920–)

Leonard Eron was born in New Jersey, completed his undergraduate studies in 1941, and served in the U.S. Army during World War II, until his discharge in 1945. He completed an M.A. degree from Columbia University in 1946 and his doctorate in psychology from the University of Wisconsin in 1949. His academic career has spanned many decades. He retired from the University of Illinois at Chicago and was named professor emeritus in 1989 and then joined the faculty at the University of Michigan until his retirement in 2003.

For almost fifty years, Professor Eron's research has focused on how children learn to be aggressive. He has received numerous grants, and his studies have included controlled laboratory experiments as well as large-scale longitudinal field investigations. One of the most important and well-known longitudinal studies is the

Columbia County New York Study, which began in 1960 and followed 856 boys from age eight. Follow-up studies were completed when the boys were nineteen and thirty years old, and Eron recently completed a forty-year follow-up in collaboration with Rowell Huesmann.

Professor Eron has testified before Congress on numerous occasions. In 1992, he told Congress that television violence has an effect on boys and girls of all ages, at all intelligence levels, and at all socioeconomic levels. Moreover, these effects are not just limited to children who are already likely to be aggressive and are not just found in the United States.

Professor Eron has made several important contributions to the study of television violence. One is that aggression is a learned behavior. Another is the findings from the longitudinal studies he has conducted, including a comparative study of aggression and television viewing in five countries (the United States, Finland, Poland, Australia, and Israel). His last, but certainly not least contribution was his participation in a recent longitudinal study focused on youngsters growing up in the 1970s and 1980s. All these studies clearly indicate that watching violence at early ages is related to later aggressive behavior.

Eron's research on the development of violence and aggression in children has spanned more than four decades. He has written nine books and published more than 100 journal articles on the topic. His most important publications include the 1986 book written with Rowell Huesmann, *Television and the Aggressive Child: A Cross-National Comparison* (Lawrence Erlbaum Associates); his chapter, "Theories of Aggression: From Drives to Cognitions" in Huesmann's 1994 edited book; and several articles in the *American Psychologist*, including a 1987 piece, "The Development of Aggressive Behavior from the Perspective of a Developing Behaviorism," that maps out the theoretical developments that have guided his longitudinal research.

Professor Eron has received numerous awards. He was given a Lifetime Achievement Award from Psychology in the Public Interest in 1995, a Distinguished Professional Contribution to Knowledge award by the American Psychological Association in 1980, and a Lifetime Contribution to Media Psychology Award by the American Psychological Association in 2003. He has served on numerous commissions and boards relating to children and violence; he currently serves on the board of directors for the National Foundation to Improve Television.

Seymour Feshbach (1925–)

Seymour Feshbach was born in New York City, began his undergraduate studies at the City College of New York in 1941, joined the U.S. Army in the summer of 1943, and served in World War II as an infantry lieutenant until he was discharged in the summer of 1946. He graduated from the City College of New York in 1947. He did his graduate work in psychology at Yale University, receiving his M.A. in 1948 and Ph.D. in 1951. During the Korean War, he was recalled to active duty as an infantry officer and served until fall 1952. Upon his discharge, he joined the faculty at the University of Pennsylvania and remained at Penn until 1963. After spending a year at the University of Colorado, Professor Feshbach joined the psychology department at the University of California at Los Angeles (UCLA). Although he formally retired in 1995, he continues as a recall professor, teaching whenever possible. In 1947 he married Norma Deitch (who also established an academic research career).

Dr. Feshbach is currently professor emeritus in the Department of Psychology at UCLA. He has served in numerous capacities at UCLA, including department chair and chair of the university's Academic Senate. He has been very active in the American Psychological Association, serving as a representative of Division 9 (Society for the Psychological Study of Social Issues) from 1980 to 1982, and he was elected a fellow of Division 7 (Developmental Psychology). He served as president of and was elected a fellow of the Western Psychological Association. He also served as president of the International Society for Research on Aggression in 1986. He has received numerous awards, including the Townsend Harris Medal, Distinguished Alumnus Award (City College of New York), and the Maurice and Fay Karpf Peace Prize.

Active in the ongoing study of television and media violence since the 1960s, Dr. Feshbach is perhaps best known for formulating the catharsis hypothesis. First described in an article in the *Journal of Abnormal and Social Psychology* in 1955, this theory suggests that watching violence may reduce aggression. Feshbach's best-known publication, "Television and Aggression" (written with Robert Singer and published in 1971) provides empirical support for this theory. His contribution to the 1972 surgeon general's report *Television and Social Behavior*, titled "Reality and Fantasy in Filmed Violence (Murray, Rubinstein, and Comstock, eds., Vol. 2) is also particularly noteworthy. His most seminal publication is

"The Function of Aggression and the Regulation of Aggressive Drive," which appeared in *Psychological Review* in 1964. His most recent work has focused on the antecedents and consequences of patriotism and nationalism, particularly in relation to dovish and hawkish policies.

Jib Fowles

Jib Fowles, currently retired, was professor of communication at the University of Houston at Clear Lake. He has written several books about the media, including *Why Viewers Watch* (1992, Sage), *Advertising and Popular Culture* (1996, Sage), and *The Case for Television Violence* (1999, Sage). He has also published several articles in both scholarly journals and the popular press, including *Atlantic Monthly, Advertising Age,* the *Chronicle of Higher Education,* the *New York Times,* and *TV Guide.*

Professor Fowles is one of the few who believes that television violence is not a negative force in society. In 1984 he was a witness at a U.S. Senate hearing on television violence and presented a rare dissenting voice, testifying that children often use the brutal fantasies they see on television for therapeutic purposes. As he notes in the preface to his book, *The Case For Television Violence,* he believes that "the controversy regarding television violence reflects festering wounds within American culture" and that it "can offer a vantage point on certain struggles—cultural, social and mental— buried in our way of life" (p. x).

Jonathan L. Freedman

Jonathan Freedman received his bachelor's degree from Harvard University in 1958 and Ph.D. from Yale University in 1961. He began his academic career at Stanford University in the Psychology Department. He was at Stanford from 1961 to 1968, achieving the rank of associate professor. He joined the faculty at Columbia University in 1969 as professor in the Department of Psychology and then joined the faculty of the University of Toronto in 1980 as professor of Psychology and as chair of the Department, continuing as chair until 1985. He is currently professor emeritus of psychology and the interim vice dean of graduate education and research, faculty of arts and sciences.

Professor Freedman is another in a select group of scholars who supports the idea that there is no relation between media violence and subsequent aggression. As he notes in the description of his 2002 book, *Media Violence and Its Effect on Aggression: Assessing the Scientific Evidence* (University of Toronto Press): "The scientific evidence does not support the notion that TV and film violence cause aggression in children or in anyone else." He comes to this conclusion by noting that "much of the research on media violence is seriously flawed" (Amazon.com). Professor Freedman has written several articles espousing this position. In 1988, "Television Violence and Aggression: What the Evidence Shows" appeared in *Applied Social Psychology Annual*, in 1994 *Hoffstra Law Review* published "Viewing Violence Does Not Make People More Aggressive," and in 1996 "Violence in the Mass Media and Violence in Society: The Link is Unproven" appeared in the *Harvard Mental Health Letter.*

George Gerbner (1919–)

George Gerbner was born in Hungary and emigrated to the United States in 1939, fleeing fascism and avoiding conscription into the Hungarian army on the side of the Nazis. He became a U.S. citizen and enlisted in the Office of Strategic Services (OSS) and the 101st Airborne Division. During World War II, he parachuted into Eastern Europe, behind enemy lines, where he fought against the Germans for six months. He was awarded a Bronze Star.

After earning a journalism degree from the University of California at Berkeley, Dr. Gerbner worked as a writer and journalist at the *San Francisco Chronicle.* He returned to the academic world and was awarded an M.A. degree in 1951 and his doctorate in 1955 from the University of Southern California. His dissertation, "Toward a General Theory of Communication," was named "best dissertation" that year. In 1956 he joined the faculty at the Institute for Communication Research at the University of Illinois, where his work focused on theory building and research on media content and media institutions.

In 1964 Dr. Gerbner became professor of communication and dean of The Annenberg School for Communication at the University of Pennsylvania, forging what came to be considered one of the country's best graduate programs in communication. In 1968 he was awarded the only study funded as part of the National Commission on the Causes and Prevention of Violence to analyze the content of television programs. This research was later funded by the Surgeon General's Scientific Advisory Committee on Television and Social Behavior and the National Institute of Mental Health. This marked the beginning of the Cultural Indicators project, the longest continuously running research on television in the world. Professor Gerbner served as dean of The Annenberg School until 1989, when he was named Bell Atlantic Professor of Telecommunications in the Department of Broadcasting, Telecommunications, and Mass Media at Temple University in Philadelphia. In 1990 he founded and became president of the Cultural Environment Movement, a global coalition of organizations and activists devoted to changing media practices and policies. He served as the executive editor of the *Journal of Communication* for many years.

Professor Gerbner is perhaps best known for his development of cultivation theory, a perspective based on the idea that we live in a world created by the stories we tell and the importance of the media in creating the stories that form the basis of our culture. He defines and isolates three basic types of stories: how things *work* (fiction that shows us the dynamics of life), how things *are* (news that tells us about the goals and values of society), and what to *do* (sermons, instruction, and more recently commercials) that traditionally were seen in legends, art, fairytales, politics and today appear in the stories told on and by television (Morgan 2002). Cultivation theory is not a linear model but rather a process, typically focusing upon the commonality in what people think about or know. Moreover, the study of cultivation takes a different approach than many other studies of media effects. Specifically, in the research that studies cultivation, or what television contributes to viewer's conceptions of the world, people are not asked what they think about television but what they think in general (Morgan 2002).

The violence profiles were an important part of the Cultural Indicators project for more than thirty years and have provided a continuous and consistent monitoring of violence and other recurrent aspects of the symbolic environment, such as images relating to gender roles, aging, and race. Professor Gerbner's research typically encompasses some element or issues of public policy. This focus is easily seen in the years of research on violence in which violence is examined as a demonstration of power, specifically looking at the demographic profile of who gets hurt and who does the hurting and focusing upon its long-term consequences. Regarding violence, Gerbner has said, "There may have been more violent periods than the present, although I am not sure of that, but I'm sure that there has never been an era when every home was drenched with violent imagery. It is mass-produced, happily sanitized, violent imagery with which our children grow up" (Lent 2002, 31). Professor Gerbner often testifies before Congress, using the violence profiles to provide evidence that there was very little change from one television season to the next in terms of the amount of violence.

Professor Gerbner's most important writings relating to television violence include his 1969 article in *AV Communication Review*, "Toward 'Cultural Indicators': The Analysis of Mass Mediated Message Systems"; and the 1976 *Journal of Communication* article (written with Larry Gross), "Living with Television: The Violence Profile." The many different facets of cultivation theory are seen in *Cultivation Analysis: New Directions of Media Effects Research* (edited by Signorielli and Morgan, 1990) and in *Television and Its Viewers: Cultivation Theory and Research* (edited by Shanahan and Morgan, 1999).

Rowell Huesmann (1943–)

Rowell Huesmann completed his undergraduate education in psychology and mathematics at the University of Michigan in 1964, his M.S. degree in psychology from the Carnegie Institute of Technology in 1967, and his doctorate in systems and communications psychology in 1969 from Carnegie-Mellon University. Since 1969, he has been on the faculty at Yale University, the University of Illinois at Chicago, and the University of Michigan. Since 1992 he has been professor of communication studies and psychology, senior research scientist, and director of the Aggression Research Program at the Institute for Social Research at the University of Michigan.

Dr. Huesmann has played a critical role in uncovering the effects of media violence on aggressive behavior. His research has spanned thirty-five years and is characterized by solid methods and state-of-the-art statistical analyses. His research has consistently been funded by numerous agencies such as the National Institute of Mental Health. He is best known for two longitudinal studies that were conducted with Leonard Eron: the Columbia County, New York, study that followed a sample of boys from the time they were eight years old until they were forty years old and a cross-national study in which media violence and aggressive behavior were studied in samples from five countries (the United States, Finland, Poland, Israel, and Australia). These studies and numerous other studies with a wide range of samples of participants, show that children who watch a considerable amount of violent television as they are growing up tend to become more aggressive adults.

Dr. Huesmann has published three books and more than 130 articles, most of which look at the relationships between violent media and aggression. His best known and most important publications include an article in the *American Psychologist* (1972), "Does Television Violence Cause Aggression?"; his book (with Leonard Eron), *Television and the Aggressive Child: A Cross-National Comparison* (1986, Lawrence Erlbaum Associates); and a recent article in *Developmental Psychology* (2003), "Longitudinal Relations between Childhood Exposure to Media Violence and Adult Aggression." Equally important is his script theory, which provides a solid theoretical explanation for the relationship between television viewing and aggressive behavior. This theory is illustrated in the 1987 article in the *Journal of Social Issues* entitled "Psychological Processes Promoting the Relation between Exposure to Media Violence and Aggressive Behavior by the Viewer."

Professor Huesmann has served as editor, associate editor, and consulting editor for several academic journals. After fifteen years as an associate editor, he was appointed editor of *Aggressive Behavior* (the official journal of the International Society for Research on Aggression) in 2004. He was associate editor of the *Journal of Abnormal Psychology* from 1977 to 1980 and has served as a consulting editor on a number of other journals, including *Aggression and Violent Behavior*. In 1986, he was the guest editor for an issue of the *Journal of Social Issues* focusing on media violence and antisocial behavior, and in 1988, he edited a special issue of *Aggressive Behavior* on alternative theoretical perspectives on aggression.

Dr. Huesmann has headed and served on numerous important committees on violence and aggression. In 2000–2001, he was appointed chair of the Surgeon General's Committee on Media Violence, and in 1999–2000, he was a member of the National Institutes of Health (NIH) Task Force on New Directions in Violence Research. He served as president of the International Society for Research on Aggression in 1997–1998 and as chair of the American Psychological Association's Human Capital Initiative on Violence from 1994 to 1997. He was recently named a member of the MacArthur Network on Middle Childhood. He has served in many leadership roles as part of his academic appointments, including being a member of the executive committee and the director of graduate studies of the Department of Communication Studies at the University of Michigan.

Professor Huesmann has received numerous awards, including several Excellence in Research awards from the University of Michigan. He was named LIFE Faculty Lecturer at the Max Planck Institute in Berlin and was elected a life fellow of Clare Hall College of Cambridge University. He has recently been nominated to receive an APA Lifetime Contribution to Media Psychology award. He has testified on numerous occasions before Congress, beginning in 1972 before Senator Pastore's hearings on the Surgeon General's Report by the Scientific Advisory Committee on Television and Social Behavior. He has often spoken on National Public Radio about media violence and throughout his illustrious career had made substantial contributions to the numerous American Psychological Association initiatives on media violence and its effects.

Dale Kunkel (1954–)

Dale Kunkel was born in Southern California. He received his B.A. in communication studies from the University of California at Los Angeles in 1977, as well as an M.A. in 1982 and a Ph.D. in 1984 from The Annenberg School of Communication at the University of Southern California in the area of communication theory and research. In 1984–1985, he was awarded a Congressional Science Fellowship from the Society for Research in Child Development, serving as an adviser on children and media. He taught at Indiana University (1989–1991) and at the University of California at Santa Barbara (UCSB) (1991–2004). From 2002 until mid-2004, he was the director of the UCSB's Washington Program, located in Washington, DC. He is currently professor of communication at the University of Arizona.

Professor Kunkel was one of the principal investigators of the National Television Violence Study, working on the content analysis conducted at the University of California at Santa Barbara from 1994 until 1997. He has also conducted several projects for the Kaiser Family Foundation. One of these projects was an extensive examination of the accuracy of the television ratings generated to use with the V-chip. This study found that although the age-based ratings were generally accurate, content-based ratings were typically not applied to all of the programs that would warrant such ratings.

Dr. Kunkel has testified before Congress on numerous occasions. His 1999 testimony before the U.S. Senate Committee on Commerce, Science, and Transportation (Chair, Senator John McCain) focused on his findings from both the NTVS and Kaiser Family Foundation studies in regard to proposed legislation, the Children's Protection from Violent Programming Act, which mandated a "safe harbor" approach to regulating television violence. In his most recent congressional testimony for hearings on Neurobiological Research and the Impact of Media in front of the U.S. Senate Subcommittee on Science, Technology, and Space of the Committee on Commerce, Science, and Transportation (April 10, 2003), Kunkel noted the need for a program of research to explore existing differences in depictions of violent behavior, particularly as they may relate to brain-mapping research. He has also testified before the Federal Communications Commission and the U.S. House of Representatives.

Dr. Kunkel is an expert in the study of telecommunications policy, particularly media policy as it relates to children. Many of his publications reflect this perspective, including a chapter, "The Road to the V-Chip: Media Violence and Public Policy," that appeared in *Media Violence and Children: A Complete Guide for Parents and Professionals,* edited by Douglas A. Gentile (Westport, CT: Praeger, 2003); and a 2003 piece in the *Journal of Applied Developmental Psychology,* "The Truest Metric for Evaluating the Children's Television Act." Professor Kunkel has also conducted research relating to children's advertising as seen in his chapter, with Mary McIlrath, "Message Content in Advertising to Children," in *Faces of Televisual Media: Teaching, Violence, Selling to Children,* edited by Edward L. Palmer and Brian M. Young (Lawrence Erlbaum Associates, 2003). It is one of the many areas in which he has made a sizable contribution to the study of and understanding of media violence.

Kunkel has received numerous grants to conduct his research, including funding from the Kaiser Family Foundation. Most recently he received a grant, with Rebecca Collins of the RAND Corporation, from the National Institute of Child Health and Human Development to study "TV Viewing and Adolescents' Sexual Attitudes and Behavior." Dr. Kunkel's advice is also sought from numerous groups. He has served on the scientific review board for media-related research funded by the National Institutes of Health and is on the editorial board of several journals, including the *Journal of Broadcasting & and Electronic Media,* the *Journal of Communication,* and *Communication Law and Policy.*

Edward J. (Ed) Markey (1946–)

Ed Markey (D-MA) was born in Malden, Massachusetts, and received his B.A. degree from Boston College in 1968 and his J.D. from Boston College Law School in 1972. He served in the U.S. Army Reserves from 1968 to 1973. He was elected to the Massachusetts House of Representatives in 1972, serving until 1976. In 1976 he was elected to the U.S. House of Representatives and continues to serve in that capacity. His district includes a wide mix of constituencies, including both blue-collar workers and those living in the high-tech suburbs of Boston. He is the highest ranking Democrat on the House Subcommittee on Telecommunications and the Internet. Markey is the third most senior Democrat on the Energy and Commerce Committee. In the 108th Congress, he was appointed to the Select Committee on Homeland Security.

Representative Markey is a champion of the conservation of environmental resources, health reform, and consumer rights. He also seeks to eliminate large monopolies. He has continually received high marks for his legislative record. A number of organizations, including the Children's Defense Fund, the National Education Association, the Conservation Law Foundation, the Consumer Federation of America, and Taxpayers for Common Sense, consistently rate him a "legislative hero."

Markey is one of the few congressmen who has been consistently concerned about media, particularly television violence. As a member of several committees related to telecommunications, he is in a good position to try to further this agenda. Along with Senator Paul Simon (who died in 2003), Markey sponsored numerous congressional hearings. He worked in support of the late Senator Paul Simon's bill, eventually passed in 1990 as the Television Violence Act, that gave the networks immunity from antitrust laws so they could meet to discuss and implement ways to reduce the amount of violence on television. In the spring of 1993, when it was obvious that the networks were making little progress in reaching accords on how to reduce television violence, Markey and Simon sponsored a series of congressional hearings. The end result of these hearings was the eventual mandating of the V-chip in newly manufactured television sets (which became law as part of the Telecommunications Act of 1996) and the implementation of the television rating system that is now in place. In 1994, Markey provided support for Senator Simon's strong suggestion that the broadcast and cable networks sponsor independent monitoring programs. Two programs were funded based on this initiative—the National Television Violence Study (funded by the cable networks) and the UCLA Television Violence Monitoring Study (funded by the broadcast networks). Senator Markey can be counted on as a successful and tireless proponent of making television better for children.

John Murray (1943–)

John P. Murray was born in Cleveland, Ohio. He received his B.A. degree in 1965 from John Carroll University, majoring in psychology with a minor in sociology. He attended Catholic University in Washington, D.C., for his M.A. (1967) and his Ph.D. (1970) in developmental psychology. Professor Murray also completed postdoctoral studies in pediatric psychology at the University of North Carolina Medical School at Chapel Hill in 1973.

Currently, Murray is a professor and the director of the School of Family Studies and Human Services at Kansas State University. He has been involved in the study of media violence for more than thirty years, serving as research coordinator for the Surgeon General's Scientific Advisory Committee on Television and Social Behavior during the late 1960s and early 1970s. He was one of the principals who wrote and coordinated the first surgeon general's report on television, which was released in 1972.

Murray also taught in the School of Behavioural Sciences at Macquarie University in Sydney, conducting research on the effects of the introduction of television into the Australian outback. In addition to his current position at Kansas State University, he has had appointments at the University of Michigan and the Boys Town Centre for the Study of Youth Development.

Professor Murray's most important publications include "Television and Violence: Implications of the Surgeon General's Research Program," which was published in *American Psychologist* in 1973; Volume 2 (*Television and Social Behavior*) of *Television and Social Learning,* compiled with Eli Rubinstein and George Comstock and published in 1972 by the U.S. Government Printing Office; and a piece in the *Journal of Communication,* written in 1978 with Susan Kippax, entitled "Children's Social Behavior in Three Towns with Differing Television Experience."

Murray's most important contributions to the study of media violence include his work from 1969 to 1972 as research coordinator for the Surgeon General's Scientific Advisory Committee on

Television and Social Behavior; his study of the introduction of television into a rural town in the Australian outback; and his most recent work on brain mapping of television violence viewing in children, his current research at Harvard University Medical School and Boston Children's Hospital. This research has found that watching television violence may activate those areas of the brain involved in arousal and attention; it was published in *Psychiatric Times* as "TV Violence and Brain Mapping in Children" in 2001.

Professor Murray is a fellow of the American Psychological Association and served as president of its Division of Child Youth and Family Services. Dr. Murray has published ten books and more than eighty articles on children and television, including a 1980 reference book, *Television and Youth: Twenty-five Years of Research and Controversy;* the 1992 American Psychological Association Report *Big World, Small Screen: The Role of Television in American Society;* and most recently, *Television and Children: Fifty Years of Research,* an edited volume (with Norma Pecora and Ellen Wartella) published by Lawrence Erlbaum Associates in 2004.

National Television Violence Study Consortium

The National Television Violence Study was a three-year effort that assessed violence on television from 1994–1995 until 1996–1997. It was funded by the National Cable Television Association and began in June 1994. The group included media scholars from four universities (the University of California at Santa Barbara [UCSB], University of Texas at Austin, University of Wisconsin at Madison, and the University of North Carolina at Chapel Hill), representatives from national policy organizations who formed an oversight council, and project administrators (Dr. Joel Federman of the Center for Communication and Social Policy at UCSB) and coordinators (NTVS 1997). In addition, during the first year of the project, the entire endeavor was administered by MediaScope under the direction of Marcy Kelly (president).

Each of the universities played a unique role in the study. Each focused on a different aspect of television violence. This short description of the project and its personnel will focus on the project directors and major contributors to the research. Moreover, several of those involved with the NTVS have been selected for individual entries in this chapter of biographies.

The largest and perhaps best-known research of the NTVS was the content analysis conducted at the University of California at Santa Barbara. This content analysis made a unique contribution to the knowledge about violent content on television because of its sampling procedures and because it examined in detail the context of violence seen in these programs. The study examined physical violence in three yearly samples (1994–1995, 1995–1996, and 1996–1997) of composite weeks of programming across twenty-three channels operating between 6:00 AM and 11:00 PM each day. The sample (N=8,200) included broadcast (commercial networks, independent stations, and public television) and cable channels (basic and premium, HBO). The program genres included television series, daytime programs, movies, specials, children's programs, and music videos. In short, all genres except game shows, religious programs, "infomercials" or home shopping channels, sports, instructional programs, and news were included. Moreover, the coding schemes (variables) included in this study were grounded in previous research and theory. Overall, the data set generated by the group at UCSB was extremely extensive and rich in detail. The primary researchers at UCSB were Dr. Barbara J. Wilson, Dr. Dale Kunkel, Dr. Dan Linz, Dr. W. James Potter, Dr. Edward Donnerstein, Dr. Stacy L. Smith, and Dr. Don Roberts, as well as a number of graduate students. In addition to writing the final reports published by Sage, this group has generated numerous journal articles isolating different elements of the portrayal of violence (please look for entries by these authors in the annotated bibliographies).

The University of Texas (UT) at Austin conducted a similar content analysis of reality programs in each of the three years of the study. These programs were defined as nonfictional programs that presented current or historical events or circumstances in a realistic context (i.e., as it actually happened, either a real-time tape of the event or a realistic enactment). The sample did not include regularly scheduled local or national news programs. The programs included were tabloid news shows, police shows, interview and talk shows, and documentaries. The nonfictional reality programs were pulled from the larger sample analyzed at UCSB. There were 393 programs in the 1994–1995 sample, 494 in the 1995–1996 sample, and 526 in the 1996–1997 sample. The primary researchers for the UT study were Dr. Charles Whitney, Dr. Ellen Wartella, Dr. Dominic Lasorsa, and Dr. Wayne Danielson, as well as several graduate students.

The University of Wisconsin (UW) at Madison's contribution to the NTVS was to examine the role of violence ratings and advisories, looking specifically at how the ratings affected parents' and children's viewing decisions. In the first year of the study, the Wisconsin team looked at what ratings and advisories were available and conducted an experiment, using a sample of children in Madison, Wisconsin, to determine how children and their parents and/or other adults perceived and understood, as well as used, the ratings and advisories (NTVS 1997). In the second year of the study, the Wisconsin team expanded their experimental framework to a sample of youngsters in Milwaukee, a more ethnically diverse population (NTVS 1998). Finally in the third year of the study, the team conducted a content analysis of programs that were tagged with the newly implemented TV parental guidelines. The sample focused on the age-based ratings that were implemented on January 1, 1997, and then on the content-based ratings that were implemented on October 1, 1997. The researchers responsible for the UW portion of the study were Dr. Joanne Cantor, Dr. Kristen Harrison, and Dr. Amy Nathanson, as well as graduate students at the University of Wisconsin.

The team assembled at the University of North Carolina at Chapel Hill studied the effectiveness of antiviolence public service announcements and educational programs that were produced by the television industry. During the first year of the study, this team conducted seven separate studies to systematically test the effectiveness of fifteen antiviolence PSAs, using interviews and focus group methods. During the second year of the study, this group looked at PSAs in terms of the target audience and conducted a content analysis of 100 antiviolence PSAs that were aired in 1994 or 1995 to isolate the types of messages seen in these announcements (NTVS 1998). Finally, during the third year of the study, the group used a sample of adolescents to examine whether PSAs that showed the negative physical consequences of using handguns were more effective than PSAs that did not show the negative consequences (NTVS 1998). The UNC-CH researchers included Dr. Jane Brown and Dr. Frank Biocca and several of their students.

John O. Pastore (1907–2000)

Senator John O. Pastore (D-RI), the son of Italian immigrants, was born in Providence, Rhode Island, and became one of the most respected senators from Rhode Island. He rose from very humble beginnings, starting work even before graduating from high school.

He began his postsecondary education by attending night classes at the Young Men's Christian Association (YMCA) in Providence that were sponsored by Boston's Northeastern University. By 1931, he had received his law degree and begun a private law practice.

Pastore began his career in politics in 1934, when he was elected to the Rhode Island General Assembly for two terms. He was Rhode Island's assistant attorney general in 1937–1938 and in 1940–1944. He was elected lieutenant governor in 1944 and in 1945 became governor. Pastore was reelected and served as governor until he won a seat in the Senate in 1950. He was the first American of Italian descent to be elected to the U.S. Senate. In his twenty-five years in the Senate, he worked for passage of the first nuclear test ban treaty and headed committees dealing with atomic energy and TV regulation. He retired from the Senate in 1976.

Pastore became interested in the topic of media violence in the late 1960s and became one of the most outspoken critics of media violence. He was responsible for persuading Congress to appropriate $1 million dollars in 1969 for the surgeon general's study on television and social behavior. In 1972 he worked for additional funding for television-related research from the National Institute of Mental Health and requested the establishment of an annual violence index that could map and publish the degree of violence on television on a yearly basis in order to keep this topic in the public arena and on the public agenda. The field of communication and the study of media violence were furthered through his efforts to secure funding for research.

W. James Potter

W. James (Jim) Potter received his B.A. in 1971 from Pacific Lutheran University, an M.S. in mass communication studies in 1973 from Clarion State University, and doctorates in instructional research in 1979 from Indiana University and in communication theory in 1981 from Florida State University. He has been on the faculty of several universities, including Western Michigan University, Florida State University, Indiana University, Stanford University, and UCLA. From 1991 to 1994, while on the faculty of Indiana University, he served as editor of the *Journal of Broadcasting & Electronic Media*. Since 2001 he has been a professor in the Department of Communication at the University of California at Santa Barbara.

Professor Potter has written several books relating to media violence and media literacy and is currently editing an encyclopedia of media violence to be published by Sage Publications. His books, *On Media Violence* (1999) and *The 11 Myths of Media Violence* (2003), provide a comprehensive and readable overview of the area. *The 11 Myths of Media Violence,* in particular, takes an innovative look at a complex subject by focusing upon eleven misunderstandings that undermine people's understanding of the complexity of media violence as well as examining the issue from a public policy perspective. His book, *Media Literacy* (2001) is a user-friendly guidebook to understanding the media and how they operate. In addition, Professor Potter has published more than forty scholarly publications in referred journals and contributed fifteen chapters in edited books.

Professor Potter was one of the principal investigators of the National Television Violence Study funded by the National Cable Television Association. In the acknowledgments for his book, *On Media Violence,* he describes this collaboration as "the most intense, mind-expanding, maddening, rewarding, frustrating, and exhilarating experience" of his entire career (1999, vii).

Professor Potter has made a solid contribution to the understanding of media violence through his collaboration with the NTVS, his research on the importance of context to understanding the impact of media messages on viewers, and particularly his books, which challenge readers to think about and/or think differently about media violence in all its nuances.

Eli A. Rubinstein (1919–)

Eli Rubinstein was born in New York City and received his B.S. degree from City College of New York in 1939 and his M.A. (1948) and Ph.D. (1951) from Catholic University in Washington, D.C. As most of the young men of his generation he served with the armed forces during World War II. Dr. Rubinstein joined the faculty as professor of psychiatry at the State University of New York (SUNY) at Stony Brook in 1971. Upon retirement from SUNY–Stony Brook, Dr. Rubinstein became a visiting professor at the School of Journalism and Mass Communication at the University of North Carolina at Chapel Hill.

In 1969 Dr. Rubinstein, the assistant director for behavioral sciences at the National Institute for Mental Health, was tapped to oversee the surgeon general's study "Television and Social Behavior." He began his task by having to work with an advisory committee, selected by the surgeon general, that was thought to be biased because the television industry secretly blackballed seven social scientists who were being considered for committee membership. Nevertheless, Dr. Rubinstein oversaw the selection of research studies that would be funded as part of this project and, almost three years later, worked with the committee and his administrative colleagues, John Murray and George Comstock, to prepare a unanimous report that was submitted in time to meet the December 31, 1971, deadline for submission. The report, *Television and Growing Up: The Impact of Televised Violence*, consisted of a lengthy summary volume and five volumes of the technical reports submitted by each researcher. The report, unfortunately, was extremely complex and ambiguous because it sought to satisfy the different constituencies on the advisory committee (Liebert, Sprafkin, and Davidson 1982).

While at SUNY–Stony Brook, Dr. Rubinstein continued his interest in mass media-related studies. He conducted, with Joyce Sprafkin and Theresa Silverman, one of the first studies focusing on sexual behaviors on television, "Physical Contact and Sexual Behavior on Prime-Time TV (*Journal of Communication,* 1979) and was a member of the 1986 American Psychological Association Task Force whose review of the literature on television and society resulted in the book, *Big World, Small Screen* (University of Nebraska Press, 1992). He has also served on the editorial board of the *Journal of Communication.*

Paul Simon (1928–2003)

Senator Paul Simon (D-IL) was born in Eugene, Oregon, and attended Blair College and the University of Oregon. Between 1951 and 1953, he served in the U.S. Army as a special agent along the Iron Curtain in Europe in the Counter-Intelligence Corps. He began his political career when he was elected to the Illinois House of Representatives in 1954 and was elected to the Illinois Senate in 1962. In 1968 he was elected lieutenant governor of Illinois, the first time the governor and lieutenant governor of Illinois were not in the same political party. He used his term as lieutenant governor to become the people's ombudsman and worked to make government better for its citizens. He was elected to the U.S. House of Representatives in 1974 and spent ten years serving the 22nd and 24th Congressional Districts. He was elected to the U.S. Senate in 1984 and sought to be the Democratic nominee for president in 1988. In 1990 he was reelected to the U.S. Senate. He retired from the Senate in 1997 and joined the faculty at Southern Illinois University (SIU) in Carbondale, teaching classes in journalism, political science, and history. He founded the Public Policy Institute at SIU, looking to find new ways to solve old problems. Senator Simon died on December 9, 2003.

Senator Simon was an extremely proficient and hard-working senator, known for providing exceptional service to his constituents. His office typically handled more cases than any other office. He held more town meetings (over 600) than any other Illinois senator. He was unusual in that he made his (and his wife's) financial records public for more than forty years.

Throughout his political career, Senator Simon received numerous awards, beginning with each of his years in the Illinois Congress, when he received the "Best Legislator Award" from the Independent Voters of Illinois. He was awarded fifty-five honorary degrees. He was also a prolific writer, writing twenty-two books, only four of which were coauthored.

Senator Simon was a very active legislator. He was particularly involved in enacting laws relating to job training and education. Among the legislation he wrote and/or sponsored were the School-to-Work Opportunities Act, the Job Training Partnership Act amendments, and the National Literacy Act. His concern about children can also be seen in his sponsorship of the Missing Children Act and subsequent legislation that established the National Center for Missing and Exploited Children. He also was the primary Democrat sponsor of the balanced budget amendment (Odle 2003).

Senator Simon played a particularly important role in the ongoing work related to media violence, particularly television violence, hoping to reduce the amount of violence on television. In the late 1980s, he introduced legislation to Congress asking that the networks be granted immunity from antitrust laws so they could work together to develop ways to reduce the amount of violence on television. This legislation was finally passed in 1989 and signed into law in 1990 as the Television Violence Act (also known as the Television Improvement Act), providing immunity to the networks for three years. In the spring of 1993, when it was obvious that the networks were making little progress in reaching accords on how to reduce television violence, he sponsored (along with Representative Edward Markey, D-MA) a series of congressional hearings. The result of these hearings was the eventual mandating of the V-chip in newly manufactured television sets (which became law as part of the Telecommunications Act of 1996) and the television rating systems that are now in place. He also provided the impetus for the broadcast and cable networks to sponsor independent monitoring programs in 1994: the National Television Violence Study (funded by the cable networks) and the UCLA Television Violence Monitoring Study (funded by the broadcast networks). Senator Simon was, in short, one of the most successful and tireless proponents of making television better for children by trying to set the wheels in motion that would reduce the amount of violence in television programming.

Dorothy Singer (1927–)

Dorothy G. Singer was born in New York City and received her B.A. from Hunter College, her M.A. from New York University, and her Ed.D. from Columbia University. She is a senior research scientist in the Department of Psychology at Yale University and since 1976 has been codirector (with her husband, Dr. Jerome Singer) of the Yale University Family Television Research and Consultation Center. In addition she is a senior research associate at the Yale Child Study Center. She is a fellow of the American Psychology Association and on the board of directors of Division 46, the Media Division of APA. Her research interests include early childhood development, the effects of television on youth, and parent training.

Dr. Singer has been principal investigator of research projects funded by numerous agencies, including the National Science Foundation, the Spencer Foundation, Johnson & Johnson Baby Products, the William T. Grant Foundation, the Mellon Foundation, the Smith Richardson Foundation, the John D. and Catherine MacArthur Foundation, the National Institute of Early Childhood Education and others. She has authored over 150 publications and written nineteen books, some of which have been translated into Dutch, Italian, and Japanese.

Currently, Dr. Singer is involved in a parent training project that teaches parents to play with their preschoolers as a means of enhancing cognitive and social skills. In addition, she consults with parent groups, television industry executives, and government agencies concerning television and education. She is on the board of Weston Woods Institute, the Letter People, and the International Play Panel for LEGO and consults for Learning Curve International. As a developmental psychologist, she is involved in writing and developing teacher-training materials for day care centers and for parents. Another facet of her work focuses on media literacy and educating children to be critical users of television. She has coauthored curricula for grades K-12 concerning the media. She was on the advisory board of CBS to help select children's television programs. She has consulted for the Stepping Stones Museum in Norwalk, Connecticut, and the Lemelson Center at the Smithsonian.

Dorothy Singer has made substantial contributions to the understanding of media violence. With her husband, Dr. Jerome Singer, she conducted the first longitudinal field study of preschoolers' television viewing and subsequent aggressive behavior in school and at home. For more than thirty years, the Singers have continued to do related work examining the positive and negative effects of television on young people. They were also pioneers in the development of critical viewing skills curricula for school-aged children. They prepared the report to Congress from the Corporation for Public Broadcasting that led to the establishment of the "Ready to Learn" series of daily programming on PBS.

Among the many publications of Dorothy and Jerome Singer, the following are considered their most outstanding contributions in relation to media violence: their 1981 books, *Television, Imagination and Aggression: A Study of Preschoolers* (Lawrence Erlbaum Associates) and *Teaching Television: How to Use Television to your Child's Advantage* (with Diane Zuckerman, Dial Press); their 1986 publication in the *Journal of Social Issues* ("Family Experiences and Television Viewing as Predictors of Children's Imagination, Restlessness, and Aggression"); and the chapter they published in 1998, "Barney and Friends as Entertainment and Education: Evaluating the Quality and Effectiveness of a Television Series for Preschool Children," in *Research Paradigms in the Study of Television and Social Behavior*, edited by Joyce Asamen and Gordon Berry (Sage). Finally, their 2001 *Handbook of Children and the Media* (Sage) has become necessary reading for those interested in children and media.

Dorothy Singer has received numerous awards, including the Distinguished Contribution to the Science of Psychology Award by the Connecticut Psychology Association in 1997 and the award for Distinguished Scientific Contributions to the Media by Division 46 of the American Psychological Association in 2004.

Jerome L. Singer (1924–)

Jerome L. Singer was born in New York City, received his B.A. degree from the City College of New York, an M.S. from Yale University, and his doctorate in clinical psychology from the University of Pennsylvania in 1950. He is professor emeritus of psychology at Yale University, where he served for many years as director of the Graduate Program in Clinical Psychology and also as director of Graduate Studies in Psychology. Dr. Singer continues as co-director, with his wife, Dr. Dorothy G. Singer, of the Yale University Family Television Research and Consultation Center. He is a specialist in research on the psychology of imagination and daydreaming. He is a fellow of the American Psychological Association, the American Association for the Advancement of Science, and the New York Academy of Sciences. He has been president of the Eastern Psychological Association, president of the Division of Personality and Social Psychology of the American Psychological Association, chair of the Board of Scientific Affairs of the American Psychological Association, and president of the Division of Psychology of the Arts of APA. Professor Singer has served as principal investigator for many federal and private foundation grants.

Dr. Singer was senior consultant to the Open Laboratory on Conscious and Unconscious Mental Processes supported by the MacArthur Foundation at the University of California's Langley Porter Psychiatric Institute in San Francisco. He is currently coeditor of the journal *Imagination, Cognition, and Personality.* He is on the board of directors of Playing for Keeps, a nonprofit organization that promotes constructive play. He has received numerous awards, the most recent being the Scroll of Honor from the Yale Science and Engineering Society in 2004.

Jerome Singer has made substantial contributions to the understanding of media violence. With his wife, Dr. Dorothy Singer, he conducted the first longitudinal field study of preschoolers' television viewing and subsequent aggressive behavior in school and at home. For more than thirty years, the Singers have examined the positive and negative effects of television on young people. They were pioneers in the development of critical viewing skills curricula for school-aged children and prepared the report to Congress that led to the establishment of the "Ready to Learn" series of daily programming on PBS.

Dr. Jerome Singer has authored more than 250 technical articles on thought processes, imagery, personality, and psychotherapy, as well as on children's play and the effects of television and has written or coedited more than fifteen books. Among the many publications by Dorothy and Jerome Singer, the following are considered their most outstanding contributions in relation to media violence: their 1981 books, *Television, Imagination and Aggression: A Study of Preschoolers* (Lawrence Erlbaum Associates) and *Teaching Television: How to Use Television to your Child's Advantage* (with Diane Zuckerman; Dial Press); their 1986 publication in the *Journal of Social Issues* ("Family Experiences and Television Viewing as Predictors of Children's Imagination, Restlessness, and Aggression"); and the chapter they published in 1998, "Barney and Friends as Entertainment and Education: Evaluating the Quality and Effectiveness of a Television Series for Preschool Children," in *Research Paradigms in the Study of Television and Social Behavior,* edited by Joyce Asamen and Gordon Berry (Sage). Finally, their 2001 *Handbook of Children and the Media* (Sage) has become necessary reading for those interested in children and media.

Victor C. Strasburger, M.D. (1949–)

Victor Strasburger, born in Baltimore, Maryland, is a summa cum laude graduate of Yale College and a member of Phi Beta Kappa. He graduated from Harvard Medical School and completed his residency in pediatrics at Children's Hospital in Seattle, Children's Hospital in Boston, and Paddington Green Children's Hospital in London. In addition, he completed a fellowship in adolescent medicine at Harvard Medical School. Dr. Strasburger is the chief of the Division of Adolescent Medicine, a professor of pediatrics, and a professor of family and community medicine at the University of New Mexico School of Medicine.

Dr. Strasburger has written eight books and more than 120 papers and articles on the topic of adolescent medicine, particularly the effects of television on children and adolescents. His most popular book, *Getting Your Kids to Say No in the 1990s When You Said Yes in the 1960s* (1993, Simon and Schuster), looks at the dilemmas many parents face in raising their children. His textbook, *Children, Adolescents, and the Media,* written with Barbara Wilson, Ph.D. (2002, Sage), has become a bestseller in courses on children, adolescents, and media while also providing parents and educators an opportunity to learn more about the complexities of this topic. Another important publication relating to children and media is the special issue of *Adolescent Medicine: State of the Art Reviews* (coedited with George Comstock, Ph.D., and published in 1993), which brought together articles from experts in the field "to help medically oriented practitioners separate fact from controversy" (ix). Strasburger's article in this issue, "Children, Adolescents, and the Media: Five Crucial Issues," clearly shows how media use is the most important and modifiable influence on adolescents and children. Other important publications include his 1995 book, *Adolescents and the Media: Medical and Psychological Impact* (Sage), and a 2004 article in *Current Problems in Pediatric and Adolescent Health Care*, "Children, Adolescents, and the Media."

Dr. Strasburger has been very active in the American Academy of Pediatrics (AAP), serving as the chair of the Section on Adolescent Health and a member of the Committee on Communications. Beginning in 1983, he has played a crucial role in mobilizing AAP to act on this issue in order to try to educate both pediatricians and parents. He has also worked with the American Medical Association and the National PTA on issues relating to children and the media. He has appeared on *The Today Show, The Oprah Winfrey Show,* and *CBS This Morning,* taking this message to a nonacademic audience.

He has received numerous awards throughout his career. In 2000, he was the recipient of the Adele Delenbaugh Hofmann Award (American Academy of Pediatrics) for outstanding lifetime achievement in adolescent medicine and the first person to receive the Holroyd-Sherry Award for media advocacy work.

Elizabeth Thoman (1943–)

Elizabeth Thoman received her B. A. in English from Marycrest College (Iowa) and an M.A. in communications management from The Annenberg School for Communication at the University of Southern California in 1978. In 1964 she became a member of the Sisters of the Humility of Mary in Davenport, Iowa, a Catholic religious order that works for educational empowerment and justice for adults and children. Ms. Thoman is the founder of the Center for Media and Values, now the Center for Media Literacy, one of the most important organizations in working toward increasing media literacy both in the home and in the schools.

As one of the founders of the media literacy movement in the United States, Ms. Thoman has made a unique and important contribution to the field of mass communication. She was the founding editor and publisher of *Media and Values,* a quarterly magazine that was published by the Center for Media and Values. Over a sixteen-year period, sixty-three issues of this periodical covered just about every major issue in the contemporary mass communication world. Some of the more significant issues were "Redesigning Women" (no. 49, Fall 1989), "Impact of Images" (no. 57, Winter

1992), and on violence, "Militarism in the Media" (no. 39, Summer 1987) and "Media and Violence" (nos. 62–63, Summer–Fall 1993). In addition, the Center for Media Literacy produces a Media Literacy Workshop Kit designed for parent and/or religious groups as well as for teachers. These kits provide a "startup" curriculum and ideas for helping children and their parents become more media-literate. Last, but certainly not least, the center has both produced and distributed a number of educational videos (see Chapters 7 and 8 in this volume).

Ms. Thoman was responsible for bringing the media literacy movement in the United States beyond a mere understanding of media to looking at the media from a social change approach. That approach makes the study and practice of media literacy in the United States unique. In particular, her approach to understanding media violence fosters greater public awareness of this issue.

Jack Valenti (1921–)

Jack Valenti was born in Houston, Texas, and graduated from Sam Houston High School in 1936, when he was only fifteen years old. Upon his graduation, he became an office boy with the Humble Oil and Refining Company (now Exxon) and soon joined their advertising department. He received his B.A. degree from the University of Houston in 1946 (studying at night and working during the day) and an M.B.A. from Harvard University in 1948. During World War II (1942–1945), he was a pilot with the Army Air Corp, where as the pilot-commander of a B-25 attack bomber, he flew fifty-one combat missions with the 12th Division, U.S. Air Force in Italy. He was awarded numerous medals, including the Distinguished Flying Cross. In 1952 he opened an advertising/political consulting agency, Weekly and Valenti.

In 1955, Valenti met U.S. Senator Lyndon B. Johnson. As a result of that contact, Valenti's agency was in charge of press relations and part of the motorcade during President John F. Kennedy's fateful trip to Dallas in November 1963. Mr. Valenti was immediately hired by President Johnson as a special assistant and was on Air Force One on the ride back to Washington, D.C.

In 1966 Valenti resigned his Washington position to become president and chief executive of the Motion Picture Association of America (MPAA), the third person to serve in that capacity. During his tenure as head of the MPAA, Valenti has been a top Washington lobbyist on behalf of Hollywood's motion picture studios.

He has played an important role in designing, defining, and implementing the rating systems that are currently in use for motion pictures and television programs. The film-rating system was designed in conjunction with the National Association of Theater Owners, as well as the Screen Actors Guild, the Directors Guild of America, the Writers Guild of America and numerous religious, public policy, and child advocacy organizations. The TV-rating system, which is similar to the film ratings, was designed using a similar model of cooperation. Mr. Valenti is a fierce critic of government censorship and has worked diligently in support of laws to force the implementation of antipiracy technology by consumer electronics vendors. He is particularly adamant about the need for copyright laws to protect the industry.

Mr. Valenti has written four books, three of which are nonfiction, *The Bitter Taste of Glory* (World Publishing, 1971); *A Very Human President* (W. W. Norton, 1976); *Speak Up with Confidence: How to Prepare, Learn and Deliver an Effective Speech* (William Morrow, 1982). His latest book, a political novel, *Protect and Defend* (Doubleday) was published in 1992. In addition, he has written numerous essays for many newspapers and magazines, including the *Washington Post*, the *New York Times*, the *Los Angeles Times, Atlantic Monthly*, and *Reader's Digest*. Interestingly, Mr. Valenti is one of the few in people in public life who actually writes his own speeches.

Mr. Valenti has received numerous awards. He was awarded the Legion d'Honneur (the French Legion of Honor) by the French government. In 1993 he was awarded the ShowEast Lifetime Achievement award. Last, but certainly not least, he was awarded his own star on the Hollywood Walk of Fame and life membership in the Directors Guild of America. In 2004, after thirty-eight years of service, he announced his resignation as president and chief executive officer of the Motion Picture Association of America.

Ellen Wartella (1949–)

Ellen Wartella was born in Wilkes-Barre, Pennsylvania, and did her undergraduate work at the University of Pittsburgh, graduating in 1971 (cum laude). She completed her Ph.D. on the effects of television on children in 1977 at the University of Minnesota. She began her academic career at Ohio State University (1976–1979) and then joined the faculty at the Institute for Communication Research at the University of Illinois at Champaign-Urbana (1979–1993). She also completed NIMH-sponsored postdoctoral studies in developmental psychology at the University of Kansas during the 1980–1981 academic year and was a fellow at the Gannett Center for Media Studies at Columbia University during the 1985–1986 academic year. She was dean of the College of Communication, the Walter Cronkite Regents Chair in Communication, and the Mrs. Mary Gibbs Jones Centennial Chair in Communication at the University of Texas at Austin from 1993 through spring of 2004. On July 1, 2004, Dr. Wartella was appointed as the Executive Vice Chancellor and Provost of the University of California, Riverside.

Beginning in graduate school, Dr. Wartella's primary research focus has been children and television. She takes a developmental perspective and most recently has been a pioneer in the application of activity theory, an approach that melds social and cultural issues (environmental factors) along with the traditional developmental perspective. Her early work focused on children and advertising, and she has testified several times on the subject before the Federal Trade Commission. Ellen Wartella is a well-respected spokesperson and advocate for children's media interests.

Dr. Wartella was one of the key investigators of the National Television Violence Study, heading up the portion of the project completed at the University of Texas at Austin. This part of the study encompassed the development of contextual code and the actual coding of violence in reality programs.

Dr. Wartella has written several books and published numerous articles. Her research has typically focused on several different perspectives relating to children and the media, including a historical piece in the *Journal of Communication* (written with Byron Reeves, 1985), "Historical Trends in Research on Children and the Media: 1900–1960"; and a chapter on public policy in Philip Gaunt's 1993 book, *Beyond Agendas: New Directions in Communication Research*, "Communication Research on Children and Public Policy." She has also contributed to the literature about media violence. A 2003 journal article she wrote with several other scholars in communication and psychology, "The Influence of Media Violence on Youth" (*Psychological Science in the Public Interest*) discusses how there is unequivocal evidence that, in both immediate and long-term contexts, media violence increases children's likelihood of exhibiting aggressive and violent behavior.

Dr. Wartella has made numerous contributions in the public service arena. She is a member of several boards, including the National Academies of Sciences Board on Children. She was chair of the Hogg Foundation for Mental Health and a member of the board of Sesame Workshop (formerly the Children's Television Workshop), the Council of Better Business Bureaus, the Children's Advertising Review Unit, and the Center for Media Education. She has received numerous awards, including being named a fellow of the International Communication Association.

References

Baker, Robert K., and Sandra Ball. 1969. *Violence and the Media.* Washington, DC: U.S. Government Printing Office.

Ball-Rokeach, Sandra J. 1971. "The Legitimization of Violence." In J. F. Short and M. E. Wolfgang, eds., *Collective Violence.* Chicago: Aldine.

Ball-Rokeach, Sandra J., Milton Rokeach, and Joel W. Grube. 1984. *The Great American Values Test: Influencing Behavior and Belief through Television.* New York: Free Press.

Charren, Peggy, and Kim Hays. 1982. "Changing Television: Why the Right Does it Wrong. In Herbert F. Vetter, ed., *Speaking Out Against the New Right.* Boston, MA: Beacon. See also http://www.harvardsquarelibrary.org/speakout/charren.html.

Lent, John A. 2002. "Interview with George Gerbner." In Michael Morgan, ed., *Against the Mainstream: The Selected Works of George Gerbner,* pp. 21–36. New York: Peter Lang.

Liebert, Robert M., Joyce N. Sprafkin, and Emily S. Davidson. 1982. *The Early Window: Effects of Television on Children and Youth.* New York: Pergamon.

Morgan, Michael. 2002. "On George Gerbner's Contributions to Communication Theory, Research, and Social Action." In Michael Morgan, ed., *Against the Mainstream: The Selected Works of George Gerbner,* pp. 1–20. New York: Peter Lang.

Odle, Linda. 2003. Paul Simon's biography. http://www.siu.edu/~ppi/psbio.htm.

National Television Violence Study. 1998. Edited by the Center for Communication and Social Policy. University of California, Santa Barbara. Thousand Oaks, CA: Sage.

National Television Violence Study. 1997. Thousand Oaks, CA: Sage.

Potter, W. James. 1999. *On Media Violence.* Thousand Oaks, CA: Sage.

Shanahan, James, and Michael Morgan. 1999. *Television and Its Viewers: Cultivation Theory, and Research.* London: Cambridge University Press.

Shanahan, James, Dietram Scheufele, Fang Yang, and Sonia Hizi. 2004.

"Cultivation and Spiral of Silence Effects: The Case of Smoking." *Mass Communication and Society* 7: 413–428.

Signorielli, Nancy. 1996. *Women in Communication: A Bibliographic Sourcebook.* Westport, CT: Greenwood.

Signorielli, Nancy, and Michael Morgan, eds. 1990. *Cultivation Analysis: New Directions in Media Effects Research.* Newbury Park, CA: Sage.

6

Facts and Figures

This chapter provides facts and figures relating to media violence. It consists of a number of tables presenting data about the portrayal of violence on television. The data in these tables come from two sources: the Cultural Indicators project data banks and the report of the third year of the National Television Violence Study (1998).

The chapter begins with an update of some of the analyses traditionally conducted as part of the Cultural Indicators project. Tables 1–9 present Indicators of Violence and the Violence Index from data collected in five different decades (from 1967 to 2003) of research. Tables 10–18 give information about the characters involved in violence. The demographic analysis shows who is more likely to get hurt/killed or to hurt/kill others. This analysis looks at differences among men, women, whites, and people of color in regard to their chances or likelihood of being involved in violence.

The last set of tables (Tables 19–23) reproduce some key findings of the National Television Violence Study. One table looks at differences in the portrayal of violence between programs telecast during the prime-time hours (8 to 11 PM) and other times of the day or evening. It makes this comparison for broadcast television channels, as well as basic and premium cable channels. Other tables from the NTVS look at data about the portrayal of violence that is designated as "high risk" for both young children and adolescents. These tables compare different genres of programs seen during different times during the day, as well as the programs telecast on different types of channels.

Each set of tables is preceded by a discussion of the information presented in the tables. It briefly tells how the data in the tables

135

were collected in each of the two represented projects and gives a short description of what the tables tell us about television violence.

Update of Cultural Indicators Project Analyses

The first set of tables updates the typical analyses conducted and published as the Violence Profile of the Cultural Indicators project. These tables list several key overall measures of violence that are combined to form the Violence Index (see, for example, Gerbner et al. 1978). The last Violence Profile was prepared and distributed in 1993 (see, Gerbner, Morgan, and Signorielli 1993). The data used in this analysis span almost forty years, from 1967 to 2003, and come from two sources. The first source for the data was the Cultural Indicators project (1967 to 1992) when it was located at the Annenberg School for Communication at the University of Pennsylvania. These data were generated with funding provided by numerous agencies and grants, including the National Commission on the Causes and Prevention of Violence, the Surgeon General's Television and Social Behavior program, the National Institute of Mental Health, the American Medical Association, and other agencies. I am indebted to George Gerbner and the rest of my colleagues with whom I worked on the Cultural Indicators project for making this data set available for my continued research. The second source data were collected at the University of Delaware between 1993 and 2003. These data were collected as part of ongoing class research projects, and I wish to thank my numerous students for their help in this process. Although the data were generated at two different venues, they are comparable because the University of Delaware data collection procedures replicated the definitions and methods originally developed and used in the Cultural Indicators project at the University of Pennsylvania.

Background Information on the Violence Profile and Violence Index

The Violence Index looks at violence as a social relationship—it considers who does the hurting or killing and who, in turn, gets hurt or killed. In this perspective, the violence we see on television may be seen as symbolic in nature and is typically used to demonstrate power. It shows who can get away with what against whom. The measures included in the Violence Profile are based on a definition of violence that focuses on reliable and consistent observations of physical violence: hurting or killing or the plausible threat of being hurt or killed.[1] The data do not include idle threats ("I'm going to get you someday"), verbal abuse, or gestures (e.g., shaking a fist at someone) that do not actually result in hurting and/or killing or actually threaten characters. Violence, if it meets the criteria of actual or real threats of physical violence, is included, whether it takes place in a realistic/serious context or a fantasy/humorous context. Comic or humorous violence is included because several studies have shown that humor and fantasy may be simple and effective ways to convey serious lessons (see, for example, Ellis and Sekyra 1972; Haynes 1978). Humor, in fact, may be the sugar coating that makes the violence more acceptable or enjoyable than other, more serious presentations of violence. "Accidental" violence (car crashes) or "acts of nature"(tornadoes, hurricanes, earthquakes) are also included because television violence is created or written/edited into a script. As such, it is always purposefully included and always claims victims, thus demonstrating power. Even some of the more recently telecast "reality" programs may include real violence that is purposely selected and edited by the producers or directors (gatekeepers) of the program and thus also tells a story of victimization.

The data are collected using the methods of a research procedure called content analysis. The first step in this procedure is to define the units or elements of analysis that will form the basis of the data collection. In this study, three separate units or elements of analysis are isolated and included. First, the analysis looks at the entire program; second, it looks at the leading characters in the programs; and third, it isolates specific violent actions or episodes (scenes of violence confined to the same characters). All of the measures or variables included in the analysis are clearly defined and the data generated using them are tested for reliability and consistency. Each measure included in the Violence Index and in the other analyses meets the standards for reliability that are judged to be acceptable in content analysis procedures (see, for example, Krippendorff 1980).

The data are gathered in the analysis of annual week-long samples of prime-time network broadcast programs. The samples were taken every fall (in late September and early October) between 1967 and 2003. The data gathered between 1967 and 1992 were generated at the University of Pennsylvania, and the more recent data, those gathered between 1993 and 2003, were generated at the University of Delaware. Programs were not sampled during sweeps months (November or February) because these programs are have been specially selected by the networks to generate larger audiences. In 1993 the samples were expanded to include three additional types or genres of programs—reality programs; award, game, and variety programs; and news magazine programs. Consequently, the tables for these types of programs only include data for two different decades. Overall, there are 37 separate samples with a total of 2,836 programs and 10,294 leading characters.

The Violence Index looks at several different sets of observations and variables that are combined into a single indicator that measures and is sensitive to several different ways to isolate and look at violence within the programs. It consists of three sets of observations, called Prevalence, Rate, and Roles.

Prevalence: the percentage of programs that contain any violence (%P).

Rate: the rate of violent actions within the programs, calculated in two ways—the average number of violent actions per program (R/P) and the average number of violent actions per hour of programming (R/H). The rates are doubled in the calculation of the Violence Index because their absolute size is small compared to the measure of the prevalence of violence.

Roles: the percentage of leading characters who are involved in violence (%V)—including those who commit violence (hurt or kill others), those who are victimized (are hurt or killed), or both. The percent of those who are involved in killing is added to the index two times because of the significance of killing and the story about victimization that killing tells.

These observations are combined into a summary figure, the Violence Index

$$(VI = \%P + 2(R/P) + 2(R/H) + \%V + \%K)$$

This index is sensitive to a wide and varied range of the many characteristics of television programs. In each sample, the individual measures included in the Violence Index have achieved high levels of intercoder reliability (consistency). Moreover, the index was subjected to a special analysis in the early 1980s and found to meet the statistical and empirical requirements one would expect from an index: unidimensionality (measuring one thing) and internal consistency or homogeneity (see, Signorielli, Gross, and Morgan 1982). The Violence Index can be used to make comparisons over time (across decades) and among different genres of programs (situation comedies, action adventures, reality, newsmagazines, etc.) or time of broadcast (early evening vs. late evening). This section is made up of nine separate tables, one for each separate analysis of the different types of programs found in network broadcast television's prime-time hours as well as tables that compare early evening and late evening programs.

Table 1: All programs

Table 2: Situation comedies

Table 3: Action adventure and crime

Table 4: Dramas (e.g., *ER*)

Table 5: Reality (e.g., *Cops*)

Table 6: Award, Game, Variety

Table 7: Newsmagazines (e.g., *60 Minutes, Dateline*)

Table 8: Early evening programs (broadcast between 7 PM and 9 PM)

Table 9: Late evening programs (broadcast between 9 PM and 11 PM)

In addition to the measures used to calculate the Violence Index, the tables include a measure of the percentage of programs that have violence that is a significant or major element or part of the plot or story line. This percentage provides yet another way to examine the amount of violence on prime time since the 1960s by eliminating those programs in which violence is not a particularly significant or important element of the story and concentrating on programs in which violence plays a critical role. The Violence Index, however, is calculated using the same formulation (percent of programs that have any violence) set out and used in the original reports of the Cultural Indicators project.

Trends in the Portrayal of Violence

The level of violence in prime-time network broadcast programs (see Table 1) has dropped since the late 1960s, when this program of research began. The percent of programs with violence was highest during the late 1960s and during the 1980s; it was lowest during the first four years of the twenty-first century (2000 to 2003). The percentage of programs with violence that is significant to the story shows a similar pattern, except for the slight rise in the samples gathered between 2000 and 2003, in which 37 percent of the programs have violence that is important for the story. The rates per program and per hour show some fluctuation by decade. Interestingly, the rate per program (R/P) in the most recent samples of programs is at one of the highest levels it has ever been (4.81 acts of violence per program); similarly, the rate per hour (R/H) was at its second highest level during the early 2000s (5.24 acts of violence per hour). Nevertheless, the average rate of violent actions per program did not change so much from decade to decade that the differences were statistically significant.[2] What has changed most dramatically, however, is the percentage of characters who are involved in violence. Involvement has decreased considerably since the 1960s. In the 1960s through the 1980s, roughly half of all the leading characters had some involvement in violence—they were either hurt/killed themselves or hurt/killed other people. Since the 1980s, however, the percentage of involvement has decreased to a third or fewer of the characters hurting/killing others or being hurt/killed themselves. These differences are statistically significant; the statistical analysis shows that percentages of characters involved in violence in the 1990s and 2000s are substantially different from those for the 1960s, the 1970s, and the 1980s.[3] Overall, the differences in the Violence Index primarily reflect the trends in character's involvement, with the index being at its lowest level in the most recent samples of programs.

Situation comedies (Table 2), as we would expect, have the least amount of violence, the smallest Violence Indices, the fewest programs with violence that is a significant part of the story, and the smallest percentage of characters who are involved in violence. Again, there are no differences from decade to decade for the rate of violence actions per program, but there are significant differences in the percentage of characters involved in violence. Again, percentages of involvement in the most recent samples (2000s) are statistically smaller than the percentages for the other decades.[4]

Table 1. Measures of Violence:
All Programs, Prime Time (1967–2003)

	1960s	1970s	1980s	1990s	2000s	Total
Samples (100%)						
Number of Programs	185	625	689	883	454	2,836
Number of Leading Characters	558	1,985	2,060	3,543	2,148	10,294
Number of Hours of Programming	163.75	585.83	600.45	728.27	411.63	2,489.9
Prevalence (%)						
Programs with Violence (%P)	73.5	70.7	72.3	64.2	60.4	67.6
Violence Significant to Plot	50.8	50.9	47.5	31.8	37.2	41.9
Rate						
Number of Violent Acts	781	3,043	3,325	3,727	2,184	13,060
Rate per Program (R/P)	4.22	4.87	4.83	4.22	4.81	4.61
Rate per Hour (R/H)	5.19	5.54	5.11	5.31	5.24	4.77
Roles						
Percent of Leading Characters						
Involved in Violence (%V)	59.0	53.7	52.5	33.5	29.9	41.8
Involved in Killing (%K)	13.8	12.1	9.0	6.2	7.6	8.6
Violence Index	165.12	157.32	153.68	122.96	118.00	136.76

Table 2. Measures of Violence:
Situation Comedies, Prime Time (1967–2003)

	1960s	1970s	1980s	1990s	2000s	Total
Samples (100%)						
Number of Programs	70	240	261	413	149	1,133
Number of Leading Characters	194	639	623	1,511	628	3,595
Number of Hours of Programming	35.5	124.0	132.0	208.5	79.5	579.5
Prevalence (%)						
Programs with Violence (%P)	44.3	42.1	41.8	46.0	40.9	43.4
Violence Significant to Plot	12.9	13.8	10.0	6.3	5.4	9.0
Rate						
Number of Violent Acts	102	326	331	588	201	1,548
Rate per Program (R/P)	1.46	1.36	1.27	1.42	1.35	1.37
Rate per Hour (R/H)	2.87	2.63	2.51	2.82	2.53	2.67
Roles						
Percent of Leading Characters						
Involved in Violence (%V)	30.4	26.1	28.1	23.6	18.9	24.4
Involved in Killing (%K)	1.5	0.0	0.5	0.3	0.8	0.4
Violence Index	84.86	76.18	77.96	79.38	68.36	76.28

Table 3. Measures of Violence:
Action-Adventure Programs, Prime Time (1967–2003)

	1960s	1970s	1980s	1990s	2000s	Total
Samples (100%)						
Number of Programs	85	275	235	172	87	854
Number of Leading Characters	273	972	756	714	413	3,128
Number of Hours of Programming	93.25	328.90	262.80	199.40	98.00	983.00
Prevalence (%)						
Programs with Violence (%P)	97.6	96.0	98.3	94.8	93.1	96.3
Violence Significant to Plot	88.2	87.6	91.1	74.4	86.2	85.8
Rate						
Number of Violent Acts	598	2,259	2,239	1,733	1,057	7,886
Rate per Program (R/P)	7.04	8.21	9.53	10.08	12.15	9.23
Rate per Hour (R/H)	6.41	6.87	8.52	8.69	10.72	8.02
Roles						
Percent of Leading Characters						
Involved in Violence (%V)	82.8	76.0	82.4	64.6	61.5	73.6
Involved in Killing (%K)	26.0	21.8	19.6	18.2	25.2	21.3
Violence Index	233.30	223.96	236.40	215.14	225.54	225.70

Table 4. Measures of Violence:
Dramas, Prime Time (1967–2003)

	1960s	1970s	1980s	1990s	2000s	Total
Samples (100%)						
Programs	30	110	193	174	111	618
Number of Leading Characters	91	374	681	877	576	2,599
Number of Hours of Programming	35.00	132.90	205.60	208.00	131.50	713.00
Prevalence (%)						
Programs with Violence (%P)	73.3	70.0	81.9	74.7	75.7	76.2
Violence Significant to Plot	33.3	40.0	45.1	40.8	45.0	42.4
Rate						
Number of Violent Acts	81	458	755	576	492	2,362
Rate per Program (R/P)	2.70	4.16	3.91	3.31	4.43	3.82
Rate per Hour (R/H)	2.31	3.45	3.67	2.77	3.74	3.31
Roles						
Percent of Leading Characters						
Involved in Violence (%V)	48.4	42.8	41.6	32.6	32.6	37.0
Involved in Killing (%K)	3.3	7.8	5.1	6.3	7.8	6.4
Violence Index	135.02	135.82	143.76	125.76	132.44	133.86

However, action-adventure and crime programs (Table 3) have the largest Violence Indices and the highest proportion of programs with violence, particularly violence that is a significant element of the plot. Interestingly, the rates of violent actions per program and per hour are higher in the samples from the 1990s and from the first few years of the twenty-first century. Moreover, the differences in the rate per program for programs from 2000 to 2003 are statistically different from the rate per program for the 1960s and the 1970s.[5] Yet fewer characters were involved in violence during the 1990s and the 2000s than in the preceding three decades. Dramas (Table 4), which include programs such as *ER*, have a moderate amount of violence. Throughout the period since the 1960s, about three-quarters of these programs had some violence, and about four in ten had violence that was a significant part of the plot. The rates of violence, however, were not particularly high—about three or four acts of violence per program and per hour of programming—and the differences were not statistically significant. At the same time, characters' involvement in violence was significantly lower during the 1990s and the 2000s.[6] Interestingly, the percentage of characters' involvement in killing has increased from the 1980s; between 2000 and 2003 the percent of characters involved in killing (7.8 percent) was the same as it was in the programs of the 1970s (7.8 percent).

Table 5. Measures of Violence: Reality Programs, Prime Time (1993–2003)

	1990s	2000s	Total
Samples (100%)			
Number of Programs	30	39	69
Number of Leading Characters	124	178	302
Number of Hours of Programming	24.50	36.50	61.0
Prevalence (%)			
Programs with Violence (%P)	90.0	50.0	72.7
Violence Significant to Plot	86.7	43.6	62.3
Rate			
Number of Violent Acts	448	159	607
Rate per Program (R/P)	14.93	4.08	8.80
Rate per Hour (R/H)	18.29	4.36	9.95
Roles			
Percent of Leading Characters			
Involved in Violence (%V)	38.7	27.5	32.1
Involved in Killing (%K)	13.7	3.9	7.9
Violence Index	208.84	98.28	150.00

Table 6. Measures of Violence:
Award, Game, Variety Prime-Time Programs (1993–2003)

	1990s	2000s	Total
Samples (100%)			
Number of Programs	19	29	48
Number of Leading Characters	50	141	191
Number of Hours of Programming	16.00	26.55	42.55
Prevalence (%)			
Programs with Violence (%P)	63.2	17.2	35.4
Violence Significant to Plot	10.5	10.3	10.4
Rate			
Number of Violent Acts	101	171	272
Rate per Program (R/P)	5.32	5.90	5.67
Rate per Hour (R/H)	6.31	6.44	6.39
Roles	%	%	%
Percent of Leading Characters			
Involved in Violence (%V)	36.0	9.2	16.2
Involved in Killing (%K)	0.0	0.0	0.0
Violence Index	122.46	51.08	75.72

Probably the least consistent genre of programming is reality (Table 5) programs, which is probably due to the fact that the nature of reality programming changed considerably from when these programs first made their debut during the early 1990s to the reality programs of the early twenty-first century. In the 1990s, reality programs typically were related to crime and law enforcement, with programs such as *Cops* and *America's Most Wanted.* In the past few seasons, however, reality programs have taken a different focus, including programs such as the *Survivor* series, *Big Brother* (a program that includes footage from "typical" days of young adults), and recently *The Bachelor* and similar programs geared toward finding "romance" or "a relationship." This shift in focus meant that reality programs in the 1990s were more violent than those in the 2000s.[7] Game and variety programs (Table 6), much like the reality programs, show a lot of variation from decade to decade. Newsmagazines (Table 7), however, were fairly consistent in their portrayal of violence, with not much change from the 1990s to the early twenty-first century. Interestingly, while characters' overall involvement increased somewhat during this time period, the average number of violent actions decreased. Finally, Tables 8 and 9 show that there is not much difference in the amount of violence in programs aired in the early or late evening hours. Early

Table 7. Measures of Violence:
News Magazine Programs, Prime Time (1993–2003)

	1990s	2000s	Total
Samples (100%)			
Number of Programs	75	39	114
Number of Leading Characters	266	210	476
Number of Hours of Programming	71.75	39.00	110.75
Prevalence (%)			
Programs with Violence (%P)	60.0	51.3	57.0
Violence Significant to Plot	37.3	41.0	38.6
Rate			
Number of Violent Acts	281	104	385
Rate per Program (R/P)	3.75	2.67	3.38
Rate per Hour (R/H)	3.92	2.67	3.48
Roles			
Percent of Leading Characters			
Involved in Violence (%V)	6.8	9.5	8.0
Involved in Killing (%K)	3.4	1.0	2.3
Violence Index	85.54	72.48	81.02

Table 8. Measures of Violence:
Early Evening Prime-Time Programs (1967–2003)

	1960s	1970s	1980s	1990s	2000s	Total
Samples (100%)						
Number of Programs	112	297	303	425	227	1,364
Number of Leading Characters	335	906	798	1,682	1,073	4,794
Number of Hours of Programming	84.25	246.20	218.30	321.20	207.10	1077.05
Prevalence (%)						
Programs with Violence (%P)	72.3	64.6	69.6	62.8	53.7	64.0
Violence Significant to Plot	52.7	44.1	43.6	29.4	27.8	37.4
Rate						
Number of Violent Acts	485	1,156	1,211	1,852	1,208	5,912
Rate per Program (R/P)	4.33	3.89	4.00	4.36	5.32	4.33
Rate per Hour (R/H)	5.76	4.70	5.55	5.77	5.83	5.49
Roles						
Percent of Leading Characters						
Involved in Violence (%V)	59.7	46.4	55.6	33.2	27.6	40.0
Involved in Killing (%K)	16.1	6.7	6.9	4.9	7.2	6.9
Violence Index	168.28	134.88	151.20	121.16	110.80	130.54

Table 9. Measures of Violence:
Late Evening Prime-Time Programs (1967–2003)

	1960s	1970s	1980s	1990s	2000s	Total
Samples (100%)						
Number of Programs	73	328	386	458	227	1,472
Number of Leading Characters	223	1,079	1,260	1,854	1,075	5,491
Number of Hours of Programming	79.50	339.70	381.20	407.10	204.50	1,412.0
Prevalence (%)						
Programs with Violence (%P)	75.3	76.2	74.4	65.5	67.0	70.9
Violence Significant to Plot	47.9	57.0	50.5	34.1	46.7	46.1
Rate						
Number of Violent Acts	296	1,887	2,114	1,875	976	7,148
Rate per Program (R/P)	4.05	5.75	5.48	4.09	4.30	4.86
Rate per Hour (R/H)	3.72	5.55	5.53	4.61	4.77	5.06
Roles						
Percent of Leading Characters						
Involved in Violence (%V)	57.8	59.9	50.6	33.8	32.3	43.5
Involved in Killing (%K)	10.3	16.7	10.4	7.3	8.0	10.1
Violence Index	158.94	175.40	157.42	124.00	125.44	144.34

evening programs are not less violent than those seen later in the evening, even though one might expect to find less violence in the early evening because more children, particularly young children, typically watch television in the early evening rather than in the hours later in the evening.

Characters' Involvement in Violence: Demographic Differences

The next set of tables (Tables 10–18) look at some of the demographic differences in characters' involvement in violence. These tables compare gender (men and women) and race (white and minorities). There are several measures of involvement. Overall involvement in violence takes two things into account. It measures whether the character is a perpetrator or commits violence by hurting and/or killing other characters and also considers whether the character is a victim of violence—whether the character gets hurt or killed. These tables present five different measures of involvement in violence: (1) overall involvement in violence—the percentage of characters who are either perpetrators or victims; (2)

involvement as perpetrators—the percentage of characters who hurt or kill other characters; (3) involvement as victims—the percentage of characters who are hurt or are killed; (4) the percentage of characters who are both perpetrators and victims; they are the characters who both hurt or kill and in turn are hurt or killed themselves; and (5) a ratio of whether the characters are more likely to be perpetrators or victims of violence. Because television typically favors victims over perpetrators, this last number gives the number of victims for every ten perpetrators.

This section is made up of the following nine tables that show the involvement in violence for different subgroups of characters.

Table 10:   Leading characters' involvement in violence

Table 11:   Male characters' involvement in violence

Table 12:   Female characters' involvement in violence

Table 13:   White characters' involvement in violence

Table 14:   Minority characters' involvement in violence

Table 15:   White male characters' involvement in violence

Table 16:   White female characters' involvement in violence

Table 17:   Minority male characters' involvement in violence

Table 18:   Minority female characters' involvement in violence

These tables also show that the percentage of characters involved in violence has decreased during the past forty years. In the 1960s and 1970s and into the 1980s, about half of the characters were typically involved in some type of violence. In the more recent samples, however, involvement has decreased to about a third or fewer of the characters. The ratios that compare being a perpetrator to being a victim of violence show, for the most part, that the differences are relatively small. For example, in the 1960s and 1970s, female leading characters were somewhat more likely to be victims than perpetrators. In the 1960s, there were twelve female victims for every ten female perpetrators, and in the 1970s there were thirteen female victims for every ten female perpetrators. In the more recent samples, however, female characters are

Table 10. Leading Characters' Involvement in Violence (1967–2003)

	1960s	1970s	1980s	1990s	2000s	Total
Number of Leading Characters	558	1,985	2,060	3,543	2,148	10,294
Involvement in Violence (%)						
Either Perpetrator or Victim	59.0	53.7	52.5	33.5	29.9	41.8
Only Perpetrators	42.8	40.4	40.4	22.9	21.9	30.6
Only Victims	49.3	44.8	43.4	22.9	21.5	32.4
Both Perpetrator and Victim	33.2	31.5	31.4	12.6	13.5	21.3
Number of Victims for Every 10 Perpetrators	11.5	11.1	10.8	10.0	-10.2*	10.6

Note: *reversed—there are more perpetrators than victims.

Table 11. Male Characters' Involvement in Violence (1967–2003)

	1960s	1970s	1980s	1990s	2000s	Total
Number of Male Characters	408	1,400	1.348	2,112	1,284	6,552
Involvement in Violence (%)						
Either Perpetrator or Victim	64.5	59.1	58.1	38.4	33.6	47.6
Only Perpetrators	48.5	46.5	46.5	26.5	25.0	36.0
Only Victims	55.4	49.7	49.8	27.8	23.6	37.9
Both Perpetrator and Victim	39.5	37.1	38.2	16.2	15.1	26.4
Number of Victims for Every 10 Perpetrators	11.4	10.7	10.7	10.5	-10.6*	10.5

Note: *reversed—there are more perpetrators than victims.

Table 12. Female Characters' Involvement in Violence (1967–2003)

	1960s	1970s	1980s	1990s	2000s	Total
Number of Female Characters	150	582	705	1,423	859	3,719
Involvement in Violence (%)						
Either Perpetrator or Victim	44.0	40.4	41.6	26.3	24.1	31.6
Only Perpetrators	27.3	25.3	28.7	17.5	17.0	21.1
Only Victims	32.7	33.0	31.1	15.7	17.9	22.5
Both Perpetrator and Victim	16.0	17.9	18.2	7.0	10.8	12.1
Number of Victims for Every 10 Perpetrators	12.2	13.1	10.8	-11.7*	10.5	10.7

Note: *reversed—there are more perpetrators than victims.

Table 13. White Characters' Involvement in Violence (1967–2003)

	1960s	1970s	1980s	1990s	2000s	Total
Number of White Characters	500	1,780	1,814	2,907	1,698	8.699
Involvement in Violence (%)						
Either Perpetrator or Victim	58.6	53.6	52.6	32.9	29.0	42.0
Only Perpetrators	43.0	40.2	40.5	22.2	20.9	30.6
Only Victims	48.2	44.6	43.3	22.7	20.5	32.5
Both Perpetrator and Victim	32.6	31.2	31.2	12.2	12.5	21.3
Number of Victims for Every 10 Perpetrators	11.2	11.1	10.7	10.2	-10.2*	10.6

Note: *reversed—there are more perpetrators than victims.

Table 14. Minority Characters' Involvement in Violence (1967–2003)

	1960s	1970s	1980s	1990s	2000s	Total
Number of Minority Characters	56	182	199	606	438	1,481
Involvement in Violence (%)						
Either Perpetrator or Victim	62.5	51.1	47.2	35.3	33.1	39.2
Only Perpetrators	41.1	39.0	35.7	25.6	25.1	29.1
Only Victims	58.9	44.0	40.7	23.1	24.7	29.8
Both Perpetrator and Victim	37.5	31.9	29.1	13.5	16.7	19.7
Number of Victims for Every 10 Perpetrators	15.0	11.3	11.4	-11.1*	-10.3*	10.3

Note: *reversed—there are more perpetrators than victims.

Table 15. White Male Characters' Involvement in Violence (1967–2003)

	1960s	1970s	1980s	1990s	2000s	Total
Number of White Males	361	1,245	1,177	1,721	1,013	5,517
Involvement in Violence (%)						
Either Perpetrator or Victim	64.0	58.9	58.2	37.8	32.7	47.7
Only Perpetrators	48.5	46.3	46.6	25.7	23.9	36.0
Only Victims	32.4	33.6	31.6	15.6	17.4	23.0
Both Perpetrator and Victim	38.8	36.7	38.1	15.9	14.0	26.5
Number of Victims for Every 10 Perpetrators*	-10.6*	-11.2*	-10.7*	-10.6*	-10.7*	-10.6*

Note: *reversed—there are more perpetrators than victims for this subgroup of characters; thus, in each decade white males were more likely to hurt others than be hurt themselves.

Table 16. Characters' Involvement in Violence (1967–2003)

	1960s	1970s	1980s	1990s	2000s	Total
Number of White Females	139	535	637	1,186	684	3,181
Involvement in Violence (%)						
Either Perpetrator or Victim	44.6	41.3	42.2	25.9	23.7	32.1
Only Perpetrators	28.8	26.0	29.2	17.1	16.5	21.4
Only Victims	32.4	33.6	31.6	15.6	17.4	23.0
Both Perpetrator and Victim	16.5	18.3	18.5	6.9	10.2	12.3
Number of Victims for Every 10 Perpetrators	10.7	11.3	12.9	-10.8*	11.0	10.5

Note: *reversed—there are more perpetrators than victims.

Table 17. Minority Male Characters' Involvement in Violence (1967–2003)

	1960s	1970s	1980s	1990s	2000s	Total
Number of Minority Males	47	141	135	372	265	960
Involvement in Violence (%)						
Either Perpetrator or Victim	68.1	58.9	54.1	39.8	37.4	45.3
Only Perpetrators	48.9	46.8	42.2	29.6	29.1	34.7
Only Victims	63.8	50.4	48.1	27.4	27.2	35.4
Both Perpetrator and Victim	44.7	38.3	36.3	17.2	18.9	24.8
Number of Victims for Every 10 Perpetrators	13.0	10.8	11.4	-10.8*	-10.7*	10.2

Note: *reversed—there are more perpetrators than victims of violence.

Table 18. Minority Female Characters' Involvement in Violence (1967–2003)

	1960s	1970s	1980s	1990s	2000s	Total
Number of Minority Females	9	41	62	232	172	516
Involvement in Violence (%)						
Either Perpetrator or Victim	33.3	24.4	33.9	28.0	26.2	27.9
Only Perpetrators	0	12.2	22.6	19.0	19.2	18.6
Only Victims	33.3	22.0	25.8	15.9	20.3	19.4
Both Perpetrator and Victim	0	9.8	14.5	7.3	13.4	10.3
Number of Victims for Every 10 Perpetrators	only victims	18.0	11.4	-11.9*	10.6	10.4

Note: *reversed—there are 11.9 perpetrators for every 10 victims.

about equally likely to be perpetrators or victims. The 1960s and to some extent the 1970s were also the decades in which minority characters were more likely to be cast as victims than as perpetrators. In more recent samples, however, minority characters are equally likely to be victims or perpetrators of violence. Interestingly, the analyses for white males (Table 15) show that they are the only subgroup who are always more likely to be perpetrators than victims of violence—they do more hurting and do not get hurt as often as other groups of characters.

Overall, in the television programs of the twenty-first century seen on the broadcast networks during the prime-time (8 to 11 PM) hours, men, women, whites, and minorities are equally likely to be involved in violence. Moreover, compared to earlier years, women and minorities are as likely to be perpetrators as victims of violence.

The National Television Violence Study

The National Television Violence Study (1998) began in 1994 as a three-year project funded by the National Cable Television Association (NCTA). This funding was provided in response to the 1993 congressional hearings on television violence and at the impetus of the late Senator Paul Simon (D-IL).

The National Television Violence Study was a content analysis that focused on the portrayal of physical violence on television. It examined physical violence in three yearly samples (1994–1995, 1995–1996, and 1996–1997) of programming. The way the sample was selected (sampling parameters) sets this study apart from other studies of television violence, such as the Cultural Indicators project discussed above. Specifically, the NTVS sample is larger, has an increased scope of coverage (most of the day and more than just broadcast television), and sampled programs over a longer period of time. The NTVS sampled composite weeks of programming telecast on twenty-three channels (broadcast and cable) operating between 6:00 AM and 11:00 PM each day. A composite week means that each individual program (unit) in the sample was randomly selected from all the programs that appeared between October and June of each year of the study.

The samples were gathered between October 1994 and June 1997 (N=8,200) and included broadcast (commercial networks, independent stations, and public television) and cable channels (basic and premium, such as HBO). All genres of programs except game shows, religious programs, "infomercials" or home shopping channels, sports, instructional programs, and news were included. Programs on CNN and ESPN were excluded. This sample thus presents a broader picture of violence on television than the Cultural Indicators perspective.

In this study, violence was defined as "any overt depiction of a credible threat of physical force or the actual use of such force intended to physically harm an animate being or group of beings" (NTVS 1998, 20). The study used three distinct units of analysis. First, violence was isolated at the program level. Second, violence was examined at the scene level, where a scene of violence was defined as "an interrelated series of violent incidents that occur without a meaningful break in the flow of actual or imminent violence" (NTVS 1998, 21). This portion of the study enabled the researchers to look at various combinations of the contextual features in the portrayal of violence. Third, the study isolated separate incidents of violence. An incident of violence was defined as "an interaction between a perpetrator (P), an act (A), and a target (T)" (21), or the PAT level. The NTVS did not isolate or analyze all the characters in the programs, only those found in the PATs or incidents of violence—the perpetrators and targets.

One of the primary goals of the NTVS was to isolate and identify the context in which violence appeared and to isolate those contextual elements that could pose the most harm to viewers, particularly children. The entire study was based on three premises: (1) that violence has antisocial effects; (2) that these effects fall into three areas—learning aggressive attitudes and behaviors, desensitization, and increased fear of being a victim of violence; (3) that television violence differs in the degree of risk it poses for viewers. The study participants identified nine possible contextual factors for the analysis:

1. The nature of the perpetrators—are they heroes or villains, attractive or unattractive?
2. The nature of the target—is the target attractive or well liked?
3. The reason or motive for the violence—is it self defense, justified, retaliation, malicious?
4. The presence or absence of weapons.
5. The extent and graphic nature of the violence—is there prolonged brutality?

6. The realism of violence.
7. The presence of rewards and/or punishments.
8. The consequences of violence—is harm, pain, and/or suffering apparent?
9. The presence of humor.

Six tables are reproduced from the final report of the NTVS. Five tables report the data collected during the third data collection period (1996–1997), and one table (Table 20) compares data from all three years of this study. Table 19 provides a comparison of programming seen during prime-time hours (8 to 11 PM) and programs seen at other times throughout the day. (Tables 1–18 from the Cultural Indicators perspective examine only prime-time programs.) Moreover, Table 19 compares the four types of channels (broadcast, independent, basic cable, and premium cable) included in the sample of programs. The table also presents data relating to the portrayal of the context of violence as described above. Table 20 gives a comparison of the percentage of programs with violence in three samples of programs (1994–1995, 1995–1996, and 1996–1997) by the four different types of channels.

Table 19 shows that the programs (mostly movies) seen on the premium cable channels (e.g., HBO) were typically the most violent. Overall, about nine out of ten of these programs had some violence. By comparison, about two-thirds of the programs on the broadcast channels had violence. For the most part, the premium cable programs, particularly those telecast during the prime-time hours, had more contextual elements, some of which indicated more negative presentations of violence. They had the most scenes that were realistic and showed more blood and gore. Yet these programs also included more long-term negative consequences, had fewer scenes of unpunished violence, and fewer specific PATs that did not show pain than most of the other channel types. This table also shows that broadcast television had more violence during prime time than other times throughout the day.

Table 20 shows interesting differences in the percentage of prime-time programs with violence during the three years of this study. In short, in prime time, the hours when most people watch some television, the percentage of programs with violence increased from year 1 (1994–1995) to year 3 (1996–1997), except for the very small decline for the premium cable programs. The premium cable programs consistently had the most violence, followed by the programs on the independent broadcast channels. The percentage of programs with violence on basic cable channels and on the commercial broadcast networks was very similar.

Tables 21 through 24 present data relating to portrayals of violence that are categorized as high risk, portrayals that could encourage the learning of aggression. In these tables, data relating to the context of violence are examined collectively. These are the elements of content that, when appearing in the same program and in the same violent incident, create a viewing environment that reflects more risk for the audience in regard to the possibility of learning aggressive behaviors and attitudes. These analyses are conservative because in order for a portrayal to be categorized as risky, it had to include all five of the following risk factors: an attractive perpetrator, justified violence, violence explicitly rewarded or implicitly sanctioned (not punished), violence without pain or harm, and realistic violence (NTVS 1998, 130). The analysis focused on the violent interactions rather than the programs and identified all violent interactions that involved "*an attractive perpetrator engaging in justified violence that does not get punished and that shows minimal consequences*" (132, emphasis added). Two separate composite measures were defined and isolated—one for young children (under age seven) and one for older children and adolescents. The composites differed in that the one for young children included fantasy violence and only included rewards and punishments that occurred at the same time the violent incident took place, whereas the composite for older children did not include fantasy violence and included rewards and punishments seen throughout the program. Also, the violence included in both these composite measures had to include aggressive behaviors that could actually result in physical harm. Finally, the violence could not be in a program with antiviolence themes. The high-risk findings are reported for different times of the day by the type of program (Tables 21 and 22) and by channel type (Tables 23 and 24). The tables report the number of high-risk interactions and the number of programming hours. These two measures are then compared in a "risk ratio" by dividing the number of high risk interactions by the number of programming hours. This ratio shows the likelihood that a viewer, in this case a child, would encounter high-risk portrayals of violence when watching. These tables do not report any percentages; the percentages referred to in the text were calculated by dividing the column total of high risk interactions by the total number of high risk interactions.

Tables 21 through 24 show that the high-risk interaction

Table 19. Comparison of Prime-time and Non-Prime-time Hours across Channel Types (1996–1997)

	Broadcast Network	Independent Broadcast	Basic Cable	Premium Cable	Overall Average
	%	%	%	%	%
% of Programs with Violence					
Prime-Time	67	77	64	88	67
Non-Prime-Time	47	56	66	82	60
% of Programs with Long-Term Negative Consequeces					
Prime-Time	24	24	15	62	23
Non-Prime-Time	15	11	13	29	14
% of Programs with Realistic Settings					
Prime-Time	93	71	58	81	68
Non-Prime-Time	62	38	50	82	53
% of Scenes with Unpunished Violence					
Prime-Time	59	73	78	66	71
Non-Prime-Time	72	73	71	68	71
% of Scenes with Blood and Gore					
Prime-Time	15	30	13	49	25
Non-Prime-Time	7	7	9	21	11
% of Scenes with Humor					
Prime-Time	22	34	35	20	29
Non-Prime-Time	43	58	44	43	45
% Violent PATs with No Pain					
Prime-Time	53	23	52	36	44
Non-Prime-Time	51	48	57	43	52
% Violent PATs with Unrealistic Harm					
Prime-Time	19	18	29	20	24
Non-Prime-Time	44	47	39	24	37

Source: "Table 17." *National Television Violence Study.* 1998. Vol. 3. Thousand Oaks, CA: Sage, p. 106. Reproduced with permission.

Table 20. Three-Year Comparisons for Prime Time: Percentage of Programs that Contain Violence by Channel Type

	Commerical Broadcast	Independent Broadcast	Basic Cable	Premium Cable	Overall
Year 1	53	70	54	91	59
Year 2	63	73	63	98	66
Year 3	67	77	64	87	67

Source: "Table 20." *National Television Violence Study.* 1998. Vol. 3. Thousand Oaks, CA: Sage, p. 124. Reproduced with permission.

Table 21. High-Risk Findings by Genre and Time of Day
(Children under Seven Years Old), 1996–1997

Time of Day	Drama	Comedy	Children's	Movies	Music Videos	Reality-Based	Across Genres
Before School (6–9 AM)							
# of High-Risk Interactions	5	0	109	33	5	2	154
# of Programming Hours	35	12.5	145.5	117.5	57.5	74	442
Risk Ratio	.14	.00	.75	.28	.09	.03	.35
During School (9 AM–3 PM)							
# of High-Risk Interactions	40	2	139	82	11	0	274
# of Programming Hours	135	49.5	176	330.5	95	164.5	950.5
Risk Ratio	.30	.04	.76	.25	.12	.00	.29
After School (3–6 PM)							
# of High-Risk Interactions	10	2	62	44	2	0	120
# of Programming Hours	43	26	88	177	42.5	85.5	462
Risk Ratio	.23	.08	.70	.25	.05	.00	.26
Early Evening (6–8 PM)							
# of High-Risk Interactions	14	0	33	19	2	6	74
# Programming Hours	27.5	37	40.5	83.5	13	63.5	265
Risk Ratio	.51	.00	.81	.23	.15	.09	.28
Prime Time (8–11 PM)							
# of High-Risk Interactions	8	4	16	61	7	1	97
# of Programing Hours	66	49.5	29.5	215.5	32	74	446.5
Risk Ratio	.12	.08	.54	.28	.01	.01	.21
Column Totals							
Total # of High-Risk Interactions	77	8	359	239	27	9	719
Total # of Programming Hours	306.5	174.5	479.5	924	240	461.5	2,586
Overall Risk Ratio For Genre	.25	.05	.75	.26	.11	.02	.28

Source: "Table 22." *National Television Violence Study.* 1998. Vol. 3. Thousand Oaks, CA: Sage, p. 139. Reproduced with permission.

analysis isolated 1,102 violent interactions that were judged to be high risk to viewers: 719 for children under seven (Table 21) and 383 for older children (Table 22). There were more high-risk interactions for children under seven years old (about two-thirds of all interactions) than for older children and adolescents (about one-third). Most of the high-risk interactions for children under the age of seven were found in children's programs (50 percent) and in movies (30 percent) and found throughout the day (see Table 21). Moreover, most of the children's programs are cartoons. As noted by the NTVS report, "Most of the hazardous depictions of violence for young children are found in the very programs that are targeted to this age group" (1998, 136). There were fewer high-risk interactions for older children (see Table 22). Two-thirds of these interactions were found in movies. Dramas had the next most sizable

Table 22. High-Risk Findings by Genre and Time (Older Children and Adolescents), 1996–1997

Time of Day	Drama	Comedy	Children's	Movies	Music Videos	Reality-Based	Across Genres
Before School (6–9 AM)							
# of High-Risk Interactions	6	0	0	21	3	2	32
# of Programming Hours	35	12.5	145.5	117.5	57.5	74	442
Risk Ratio	.14	.00	.00	.18	.05	.03	.07
During School (9 AM–3 PM)							
# of High-Risk Interactions	37	2	0	108	16	1	164
# of Programming Hours	135	49.5	176	330.5	95	164.5	950.5
Risk Ratio	.27	.04	.00	.33	.17	.00	.17
After School (3–6 PM)							
# of High-Risk Interactions	9	2	0	63	1	0	75
# of Programming Hours	43	26	88	177	42.5	85.5	462
Risk Ratio	.21	.08	.00	.35	.02	.00	.16
Early Evening (6–8 PM)							
# of High-Risk Interactions	11	0	2	11	2	6	32
# Programming Hours	27.5	37	40.5	83.5	13	63.5	265
Risk Ratio	.40	.00	.05	.13	.15	.09	.12
Prime Time (8–11 PM)							
# of High-Risk Interactions	13	4	0	57	5	1	80
# of Programing Hours	66	49.5	29.5	215.5	32	74	466.5
Risk Ratio	.20	.08	.00	.26	.16	.01	.17
Column Totals							
Total # of High-Risk Interactions	76	8	2	260	27	10	383
Total # of Programming Hours	306.5	174.5	479.5	924	240	461.5	2,586
Overall Risk Ratio For Genre	.25	.05	.00	.28	.11	.02	.15

Source: "Table 22." *National Television Violence Study.* 1998. Vol. 3. Thousand Oaks, CA: Sage, p. 139. Reproduced with permission.

number of high-risk interactions (20 percent), followed by music videos (7 percent). In regard to channel type, young children's high-risk programming was found mostly on basic cable children's shows (Disney, Cartoon Network, and Nickelodeon) followed by basic cable general entertainment (see Table 23). By the time of day, the most high-risk interactions were found in the before school hours (6 to 9 AM) on the independent broadcast channels where a young child could see one high-risk incident during each hour of viewing, which would translate to over 20 a week and over 1,000 a year (NTVS 1998, 142). Again, most of these programs are cartoons. Last, older children and adolescents would encounter high-risk violent interactions when watching basic cable general entertainment programs and the premium cable movie channels (see Table 24).

Table 23. High-Risk Findings by Channel Type and Time (Young Children), 1996–1997

Time of Day	BROADCAST CHANNELS			BASIC CABLE			PREMIUM CABLE	TOTAL
	Networks	Public	Independent	General Entertainment	Music	Children	Movies	
Before School (6–9 AM)								
# of High-Risk Interactions	4.00	2.00	44.00	35.00	5.0	34.00	30.00	154.00
# of Programming Hours	55.00	21.50	40.50	130.00	64.00	62.00	96.00	442.00
Risk Ratio	.07	.09	1.09	.34	.08	.55	.31	.35
During School (9 AM–3 PM)								
# of High-Risk Interactions	19.00	0.00	31.00	86.00	11.00	86.00	41.00	274.00
# of Programming Hours	124.50	40.00	109.00	259.00	119.5	127.5	171.00	950.50
Risk Ratio	.15	.00	.28	.33	.09	.67	.24	.29
After School (3–6 PM)								
# of High-Risk Interactions	15.00	0.00	41.00	20.00	2.00	23.00	19.00	120.00
# of Programming Hours	48.50	18.50	62.50	135.50	58.50	61.50	77.00	462.00
Risk Ratio	.31	.00	.66	.15	.03	.37	.25	.26
Early Evening (6–8 PM)								
# of High-Risk Interactions	7.00	0.00	10.00	19.00	2.00	31.00	5.00	74.00
# of Programming Hours	31.00	12.00	35.00	80.50	28.50	46.00	32.00	265.00
Risk Ratio	.23	.00	.29	.24	.07	.67	.16	.28
Prime Time (8–11 PM)								
# of High-Risk Interactions	13.00	0.00	13.00	13.00	8.00	23.00	27.00	97.00
# of Programming Hours	84.00	19.50	28.50	124.50	53.50	66.00	90.50	466.50
Risk Ratio	.15	.00	.46	.10	.15	.35	.30	.21
Column Totals								
Total # of High-Risk Interactions	58	2	139	173	28	197	122	719
Total # of Programming Hours	343	111.5	275.5	702.5	324	363	466.50	2,586
Overall Risk Ratio For Genre	.17	.02	.50	.25	.09	.54	.26	.28

Source: "Table 23." *National Television Violence Study,* 1998. Vol. 3. Thousand Oaks, CA: Sage, p. 143. Reproduced with permission.

Table 24. High-Risk Findings by Channel Group and Time (Older Children), 1996–1997

Time of Day	BROADCAST CHANNELS			BASIC CABLE			PREMIUM CABLE	TOTAL
	Networks	Public	Independent	General Entertainment	Music	Children	Movies	
Before School (6–9 AM)								
# of High-Risk Interactions	0	0	0	14.00	3.00	0	15.00	32
# of Programming Hours	55.00	21.50	14.50	103.00	64.00	62.00	96.00	442.00
Risk Ratio	.00	.00	.00	.13	.05	.00	.16	.07
During School (9 AM–3 PM)								
# of High-Risk Interactions	3.00	0	6.00	90.00	16.00	0	49.00	164
# of Programming Hours	124.50	40.00	109.00	259.00	119.5	127.5	171.00	950.50
Risk Ratio	.02	.00	.05	.35	.13	.00	.29	.17
After School (3–6 PM)								
# of High-Risk Interactions	1.00	0	10.00	31.00	1.00	0	32.00	75
# of Programming Hours	48.50	18.50	62.50	135.50	58.50	60.50	77.00	462.00
Risk Ratio	.02	.00	.16	.23	.02	.00	.41	.16
Early Evening (6–8 PM)								
# of High-Risk Interactions	2.00	0	12.00	10.00	2.00	2.00	4.00	32
# of Programming Hours	31.00	12.00	35.00	80.50	28.50	46.00	32.00	265.00
Risk Ratio	.06	.00	.34	.12	.07	.04	.13	.12
Prime Time (8–11 PM)								
# of High-Risk Interactions	21.00	0	13.00	18.00	5.00	2.00	21.00	80
# of Programming Hours	84.00	19.50	28.50	124.50	53.50	66.00	90.50	466.50
Risk Ratio	.25	.00	.46	.14	.09	.03	.23	.17
Column Totals								
Total # of High-Risk Interactions	27	0	41	163	27	4	121	383
Total # of Programming Hours	343	111.5	275.5	702.5	324	363	466.5	2,586
Overall Risk Ratio For Genre	.08	.00	.15	.23	.08	.01	.26	.15

Source: "Table 25." *National Television Violence Study.* 1998. Vol. 3. Thousand Oaks, CA: Sage, p. 152. Reproduced with permission.

Notes

1. Violence is defined as "the overt expression of physical force (with or without a weapon, against self or other) compelling action against one's will on pain of being hurt or killed, or actual hurting or killing" (Signorielli, Gross, and Morgan 1982, 163).

2. These differences were tested by calculating an analysis of variance for the rate per program. It was not statistically significant (F=1.08, df=4,2831; p=.36).

3. Results of the analysis of variance (F=132.45, df=4,10,289; p<.0001).

4. Results of the analysis of variance: rate per program (F=.1366, df=4,1128, ns) and involvement in violence (F=5.06, df=4,3590; p<.001).

5. Results of the analysis of variance for action programs: rate per program (F=5.03, df=4.840; p<.001) and involvement in violence (F=27.43, df=4,3123; p<.0001).

6. Results of the analysis of variance for dramas: rate per program (F=1.19, df=4, 613; ns) and involvement in violence (F=7.17, df=4,2594; p<.0001).

7. Results of the analysis of variance for reality programs: rate per program (F=5.68, df=1,67; p< .02) and involvement in violence (F=4.22, df=1,300; p<.05).

References

Ellis, G. T., and F. Sekyra, III. 1972. "The Effects of Aggressive Cartoons on the Behavior of First-Grade Children. *Journal of Psychology* 81, no. 1: 7–43.

Gerbner, G., L. Gross, M. Jackson-Beeck, S. Jeffries-Fox, and N. Signorielli. 1978. "Cultural Indicators: Violence Profile no. 9." *Journal of Communication* 28, no. 3: 176–207.

Gerbner, G., M. Morgan, and N. Signorielli. 1993. *Television Violence Profile no. 16: The Turning Point.* Philadelphia: Annenberg School for Communication.

Haynes, R. B. 1978. "Children's Perceptions of 'Comic' and 'Authentic' Cartoon Violence." *Journal of Broadcasting* 22, no. 1: 63–79.

Krippendorff, K. 1980. *Content Analysis.* Thousand Oaks, CA: Sage Publications.

National Television Violence Study. 1998. Vol. 3. Thousand Oaks, CA: Sage Publications.

Signorielli, N., L. Gross, and M. Morgan. 1982. "Violence in Television Programs: Ten Years Later." In D. Pearl, L. Bouthilet, and J. Lazar, eds., *Television and Social Behavior: Ten Years of Scientific Progress and Implications for the Eighties*, pp. 158–173. Rockville, MD: National Institute of Mental Health.

7

Organizations and Websites

There are thousands and thousands of World Wide Web (WWW) sites about media violence. A search on Google.com uncovered 4,590,000 possible sites for the key words "media violence" and "2,560,000 for "television violence." Searches using other search engines had similar results.

The following chapter lists organizations who have WWW sites related to media violence as well as some specific pages devoted to this topic. In addition to the site URL (address), the entry lists the organization's address, phone numbers, and e-mail when available. Most of these sites are developed, set up, and maintained by organizations (e.g., American Psychological Association, Center for Media Literacy) whose mission statements clearly indicate interest in this topic. While the large majority of these sites talk about the problems of media violence in society, several provide information about what their authors would call "myths" of media violence.

Each entry was generated using information from the organization's website. Each entry has a brief overview of the organization and its mission. In addition, each entry notes the title(s) of various articles presented on the website and provides their corresponding URLs. Readers are encouraged to explore the suggested sites because the Internet is far from a static resource, and as such, its information changes very frequently. The sites are listed alphabetically by organization.

Abelard
E-mail: abelard@abelard.org
Web: www.abelard.org

A website dedicated to providing tools to enhance education; numerous links lead to information about many different topics including media violence.
Children and Television Violence:
http://www.abelard.org/tv/tv.htm

Action Alliance for Children
1201 Martin Luther King Jr. Way
Oakland, CA 94612
Tel: 510-444-7136
E-mail: acc@4children.org
Web: www.4children.org

This website provides a number of links with reliable information about issues that affect families and children. It is a resource for the media as well as policymakers and those who provide services for children and families. Their award winning newsmagazine, *Children's Advocate*, focuses on trends and public policy issues.
From Children's Advocate newsmagazine: "What Do Children Learn from Media Violence?":
http://www.4children.org/news/1–97toxl.htm

American Academy of Child and Adolescent Psychiatry
3615 Wisconsin Ave, NW
Washington, DC 20016–3007
Tel: 202-966-7300
Fax: 202-966-2891
E-mail: webthing@aacap.org
Web: www.aacap.org

This organization of child and adolescent psychiatrists is committed to providing information to facilitate the understanding of mental illness and the removal of the stigmas typically associated with mental illnesses. Their concern with television violence stems from their focus on the cultural and social perspectives related to the diagnosis, treatment, and understanding of mental illness in society. Research, training, and advocacy are particularly relevant to this organization.

Facts for Families, Children and Television Violence, No. 13:
http://www.aacap.org/publications/factsfam/violence.htm
Impact of Media Violence on Children and Adolescents:
Opportunities for Clinical Interventions:
http://www.aacap.org/training/DevelopMentor/Content/
1999Fall/f1999_a3.cfm

American Academy of Pediatrics
141 Northwest Point Boulevard
Elk Grove Village, IL 60007–1098
Tel: 847-434-4000
Fax: 847-434-8000
Web: www.aap.org
Washington, DC Office:
The American Academy of Pediatrics
Department of Federal Affairs
601 13th Street, NW
Suite 400 North
Washington, DC 20005
Tel: 202-347-8600
Fax: 202-393-6137
E-mail: kidsdocs@app.org

The official website of the American Academy of Pediatricians, an
organization committed to the health, physical and mental, as well
as the well being of children and their families. The organization's
Provisional Section on Media (PSOM) serves as a resource on
media-related issues of interest and importance. In particular this
section focuses on the development of media literacy skills that can
be used by pediatricians to inform parents and children about the
potentially adverse effects of media messages.

"Some Things You Should Know About Media Violence and
Media Literacy"
http://www.aap.org/advocacy/childhealthmonth/media.htm
Policy Statement on Media Violence:
http://aappolicy.aappublications.org/cgi/content/full/
pediatrics;108/5/1222

American Booksellers Foundation for Freedom of Expression
139 Fulton Street, Suite 302
New York, NY 10038
Phone: 212-587-4025
Fax: 212-587-2436
E-mail: Chris Finan, president, chris@abffe.com
Caitlin Delohery, program director, caitlin@abffe.com
Web: www.abffe.org

The mission of the American Booksellers Foundation for Free
Expression is to promote and protect the free exchange of ideas.
This site provides information about how to protect against censorship. As one of the sponsors of "Banned Books Week," the organization continues its fight against censorship and loss of first
amendment rights.

"The Media Violence Myth," an interview with Richard Rhodes:
http://www.abffe.com/myth1.htm

American Civil Liberties Union
125 Broad Street, 18th Floor
New York, NY 10004
Web: www.aclu.org

The ACLU works to conserve and preserve first amendment
rights, including freedom of speech, freedom of religion, and freedom of the press along with our right for equal protection regard-
less of sex, race, national origin, or religion. In addition the organization works to protect our rights to privacy and due process.

"Media Violence and Free Speech" by Marjorie Heins, 1994:
http://archive.aclu.org/issues/freespeech/mediaviolence.html

American Family Association
P.O. Drawer 2440
Tupelo, MS 38803
Tel: 601-844-5036
Fax: 601-842-7798
Web: www.afa.net

Founded in 1977 by Don Wildmon, this nonprofit organization
promotes family values and is concerned with the negative influence of the media, particularly television, on society. The organization believes that the entertainment industry has contributed to
the demise of family values in society.

American Psychiatric Association
1000 Wilson Boulevard, Suite 1825
Arlington, Va. 22209–3901
Tel: 703-907-7300
E-mail: apa@psych.org
Web: www.psych.org

An organization of psychiatrists who work to better the care and treatment of those with mental disorders, including the mentally retarded and those with substance-abuse disorders. It is concerned with promoting psychiatric education and research. Its links provide valuable information for both the public and its members.
Psychiatric Effects of Media Violence:
http://www.psych.org/public_info/media_violence.cfm

American Psychological Association
750 First Street, NE
Washington, DC 20002–4242
Tel: 800-374-2721; 202-336-5500; TDD/TTY: 202-336-6123
E-mail: webmaster@apa.org
Web: www.apa.org

A scientific and professional organization that seeks to advance the study of the science of psychology. This website provides valuable information and relevant links for psychologists, students, the media, and the public about numerous issues that impact upon health and welfare. The organization has been particularly active in issues relating to media violence and has some very useful links about research in this area.
Violence on Television: What Do Children Learn? What Can Parents Do?
http://www.apa.org/pubinfo/violence.html
Family and Relationships, Get the Facts; Children and Television Violence:
http://helping.apa.org/family/kidtvviol.html
Press Release: Childhood Exposure to Media Violence Predicts Young Adult Aggressive Behavior, According to a New 15-Year Study: Children Who Identify with Aggressive TV Characters and Perceive the Violence to Be Realistic Are Most at Risk for Later Aggression: http://www.apa.org/releases/media_violence.html

American Psychological Society
1010 Vermont Avenue, NW, Suite 1100
Washington, DC 20005–4907
Tel: 202-783-2077
Fax: 202-783-2083
E-mail: aps@psychologicalscience.org
Web: http://www.psychologicalscience.org/about/

A nonprofit organization, founded in 1988, dedicated to the advancement of scientific psychology and its representation at the national level. It works as an advocate for psychological science, particularly as it relates to research, teaching, and the improvement of human welfare. Its journal, *Psychological Science*, plays a leading role in the dissemination of psychological research. The website includes links to media coverage of research studies as well as information for students and the public.

The Influence of Media Violence on Youth:
http://www.psychologicalscience.org/journals/index.cfm?journal=pspi&content=pspi/4_3

Annenberg Public Policy Center
at the University of Pennsylvania
Philadelphia Office
3620 Walnut Street
Philadelphia, PA 19104–6220
Tel: 215-898-7041
Fax: 215-898-2024
Washington, DC Office
320 National Press Building
Washington, DC 20045
Tel: 202-879-6700
Fax: 202-879-6707
E-mail: appcdc@appcpenn.org
Web: http://www.annenbergpublicpolicycenter.org/index.htm

Established in 1994, with offices in Philadelphia and Washington, D.C., this organization focuses on the relationship between the media and public policy. It sponsors research on issues related to media and public policy and also hosts conferences and lectures on related topics. One area of particular interest is research on children as well as research in health communication focusing on adolescent risk as well as political communication. Recent studies have examined privacy policies on the Internet.

Baby Bag Online
P.O. Box 176
Dana Point, CA 92629
Tel: 949-388-5257
Fax: 949-388-5258
E-mail: national@babybag.com
Web: www.babybag.com

A commercial website devoted to numerous issues relating to babies and children, including shopping, pregnancy information, child-rearing tips, health and safety, food and nutrition and general childcare and child welfare.

Facts about Media Violence and Effects on the American Family:
http://www.babybag.com/articles/amaviol.htm
Tips for Parents: Reduce Your Family's Exposure to Media Violence:
http://www.babybag.com/articles/amatips.htm
AMA Survey Shows 75 Percent of Parents Disgusted with Media Violence:
http://www.babybag.com/articles/amarele.htm

Cable in the Classroom
1724 Massachusetts Ave, NW
Washington, DC 20036
Tel: 202-775-1040
Fax: 202-775-1047
Web: http://www.ciconline.org/default.htm

Started in 1989, Cable in the Classroom provides free access to educational materials for public and private schools. The site contains several useful enrichment pages for both parents and teachers.
Media Literacy:
http://www.ciconline.org/Enrichment/MediaLiteracy/default.htm
Teaching and Learning:
http://www.ciconline.org/Enrichment/Teaching/default.htm

Campaign for a Commercial-Free Childhood
c/o Judge Baker Children's Center
3 Blackfan Circle, Boston, MA 02115
Tel: 617-232-8390 x2328
Fax: 617-232-7343
E-mail: SCEC@JBCC.harvard.edu
Web: http://www.commercialexploitation.com/

Founded in 1999, this national coalition of educators, advocates, parents, and health care professionals works to reduce marketing to children and to protect children from excessive commercialism. Pages on the website include the newsroom with recent press releases about commercialism in movies and results from recent surveys. Another page provides fact sheets for parents, teachers, and youngsters about marketing to children in various venues.

Marketing Violence to Children: http://www.commercialexploitation.com/factsheets/CCFC-Facts%20Violence.pdf

Marketing Sex to Children:
http://www.commercialexploitation.com/factsheets/CCFC-Facts%20MarketingSex.pdf

Canadian Radio-Television and
Telecommunications Commission(CRTC)
CRTC
Ottawa, Ontario
Canada, K1A 0N2
Tel: 1-877-249-2782 (toll free); TDD: 1-877-909-2782 (toll free)
E-mail: webmaster@crtc.gc.ca
Web: http://www.crtc.gc.ca/

The CRTC is an independent agency responsible for regulating Canada's broadcasting and telecommunications systems, reporting to Parliament through the Minister of Canadian Heritage. It includes numerous links to enable visitors to the site to learn more about broadcasting in Canada. The site can be accessed in both English and French.

Respecting Children: A Canadian Approach to Helping Families Deal with Television Violence:
http://www.crtc.gc.ca/eng/social/tv.htm

Chronology of Main Events and Initiatives Undertaken Related to the Issue of Television Violence:
http://www.crtc.gc.ca/ENG/INFO_SHT/TV1.HTM

**Canadians Concerned About Violence
in Entertainment (C-CAVE)**
167 Glen Road
Toronto, ON M4W 2W8
Canada
Tel: 416-961-0853
Fax: 416-929-2720
E-mail: info@c-cave.com
Web: www.c-cave.com

This is a nonprofit, national, independent, public interest organization. It seeks to increase public awareness about cultural violence in society, particularly as it relates to entertainment including television and film violence, war toys, pornography, the Internet, sports, and rock music. It promotes media literacy along with responsible government regulation.

Thirteen Strategies for Addressing Media Violence in Ontario: http://www.c-cave.com/

Globalization, Mergers and Media Violence: What Are the Links with the Commercial Exploitation of Children? http://www.c-cave.com/

Cato Institute
1000 Massachusetts Ave., NW
Washington, DC 20001
Tel: 202-842-0200
Fax: 202-842-3490
E-mail: cato@cato.org
Web: www.cato.org

This nonprofit organization was founded in 1977 with headquarters in Washington, D.C. The institute works to increase and broaden public policy debate to incorporate traditional American principles including limited government, free markets, and individual liberty. It is particularly concerned with having the lay public become knowledgeable about and involved in the appropriate role of government and questions of policy.

Rated V for Violence: Legislation Stamping Warning Labels on Electronic Media May Cause Constitutional Sticker Shock: http://www.cato.org/dailys/08–28–00.html

Center for Adolescent and Family Studies
Eigenmann Hall, 5th Floor, Rm 509
Indiana University
1900 East 10th Street
Bloomington, IN 47408
Tel: 812-855-2355
Fax: 812-855-1847
E-mail: cafs@indiana.edu

A research center in the School of Education at Indiana University that identifies and disseminates information regarding the effective treatment of at-risk adolescents and their families. CAFS serves as a resource for practitioners, teachers, and families by providing information through its website, professional papers, presentations, and other print media.

Great Ideas: Television Violence:
http://education.indiana.edu/cas/tt/v2i3/tv.html

The Center for Communication Policy, UCLA
University of California, Los Angeles
The Center for Communication Policy
Box 951586
Los Angeles, CA 90095–1586
Tel: 310-825-3711
E-mail: internet@ucla.edu
Web: http://www.ccp.ucla.edu

The site includes the report of the three-year project (1995–1997) that monitored television violence funded by the four broadcast networks (ABC, CBS, Fox, and NBC). The center monitored all television with a particular emphasis on broadcast network television, including every series, television movie, theatrical film shown on television, children's program, special and advertisement aired during a television season (over 3,000 hours). The report examines the context in which violence occurs, thus distinguishing between violence that may raise concerns and that which does not. The report is written in a clear and plain style that makes it more accessible to anyone interested in the topic, particularly the press, the government, academics, advocates, and parents.

Television Violence Reports:
http://ccp.ucla.edu/pages/VReports.asp

Center for Communication and Social Policy, UCSB
University of California, Santa Barbara
Santa Barbara, CA 93106
E-mail: Edward Donnerstein, codirector; dean, Division of Social
Sciences donnerst@alishaw.ucsb.edu
Joel Federman, codirector
federman@creative-communication.net
Heather Hinman-Espey, program associate
hespey@sscf.ucsb.edu
Web: http://www.ccsp.ucsb.edu

This university-based center was the home base for the National
Television Violence Study. The center continues its research orientation along with promoting the discussion of policy issues. It is
particularly concerned with improving conflict resolution and the
prevention of violence as well as increasing public awareness and
sensitivity about the harmful effects of violence, including sexual
violence, in the mass media.

National Television Violence Study Report and Summary:
http://www.ccsp.ucsb.edu/ntvs.htm
Violence Prevention Evaluation Project:
http://www.ccsp.ucsb.edu

Center for the Digital Future
USC Annenberg School for Communication
Center for the Digital Future
300 S. Grand Ave, Suite 3950
Los Angeles, CA 90071
Tel: 213-437-4433
E-mail: digitalcenter@digitalcenter.org
Web: http://www.ccp.ucla.edu(http://www.digitalcenter.org/

A center dedicated to the development and recommendation of
communication policy based on sound research. One recent study
is tracking the impact of the Internet on Americans over a ten-year
period.

"Results from Year Four: Impact of the Internet on Americans":
http://www.digitalcenter.org/downloads/DigitalFuture
Report-Year4–2004.pdf

Center for Media Literacy
3101 Ocean Park Boulevard, #200
Santa Monica, CA 90405
Tel: 310-581-0260
Fax: 310-581-0270
E-mail: cml@medialit.org
Web: http://www.medialit.org

The Center for Media Literacy (CML) is a nonprofit educational organization. Its primary mission is to support and promote media literacy education. It provides, on a national level, leadership, professional development, and educational resources. The organization strives to help people of all ages, but especially children and adolescents, to develop the critical thinking skills needed to live in today's media culture. CML was incorporated in 1989 and is an independent, nonpartisan and nonprofit organization. It has both produced and distributed several excellent videos related to media violence.

Their website offers a unique opportunity to learn about media literacy. It is particularly useful and accessible to teachers and parents. The site focuses on goals that provide a consistent definition of media literacy that encompasses intellectual inquiry and creative self-expression. Its philosophy of empowerment through education provides a solid anchor for the field. Some of these goals include:

- focusing on interconnections between teaching and educational resources so media education can be successfully implemented in pre K through 12 classrooms, youth groups, religious education, and after school programs.
- providing access to three decades of work in media literacy education by archiving 300 articles from Media & Values magazine (1977–1993), as well as historical documents and conference reports. Provides a chronology of the development of media literacy in the United States

TV Violence and the Art of Asking the Wrong Question, by George Gerbner:
http://www.medialit.org/reading_room/article459.html

Center for Media and Public Affairs
2100 L Street, NW
Washington, DC 20037
Tel: 202-223-2942
Fax: 202-872-4014
E-mail: mail@cmpa.com
Web: www.cmpa.com

Founded in 1985, this nonpartisan educational and research organization is involved in the study of media and public policy, with a particular focus on entertainment media and the news. Reports are presented in a bimonthly newsletter, *Media Monitor*. Studies have examined how and what the media tell us about health risks. Other recent studies have examined violence, sex, race and ethnicity in popular culture.

Violence in Popular Culture:
http://www.cmpa.com/entertainmentStudies/Violence.htm

Center for Media Studies

SCILS, Rutgers University
4 Huntington Street
New Brunswick, NJ 08901–1071
Tel: 732-932-7500 x8017
Fax: 732-932-7830
Email: njmedialit@scils.rutgers.edu
Web: www.mediastudies.rutgers.edu

This university-based center focuses on how the media impact contemporary society, looking particularly for effective ways in which the media can serve the public interest. The center seeks to support and initiate interdisciplinary studies and collaborative research and teaching within the university as well as develop outreach programs for parents and those in business and the government. Particular areas of interest include Media and Health, Media and Cultural Diversity, and Youth and Media Education.

Youth, Media Education, and Health: The New Jersey Media Literacy Project:
http://www.mediastudies.rutgers.edu/cmsyme.html

Child and Family, Canada

E-mail: ghuot@cccf.fcsqe.ca
Web: www.cfc-efc.ca

This Canadian public education website is part of the Canadian Child Care Federation. It seeks to provide an easy-to-navigate website that will provide credible resources about children and families. The site includes a useful library of relevant documents.

"Television Violence: Review of the Effects on Children of Different Ages" by Wendy L. Josephson, Ph.D.:
http://www.cfc-efc.ca/docs/mnet/00001068.htm

Children Now, Inc.
1212 Broadway, 5th Floor
Oakland CA 94612
Tel: 510-763-2444
Fax: 510-763-1974
E-mail: children@childrennow.org
Web: http://www.childrennow.org

An independent, nonpartisan research and action organization that works to improve the quality of media for children. The website has resources for journalists to help them provide better coverage about issues that affect children. Their recent study *Digital Television: Sharpening the Focus on Children* played a critical role in the adoption of new rules by the FCC to insure that children have access to educational television and that their parents can easily identify educational programs.

"Children and Television Violence, A Report" (Winter 1998): http://www.childrennow.org/media/medianow/mn winter1998.html

"Fair Play? Violence, Gender and Race in Video Games" (2001): http://www.childrennow.org/media/index.html

Children's Defense Fund
25 E Street, NW
Washington, DC 20001
Tel: 202-628-8787
E-mail: cdfinfo@childrensdefense.org
Web: www.childrensdefense.org

With roots in the civil rights movement, this independent, nonprofit organization has focused on the needs of children since 1973. The goal is to help as many children as possible, not just those from particularly needy families. The group has worked to make information available about health care and other issues of importance to the general welfare of children and their families. Their ground breaking media campaigns focusing specifically on gun control and teen pregnancy have been particularly effective.

Resources about media violence: http://www.childrensdefense.org/education/media violence/otherorganizations.asp

Coalition for Quality Children's Media and Kids First!
112 West San Francisco Street, Suite 350A
Santa Fe, New Mexico 87501
Tel: 505-989-8076
Fax: 505-986-8477
E-mail: netman@cqcm.org
Web: www.cqcm.org

Founded in 1991, this not-for-profit organization strives to work with child advocacy groups, the media industry, educators, and families to teach media literacy/critical viewing skills to children and to increase the availability and visibility of high quality children's programs. Community based volunteers rate and evaluate children's media, including videos, DVDs, television programs, software, and children's films. It holds a yearly children's film festival through collaboration with children's museums and other groups, including nonprofit film centers. Its junior film critic program teaches children to be critical media viewers and provides opportunities for them to judge films/programs for the organization. The website includes reviews of endorsed films, videos, software, etc., as well as relevant articles about the media.

Children and Media Information:
http://www.cqcm.org/kidsfirst/finfo.htm

Community Learning Network (CLN)
Web: http://www.cln.org

A site designed for K-12 teachers with over 5,300 links to educational sites. The keyword search and organization of the site into theme pages makes it easy to use. The annotated links include media-related sites including those for media violence, advertising in the media, journalism, and eating disorders. A useful site to help teachers integrate technology into their classrooms.

Television violence web page with links to other sources/pages:
http://www.cln.org/themes/media_violence.html

Computer Addiction Services
McLean Hospital
115 Mill Street
Belmont, MA 02478
E-mail: orzack@computeraddiction.com
Web: www.computeraddiction.com

Clinical Psychologist, Maressa Hecht Orzack, Ph.D., believes computer addiction and inappropriate computer use is similar to substance abuse. As society becomes more computer dependent for both information and entertainment, inappropriate computer use may become a problem affecting both children (use of video games and instant messenger) and adults who become overly involved in chat rooms and other on-line activities.

Educational Resources Information Center (ERIC)
2277 Research Boulevard, 6M
Rockville, MD 20850
Tel: 301-519-5157 and toll free 800-LET-ERIC (538-3742)
Fax: 301-519-6760
E-mail: accesseric@accesseric.org
Web: http://www.eric.ed.gov/

This major data base/information system of educational literature (from journal and conference sources) is sponsored by the U.S. Department of Education's Institute of Education Sciences. It contains more than 1 million citations dating to 1966, many of which are available for free. A major resource for those searching for academic sources.

Eric Digests: http://www.ericfacility.net/databases/ERIC_Digests/ed414078.html

Television Violence and Behavior: A Research Summary (Eric Digest), by Marilyn E. Smith, 1993:

http://www.ericfacility.net/databases/ERIC_Digests/ed366 329.html

Entertainment Software Rating Board
317 Madison Ave, 22nd floor
New York, NY 10017
Tel: 212-759-0700
Fax: 212-759-2223
Web: www.esrb.org

Established in 1994 by the Entertainment Software Association, this organization developed a rating system that is applied to computer/video games. Parents and other consumers can use the ratings to choose games that are age appropriate. Ratings include E (everyone), T (teen), M (mature), and EC (Early childhood). The ratings consist of two parts. Rating symbols indicate the appropriate age group and content descriptors flag content elements (e.g., excessive violence) of interest or concern. Site allows visitors to search for games and their ratings.

Game Rating and Descriptor Guide:
http://www.esrb.org/esrbratings_guide.asp

Family Education Network
20 Park Plaza, 12th Floor
Boston, MA 02116
Tel: 617-542-6500
Web: http://www.fen.com

An online consumer network, launched in 2000, to provide information about learning and information resources. The site has resources for parents, kids/teens, teachers, and those schooled at home as well as reference and shopping links.

"Fighting Media Violence!":
http://www.familyeducation.com/article/0,1120,67
–2376,00.html

Federal Communications Commission (FCC)
1919 M Street, NW
Washington, DC 20554
Tel: 202-418-0200
Fax: 202-418-0232
E-mail: fccinfo@fcc.gov
Web: www.fcc.gov

Established by the Communications Act of 1934, the FCC is an independent agency of the United States Government and directly responsible to Congress. It is made up of 5 commissioners appointed by the President. It regulates all interstate and international communication, including radio, television, satellite, cable, and wireless (cell phone) communication. It allocates the electromagnetic spectrum through the granting of licenses to radio and television stations and other communication organizations.

Fact Sheet: V-Chip:
http://ftp.fcc.gov/Bureaus/Mass_Media/Factsheets/factvc
hip.html
Fact Sheet: Television Use in the U.S.:
http://www.fcc.gov/Bureaus/Mass_Media/Factsheets/fact
vchp.txt

Federal Trade Commission (FTC)
600 Pennsylvania Ave.
Washington, DC 20580
Tel: 202-326-2222
Web: http://www.ftc.gov

Established in 1914, the FTC is the government agency that works
to monitor unfair trade practices and promote free-market competition. Throughout the years it has played an important role in
assessing children's television, particularly in regard to advertising practices.
    Marketing Violent Entertainment to Children: A Review of
Self-Regulation and Industry Practices in the Motion Picture,
Music Recording and Electronic game Industries.
    Press Release:
http://www.ftc.gov/opa/2003/09/violence.htm
    Executive Summary:
http://www.ftc.gov/reports/violence/execsumm.htm
    Follow Up Review (report to Congress), July 2004:
http://www.ftc.gov/os/2004/07/040708kidsviolencerpt.pdf

Film Advisory Board
7045 Hawthorn Ave. #305
Hollywood, CA 90028
Tel: 323-461-6541
Fax: 323-469-8541
Web: http://www.filmadvisoryboard.org/

Founded in 1975, the Film Advisory Board's (FAB) AWARD OF
EXCELLENCE awards and promotes quality family oriented and
children's entertainment. The board considers film, video, TV, CD-
ROM, books and music for recognition In 1988 the FAB devised a
rating system for home video based on level of maturity and content. Ratings include C (children), F (family), PD (parental discre-
tion), PD-M (parental discretion-mature–13 and over), EM

(extremely mature, 17 and older), and AO (adults only, 18 and older).
FAB Rating System:
http://www.filmadvisoryboard.org/ratings/Default.asp

Free Expression Policy Project
Brennan Center for Justice at NYU School of Law and Democracy Program
Free Expression Policy Project
161 Avenue of the Americas, 12th Floor
New York, NY 10013
Tel: 212-992-8847
Fax: 212-995-4550
E-mail: marjorie.heins@nyu.edu
Web: http://www.fepproject.org/index.html

Founded in 2000, FEPP conducts research on difficult issues relating to censorship, including free speech and copyright. It focuses on expression that is publicly funded (in libraries, museums, etc.), Internet filters and rating systems (restrict access to ideas and information), restrictive copyright laws, the consolation of mass media which may reduce public access to the airwaves. Seeks to protect artistic and intellectual freedom. It is part of the Democracy Program at the Brennan Center for Justice at New York University's School of Law.
Media Violence Fact Sheet:
http://www.fepproject.org/factsheets/mediaviolence.html

Google Search Engine
Web: http://www.google.com/

Television violence links:
http://directory.google.com/Top/Society/Issues/Violence_and_Abuse/Media/

Kaiser Family Foundation
Headquarters
2400 Sand Hill Road
Menlo Park, CA 94025
Tel: 650-854-9400
Fax: 650-854-8400

Web: http://www.kff.org
Washington, DC Office / Public Affairs Center
1330 G Street, NW
Washington, DC 20005
Tel: 202-347-5270
Fax: 202-347-5274

This site provides information about the research projects conducted by the foundation on major health care issues. The foundation works with outside organizations to conduct cutting edge research that provides information for the health care industry, the media, policymakers, and the general public. Past studies have focused on television violence and sex in the media. Their Entertainment Media Partnerships work to provide information about HIV and sexually transmitted diseases.

Reports of several violence-related research projects may be found at the website, including "A Parent's Guide to the TV Ratings and V-Chip."

Kansas State University, Dr. John Murray
Professor of Developmental Psychology
School of Family Studies and Human Services
Kansas State University
303 Justin Hall
Manhattan, KS 66506–1403
Tel: 785-532-5510
Fax: 785-532-5505
E-mail: jpm@ksu.edu

A source of information about the research conducted by John Murray and his colleagues in the School of Family Studies and Human Services at Kansas State University.
Television and Violence:
http://www.ksu.edu/humec/fshs/tele.htm
The Impact of Television Violence
http://communication.ucsd.edu/tlg/123/murray.html

Kidsnet
6856 Eastern Avenue, NW, Suite 208
Washington, DC 20012
Tel: 202-291-1400
Fax: 202-882-7315
E-mail: kidsnets@kidsnet.org
Web: http://www.kidsnet.org

KIDSNET provides information and websites to help educators, children and their families access educational information from multimedia, radio, and television sources. It has developed a computerized national clearinghouse to disseminate educational materials and pertinent information about children's television and other media sources. A goal of the organization is to encourage children and their families to become media literate as well as encourage educational excellence from broadcasters. The website provides program ratings and a media guide. KIDSNET is a nonprofit organization that has worked with community organizations, educators, health and social service professionals and media professionals since 1985.

Lion and Lamb Project
4300 Montgomery Avenue, Suite 104
Bethesda, Maryland 20814
Phone : 301-654-3091
Fax : 301-654-2394
E-mail: lionlamb@lionlamb.org
Web: http://www.lionlamb.org

An organization devoted to reducing the marketing of violent games, entertainment, and toys to children. The website pinpoints pages about media violence, including toy lists and information for parents including a parent-action kit.
Media Violence:
http://www.lionlamb.org/media_violence.htm
Media Violence: Video Games:
http://www.lionlamb.org/media_violence_video_games.htm

Magic Dragon
Web: http://www.magicdragon.com

Founded in 1995 as a subsidiary of Emerald City Publishing, Magic Dragon Multimedia provides a domain that links over 600 web pages, for small businesses, nonprofit organizations, as well as links for extensive content of selected areas. The site includes an on-line encyclopedia of fantasy, science fiction, and horror as well as mystery, crime, and thriller media and literature.

Open Questions on the Correlation between Television and Violence, by Jonathan Vos Post (1995):
http://www.magicdragon.com/EmeraldCity/Nonfiction/socphil.html

Media Awareness Network
1500 Merivale Road, 3rd floor
Ottawa, Ontario
Canada K2E 6Z5
Tel: 613-224-7721
Fax: 613-224-1958
E-mail: info@media-awareness.ca
Web: http://www.media-awareness.ca/english/index.cfm

Since 1996 this nonprofit Canadian organization has pioneered the development of media literacy programs. The website, which can be accessed in English and French, contains a comprehensive collection of information relating to media education and literacy. The site includes a section providing tips for parents about talking to kids about media; other sections discuss stereotypes, media violence, diversity, and other pertinent topics for children and their parents.

Research on the Effects of Media Violence:
http://www.media-awareness.ca/english/issues/violence/index.cfm
http://www.media-awareness.ca/english/issues/violence/effects_media_violence.cfm
http://www.media-awareness.ca/english/issues/violence/index.cfm

Media Coalition
139 Fulton Street, Suite 302
New York, NY 10038
Tel: 212-587-4025
Fax: 212-587-2436
E-mail: info@mediacoalition.org
Web: www.mediacoalition.org

Founded in 1973 this organization of booksellers, librarians, and media manufacturers and retailers works to defend First Amendment rights to sell and produce magazines, books, movies, video games, recordings, and videotapes. It defends the public's First Amendment right to have access to a broad range of entertainment and opinion. The site provides regular updates on matters relating to the First Amendment in the courts, state legislatures and Congress.

"Shooting the Messenger: Why Censorship Won't Stop Violence" by Judith Levine:

http://www.mediacoalition.org/reports/stm.htm

Media Education Foundation
60 Masonic Street
Northampton, MA 01060
Tel: 800-897-0089 or 413-584-8500
Fax: 800-659-6882 or 413-586-8398
E-mail: Webmaster@mediaed.org
Web: http://www.mediaed.org/

Founded in 1991, The Media Education Foundation produces and distributes educational documentaries that encourage debate and critical thinking about media content and media industries. Videos, designed to appeal to high school and college students, use cutting edge research to provide information about media violence, stereotypes, advertising, video games, and numerous other topics.

Media Violence: Facts and Statistics:

http://www.mediaed.org/handouts/pdfs/ChildrenMedia.pdf

Media Literacy Online Project
College of Education, University of Oregon, Eugene
Web: http://interact.uoregon.edu/MediaLit/HomePage

This website of the College of Education at the University of Oregon provides numerous links to articles dealing with media violence and other related topics.
Violence, Sex, and Media:
http://interact.uoregon.edu/MediaLit/mlr/readings/contents/violence.html
Television Violence and Children:
http://interact.uoregon.edu/MediaLit/mlr/readings/articles/kalin.html

MediaScope
100 Universal City Plaza, Bldg. 6159
Universal City, CA 91608
Tel: 818-733-3180
Fax: 818-733-3181
E-mail: facts@mediascope.org
Web: http://www.mediascope.org/index.htm

This national, nonprofit policy and research organization worked between 1992 and 2004 to examine and encourage responsible portrayals in television, advertising, films, and video games. It was particularly concerned with promoting issues of social relevance. It oversaw the first year of the National Television Violence Study.
American Public Opinion on Media Violence:
http://www.mediascope.org/pubs/ibriefs/apomv.htm

Media Watch
P.O. Box 618
Santa Cruz, CA 95061
Tel: 831-423-6355
E-mail: Info@mediawatch.com
Web: www.mediawatch.com

Established in 1984 this organization challenges stereotypes about violence, racism, and sexism in the media. It distributes educational videos and media literacy information to create more informed mass media consumers.

Motion Picture Association of America
15503 Ventura Blvd.
Encino, CA 91436
Tel: 818-995-6600
Web: www.mpaa.org

Founded in 1922, the MPAA is the advocate and voice of the American motion picture, the television, and home video industry. Its international counterpart is the MPA (Motion Picture Association). Its mandate has been expanded in recent years to reflect the increasing diversity in the industry. The website provides a useful database with information about movie ratings as well as a page devoted to the television parental guidelines. Another major concern and initiative is the antipiracy program.

TV Parental Guidelines:
http://www.mpaa.org/tv/index.htm
Movie Ratings:
http://www.mpaa.org/movieratings/index.htm

National Alliance for Non-Violent Programming
1101 N. Elm St. #407
Greensboro, NC 27401
Tel: 336-230-0408 l
Fax: 336-574-2946
E-mail: NA4NVP@aol.com
Web: http://www.jack-and-jill.org/NANP.htm

Along with Jack and Jill of America, Inc., this organization works to eliminate the current culture of disrespect and violence by teaching, promoting, and advocating media literacy and nonviolence in communities across the nation. Interesting pages include a discussion on the necessity of teaching ethics to children.

A Media Wake-Up Call:
http://www.jack-and-jill.org/NANP_media_wakeup.htm
Teaching our Children Ethics:
http://www.jack-and-jill.org/home_teaching.htm

National Association of School Psychologists
4340 East West Highway, Suite 402
Bethesda, MD 20814
Tel: 301-657-0270
E-mail: publications@naspweb.org
Web: www.nasponline.org

This organization supports and represents school psychology in order to help school children reach their potential. The site provides links to position papers as well as helpful information for parents and teachers.

Children and Fear of War and Terrorism: Tips for Parents and Teachers:

http://www.nasponline.org/NEAT/children_war

Youth Violence Intervention and Prevention:

http://www.naspcenter.org/teachers/gc_youth.html

National Association for the Education of Young Children (NAEYC)
1509 16th Street, NW
Washington, DC 20036
Tel: 1-800-424-2460
E-mail: naeyc@naeyc.org
Web: www.naeyc.org

Founded in 1926, this organization of early childhood educators seeks to improve programs for children. Focusing on children from birth to 8 years old, the group works to build support for quality early childhood education programs. The site provides links for recent relevant reports and research that can be helpful in developing policy and advocacy as well as practical short articles for parents and teachers. One particularly relevant page provides supplemental information to the articles found in the organization's journal, *Young Children.*

Position Statement: Media Violence in Children's Lives:

http://www.naeyc.org/resources/position_statements/psmevi98.htm

National Cable and Telecommunications Association
1724 Massachusetts Ave., NW
Washington, DC 20036
Tel: 202-775-3550
E-mail: webmaster@ncta.com
Web: www.ncta.com, www.controlyourtv.org

Founded in 1952, the organization is the principal trade association for the cable TV industry in the United States. It seeks, on a national level, to present a unified voice about issues of importance to the industry. The media center link on the web page provides information and press releases about important developments in the industry for NCTA members as well as the media.

This website of the industry notes that cable operators take parents' and educators' concerns about television content seriously. Overall, the industry strives to provide:

- CHOICE in television programming
- CONTROL via tools to manage what comes into the homes, and
- EDUCATION about making good decisions regarding children's media use

National Center for Children Exposed to Violence

Yale Child Study Center
230 South Frontage Road
P.O. Box 207900
New Haven, CT 06520–7900
Tel: 203-785-7047 or 877–49 NCCEV (496-2238)
Fax: 203-785-4608
E-mail: nccev@info.med.yale.edu
Web: www.nccev.org

This organization, part of the Child Study Center at Yale University, works to increase awareness of how exposure to violence affects children. It also works to try to reduce the impact of violence on children and their families as well as those who work with them. The group tries to work with communities to decrease the incidence and impact of violence on children. A particularly relevant link is the page on violence and children.

Children and Violence:
http://www.nccev.org/violence/index.html
Media Violence:
http://www.nccev.org/violence/media.html

National Coalition against Censorship (NCAC)

275 Seventh Ave.
New York, NY 10001
Tel: 212-807-6222
Web: www.ncac.org

An alliance of nonprofit organizations, founded in 1974, that educates about the dangers of censorship. These groups believe that the First Amendment freedoms of expression, thought, and inquiry must be defended. Its web page on special programs provides links relating to how to counter censorship in the schools and how to resist homophobic attacks on education and art.

Violence in the Media (NCAC on the Issues):
http://www.ncac.org/issues/violencemenu.html
"Censorship's Tools DuJour: V-Chips, TV Ratings, PICS, and Internet Filters":
http://www.ncac.org/issues/toolsdujour.html

National Coalition on Television Violence
5132 Newport Ave.
Bethesda, MD 20816
Web: www.nctvv.org

An educational and research organization that seeks to reduce violence in films and on television.

Paper written about the coalition for a University of Texas Journalism course:
http://www.utexas.edu/coc/journalism/SOURCE/j363/nctv.html
Ten common myths about the V-Chip and the facts:
http://www.nctvv.org/NCTV%20Images/V-Chip.htm.

National Institute on Media and the Family
606 24th Avenue South, Suite 606
Minneapolis, MN 55454
Tel: 612-672-5437 and toll free 888-672-5437
Web: www.mediafamily.org

Founded in 1996 this nonprofit, nonsectarian, nonpartisan and independent organization provides reliable information about the media for families and children. Examining the impact of electronic media on children, it provides information so parents and children can make informed decisions about media usage.

Fact Sheet: Children and Media Violence:
http://www.mediafamily.org/facts/facts_vlent.shtml

National PTA
330 N. Wabash Ave., Suite 2100
Chicago, IL 60611–3690
Tel: 312-670-6782
Web: www.pta.org

This nonprofit association of educators and parents is the largest volunteer child advocacy group in the United States. It seeks to promote child welfare in the schools, homes, and community. Strives to create better cooperation between parents and teachers to realize educational goals.

"Helping Children Cope with those Startling Images from Iraq" by Joanne Cantor

http://www.pta.org/parentinvolvement/parenttalk/iraq photos.asp

Nemours Foundation Center for Health Media—Kids Health
The Nemours Center for Children's Health Media
Alfred I. duPont Hospital for Children
1600 Rockland Road
Wilmington, DE 19803
Tel: 302-651-4046
Fax: 302-651-4077
E-mail: info@KidsHealth.org
Web: www.kidshealth.org

Founded in 1992 as part of the Nemours Foundation the Center is committed to improving the health of children. Activities include creating books, videos and the KidsHealth website to help families find health information. The site has pages for parents, kids, and teens.

PageWise, Inc.
815-A Brazos St. #PMB 534
Austin, TX 78701
Tel: 512-478-4566
E-mail: Editor@pagewise.com
Web: http://www.essortment.com

Website of articles for those searching for information on various topics, including media violence. The articles are written by numerous who are experts and scholars in their field.

"Television Violence and Children" by Bobbi Jo Innamorato Williams, 2002

http://wa.essortment.com/televisionviole_rfzn.htm

Parents Television Council
707 Wilshire Boulevard #2075
Los Angeles, CA 90017
Tel: 213-629-9255
E-mail: editor@parentstv.org
Web: http://www.parentstv.org/

A nonpartisan group, established in 1995, that offers private sector solutions to make television programming more socially responsible. The group works with parents to voice support of family-oriented programming and challenges the entertainment industry to make television better for all viewers, but particularly children. The website includes ways to take action as well as provides information. There are pages about ongoing campaigns such as those designed to have better programs in the early evening hours and publications including reviews of both television programs and movies.

Press Release: PTC Study Shows Sex, Violence, and Foul Language Increased 52 Percent on Reality TV Genre Since 2000
http://www.parentstv.org/PTC/publications/release/2004/0628.asp

Public Broadcasting Service (PBS)
Web: www.pbs.org

The PBS comprehensive website provides information about PBS television programs and specials as well as news, history, science, the arts, and technology. The site contains special pages for parents that provide parenting advice as well as information about games and activities for children. PBS TeacherSource provides in depth information for K-12 teachers. Pages for kids provide more activities and games.

The Station Finding information to contact stations and Program Contacts provide a forum to give feedback to specific PBS programs or ask questions of program producers.
PBS Parents:
www.pbs.org/parents
Media Awareness:
http://www.pbs.org/parents/issuesadvice/media_awareness.html

Research Matters
Harvard University
Office of News and Public Affairs
Holyoke Center 1060
Cambridge, MA 02138
Tel: 617-495-1585
Web: http://www.researchmatters.harvard.edu/index.php

The latest news from researchers at Harvard University about medical treatments, societal research, basic science, technological advances, and earth and space exploration.
How Media Violence Touches Children:
http://www.researchmatters.harvard.edu/story.php?article_id=318

Senate Judiciary Committee
The U.S. Department of Health and Human Services
200 Independence Avenue, SW
Washington, DC 20201
Tel: 202-619-0257 and toll free 877-696-6775
Web: http://judiciary.senate.gov/

"Children, Violence and the Media" (A report for parents and policymakers):
http://judiciary.senate.gov/oldsite/mediavio.htm

Surgeon General
The U.S. Department of Health and Human Services
200 Independence Avenue, SW
Washington, DC 20201
Tel: 202-619-0257 and toll free 877-696-6775
Web: www.surgeongeneral.gov

Part of the U.S. Department of Health and Human Services this website provides links to information to improve people's and the nation's health., including testimony before congress and relevant reports and publications.
Media Violence: Exposure and Content:
http://www.surgeongeneral.gov/library/youthviolence/chapter4/appendix4bsec2.html

Teen Health and the Media
Teen Futures Media Network
University of Washington
Experimental Education Unit
Box 357925
Seattle, WA 98195
Tel: 206-543-9414 and toll free 888-TEEN-NET (888-833-6638)
E-mail: thmedia@u.washington.edu
Web: http://depts.washington.edu/thmedia/

Stressing media literacy, the Teen Health and Media Website, provides information so teens can make healthy choices relating to issues critical to their health. Web pages provide information about tobacco, alcohol and other drugs, sexuality, nutrition and body image, and violence. The site also provides information about suicide prevention and other crisis-related hotlines.
Violence:
http://depts.washington.edu/thmedia/view.cgi?section=
violence

The TV Parental Guidelines
P.O. Box 14097
Washington, DC 20004
Tel: 202-879-9364
E-mail: tvomb.usa.net
Web: http://www.tvguidelines.org/

A rating system that is used in conjunction with the V-Chip, an electronic device in all television sets manufactured after 1999. The ratings give parents options to block programs they believe are unsuitable for their children to watch. The TV Parental Guidelines Monitoring Board, experts from the television industry, ensure that the ratings are applied consistently and uniformly.

TV-Turnoff Network
1611 Connecticut Ave., NW, Suite 3A
Washington, DC 20009
Tel: 202-887-0436
Fax: 202-518-5560
E-mail: e-mail@tvturnoff.org
Web: www.tvturnoff.org

Founded in 1994, TV-Turnoff Network is a nonprofit national organization that people to watch less television. Two programs, TV-Turnoff Week and More Reading, Less TV are particularly effective in helping people watch less television. The website provides specific information about this program and provides other useful information for parents and children.

Press Release: TV-Aggression Link Too Strong to Ignore, says TV-Turnoff Network:

http://tv-turnoff.org/tv_violencelinkstrongpr.htm

The UNESCO International Clearinghouse on Children, Youth and Media
Nordicom, Goteborg University, Box 713
SE 405 30 Goteborg, Sweden
Tel: +46-31-733-10-00
Fax: +46-31-733-46 55
E-mail: nordicom@nordicom.gu.se
Web: http://www.nordicom.gu.se/unesco/

The website provides information about children and the media for policy makers, academics, researchers, media professionals, and other interested groups. Special attention is devoted to media violence and media literacy. The Clearinghouse has developed several bibliographies of related research on children and the media as well as a global network of those working in this particular area.

Publications listed on the website:

Promote or Protect: Perspectives on Media Literacy and Regulations (Yearbook 2003)

Bibliography: Children and Media Violence Research (1999)

Influences of Media Violence: A Brief Research Summary

V-Chip Canada
182 Faraday St
Ottawa, Ontario
Canada
K1Y 3M6
Contact: Al MacKay, chair, The Action Group on Violence on Television
Tel: 613-799-3668
Fax: 613-728-4265
E-mail: almackay@magma.ca
Web: http://www.vchipcanada.ca/english/index.html

This website provides information and links about the use of the V-chip to help parents monitor the types of programs their children watch. It discusses how to buy a suitable television set to implement the use of the V-Chip as well as provides information about how programs are rated for violence in Canada.

The Violence Policy Center
1140 19th Street, NW
Suite 600
Washington, DC 20036
E-mail: info@vpc.org
Web: http://www.vpc.org/index.htm

A national nonprofit organization devoted to the study of gun control and to provide information about firearms to policymakers, public health professionals, journalists, and the general public. Website provides links to press releases and publications related to gun violence.

William T. Grant Foundation
570 Lexington Ave., 18th Floor
New York, NY 10022–6837
Tel: 212-752-0071
Fax: 212-752-1398
E-mail: info@wtgrantfdn.org
Web: www.wtgrantfoundation.org

The foundation seeks to help young people reach their potential. It sponsors numerous research projects, including a recent study on understanding adolescent violence and "Prime-Time Teens: Perspectives on the New Youth Media Environment" conducted in conjunction with MediaScope, Inc.

Adolescent's Sexual Health and the Internet: A Case Study of Iwannaknow.org:
www.wtgrantfoundation.org/grant_profile3079/grant_profile_show.htm?doc_id=79600

8

Video and Film Resources

There are numerous videos about violence and related topics in the media. Some have been developed, created, and produced by independent producers, whereas others have been developed, created, and produced by organizations whose missions involve the development and distribution of educational videos.

Three organizations are the primary sources for instructional/educational videos and DVDs.

Films for the Humanities and Sciences
P.O. Box 2053
Princeton, NJ 08543-2053
Tel: 800-257-5126
Fax: 609-671-0266
Email: custserv@films.com
Web: http://www.films.com

This company has been listing and/or selling videos generated by independent producers for more than twenty-five years. Its website notes that "our editorial board chooses each program on the basis of the importance of its subject, the quality of its production, and its relevance as an instructional aid. The result is a collection of the best work of the world's preeminent film makers."

The website and catalogue describes both individual videos, as well as series of videos related to a specific topic.

Center for Media Literacy
3101 Ocean Park Boulevard, #200
Santa Monica, CA 90405
Tel: 310-581-0260
Fax: 310-581-0270
E-mail: cml@medialit.org
Web: http://www.medialit.org

The Center for Media Literacy (CML) an independent, nonpartisan nonprofit educational organization was incorporated in 1989. Its primary mission is to support and promote media literacy education. It provides leadership, professional development, and educational resources on a national level. The organization strives to help people of all ages, but especially children and adolescents, develop the critical thinking skills needed to live in today's media culture. It has both produced and distributed several excellent videos related to media violence.

Media Education Foundation
60 Masonic Street
Northampton, MA 01060
Tel: 800-897-0089 or 413-584-8500
Fax: 800-659-6882 or 413-586-8398
E-mail: Webmaster@mediaed.org
Web: www.mediaed.org

This organization creates, produces, and distributes video documentaries designed to develop and encourage critical thinking and debate about media ownership, commercial media content, and the diverse representations of ideas and people.

Two additional sites for media-related videos:

Video Librarian
8705 Honeycomb Ct., NW
Seabeck, WA 98380
Tel: 800-692-2270
E-mail: vidlib@videolibrarian.com
Web: www.videolibrarian.com
Video Librarian is the video review magazine for public, school, academic, and special libraries, offering nearly 200 critical reviews per issue.

California Newsreel
500 Third Street, Suite 505
San Francisco, CA 94107
Tel: 415-284-7800
Fax: 415-284-7801
E-mail: contact@newsreel.org
Web: www.newsreel.org

California Newsreel is an organization similar to Films for the Humanities and Sciences.

This chapter will list the most relevant documentaries on media violence, beginning with those distributed by Films for the Humanities and Sciences, then the Center for Media Literacy, and finally the Media Education Foundation. The last part of the chapter will list videos from California Newsreel, as well as a number of independently produced and distributed videos and DVDs.

The entries will provide, when available, the title, distributor, length, copyright date, format, and ISBN number, as well as a brief abstract of the content. Most of the information for these listings comes from the organizations' websites, and the reader is encouraged to visit these sites for more specific information about these resources and how to order them.

Films for the Humanities and Sciences

Individual Documentaries

It's Not Okay: Speaking Out against Youth Violence
Date: 2000
Length: 40 minutes
Format: VHS and DVD
ISBN: 0-7365-3257-9

High school students discuss violence and its day-to-day impact in schools, homes, and the community. Teens present their perspectives on the causes of violent behavior, bullying, mob mentality, effects of dysfunctional families, and the fears they face going to and from school. Mental health professionals and school administrators note the need for more parental support, the elimination of media stereotypes, and social change. Objectionable language.

Media Hype: When News Coverage Goes Too Far
Date: 2002
Length: 41 minutes
Format: VHS and DVD
ISBN: 0-7365-5196-4

Bob Lichter (Center for Media and Public Affairs), Greg McCrary (Threat Assessment Group), and ABC News anchor John Stossel discuss factors contributing to the presentation and exaggeration of danger and risk in the news media. Discusses why the reporting of homicides increased by 700 percent during the 1990s, when the actual U.S. homicide rate dropped by 50 percent. Other topics include road rage, car jacking, and the industry's "if it bleeds, it leads" reporting style.

Reporting on Terrorism: The News Media and Public Health
Date: 2004
Length: 57 minutes
Format: VHS and DVD

This Fred Friendly seminar explores how the news media could prepare for or cope with a potential bioterrorist attack. A hypothetical scenario examines how patients should be handled, when the health department should be contacted, how journalists should cover the story, how the public should be told, and their possible reactions. Panelists include a newspaper editor and news personnel from CNN, personnel from the Centers for Disease Control, a police chief, the president and general manager of a television station, politicians, and a medical doctor. See www.fredfriendly.org for additional resources.

School Violence
Date: 1998
Length: 20 minutes
Format: VHS and DVD

Report on the success of New Haven, Connecticut's, community-based outreach program (partnered with the Yale University Child Study Program, the police department, and numerous agencies) to promote safety and curb violence through intervention, mentoring, and after-school programs.

Should You Let Them Watch? Assessing Media Violence
Date: 2000
Length: 13 minutes
Format: VHS and DVD
ISBN: 0-7365-3192-0

An ABC news program debate about media violence. Leonard Eron and L. Rowell Heusmann (University of Michigan), whose decades of research support the contention that media violence is harmful, take the affirmative position. The negative position is presented by Richard Rhodes (Pulitzer-Prize-winning science author) and Jonathan Freedman (University of Toronto) who contend that media violence does not promote violent behavior.

TV-TV: The Television Revolution
Date: 1995
Length: 96 minutes
Format: VHS and DVD

Stand-alone essays by media luminaries (e.g., George Gerbner, Oliver Stone, Camille Paglia, and Marshall McLuhan) discuss the far-reaching effects of television on society. Topics include how the global village encourages U.S. imperialism, pop culture, how television violence fosters a culture of fear, the use of sound bites in politics, and how news programs try to improve their audience ratings.

TV Violence and You
Date: 1995
Length: 30 minutes
Format: VHS and DVD

George Gerbner (dean emeritus, The Annenberg School for Communication, University of Pennsylvania) and other media experts discuss television violence, including why television is violent and how viewers are affected by these images. Video clips illustrate five areas, including how stereotypes and putdowns build distrust, how television affects interpersonal relationships, news, censorship, and television as big business. Contains some objectionable content.

Violence and Sex on TV
Date: 1993
Length: 28 minutes
Format: VHS and DVD

An adapted Phil Donahue program examines whether young people's consistent diet of onscreen violence has altered their view of reality. Discussions explore whether there should be government restrictions. Includes an interview with Jeanne Quinn, who believes TV violence was responsible for her son's murder.

You Can't Say That! "Politically Correct" Free Speech
Date: 2000
Length: 43 minutes
Format: VHS and DVD
ISBN: 0-7365

An evaluation of freedom of speech in which ABC News correspondent John Stossel examines constraints, including virtual "speech police" who use special forms of censorship and "sensitivity training" to protect the public from offensive language.

Youth Crises: Planning the Response to Hostage-Taking, Shootings, and Suicides
Length: 37-minute video, 1 facilitator guide, 1 implementation guide
Format: multimedia format

A comprehensive development program to help school administrators prepare an action plan to reestablish and maintain order if a school erupts in violence. Focuses on aspects of crisis management, including how to respond to the media, how to establish emergency communications, how to work with law enforcement agencies, and how to maintain student support and provide counseling.

Series

**Media Interrupted: The Dissection
of Media in American Culture**
Date: 2001
Length: Each video is 25 minutes
Format: VHS and DVD
ISBN: 0-7365-3553-5
A three-part series that examines the influence of increased media availability, including greater channel capacity and widespread Internet access. Experts, including George Gerbner (professor of communications, Temple University), Todd Gitlin (New York University), and Melanie Mannarino (*Seventeen* magazine), discuss how television, newspapers, and advertising affect what people buy and what they do, as well as how these media generate stereotypes of sex and sexuality.

Media Power Series
Date: 1997
Length: Eight 28-minute units
Format: VHS and DVD

An eight-part series that examines the role and dynamics of the media-audience relationship, particularly in shaping perceptions. It includes:
　　Mass Media in Society
　　Media Rights and Responsibilities
　　Media Ethics
　　Media Impact
　　Audience and Feedback
　　Global Media
　　Public Relations
　　Advertising

Media Impact (part of the Media Power Series)
Date: 1997
Length: 28 minutes
Format: VHS and DVD
ISBN: 0-7/365-2221-2

How film and television pervade everyday life, their seductive nature, and how viewers may find it difficult to differentiate fact from fiction. Examines how behaviors, such as smoking and violence, are popularized in the media. Illustrates how violent images may lead to desensitization in relation to real-life situations.

Mass Media in Society (part of the Media Power Series)
Date: 1997
Length: 28 minutes
Format: VHS and DVD

Industry and academic experts discuss media globalization and the future of mass media. Although in the United States the typical person watches about 4.5 hours of TV each day, the current media environment produces demographically fragmented audiences along with increased demand for interaction communication. Explores the idea of mass media and whether the mass media may become extinct.

Language of Photography Series
Date: 2001
Length: Eight 27-minute units
Format: VHS and DVD

An eight-part series in which academics, museum personnel, and world-class photographers examine the importance of visual literacy in relation to the history and mechanics of photography. Explores concerns of photographers, including digital image manipulation and consumer issues, including selective perception and information overload. It includes:
    Introduction to Photography and Visual Literacy
    Photography and the Brain
    Decoding Photographic Images
    Photographic Storytelling
    Portraits and Snapshots
    Photography: Making Art and Recording Life
    Persuasion, Propaganda, and Photography
    Truth or Fiction? Photography and Ethics

Persuasion, Propaganda, and Photography (part of the Language of Photography series)
Date: 2001
Length: 27 minutes
Format: VHS and DVD

Examines the manipulative power of photography. Illustrates how youth and physical perfection have become the focus of commercial advertising, changing the way most people view themselves and others. Explores how the media exploit sexuality and violence and demonstrates how politics and the political scene are dominated by photogenic people.

School Crime: How to Fight It
Date: 1994
Length: Three 25-minute units
Format: VHS

This three-part series examines how prevention, early intervention, and community and student support have helped the San Antonio school district fight school crime and violence. It includes:
    School Crime: Sounding the Alarm
    School Crime: Campus Combat Zone
    School Crime: Establishing Communication

School Crime: Sounding the Alarm (Part of the Series School Crime: How to Fight It)
Date: 1994
Length: 24 minutes
Format: VHS

While exploring the numerous causes of and possible solutions to school crime, the video presents a proactive approach to its elimination. It shows the role played by alcohol, drugs, media violence, and gang membership in school crime, as well as the problems of dysfunctional families in combating gang violence. Examines enforcement techniques, including profiling characteristics of gang membership so as to identify those who might be targeted to join a gang and/or become involved in violence.

Series: The Public Mind
Date: 1989
Length: Four 60-minute units
Format: VHS and DVD

A four-part series to explore, in a society dominated by images, how fact and fiction are melded to form public opinion. The series examines whether people can distinguish between fiction and the truth and whether they know they are ill informed. Host Bill Moyers notes, "Our public discourse and our ability as a political culture to face reality depend upon our information system. If it gives us an inadequate picture of reality, we wind up in trouble. Our own willingness to face reality has been deeply affected by the triumph of the visual image as the grammar of the times." It includes:
Consuming Images
Leading Questions
Illusions of News
The Truth About Lies

Consuming Images (Part of the Public Mind Series)
Date: 1989
Length: 60 minutes
Format: VHS and DVD
ISBN: 0-7365-0419-2

This video examines the cultural atmosphere of the mass-produced visual images in which American society is immersed (billboards, rock videos, and print and electronic advertisements). What do these images say about Americans? What do they say to Americans?

The Center for Media Literacy

Beyond Blame: Challenging Violence in the Media
Date:1995
Format: VHS

A media literacy program developed to explore violence in movies; on television; and in the news, music videos, and video games. Explores why viewers typically ask the wrong questions and what questions they should ask. Provides opportunities to practice basic skills, including critical thinking and problem solving. Discusses media violence in terms of an unproductive "circle of blame." Shows that media violence will only be reduced if everyone becomes involved in a learning process that goes from awareness to action.

Media Literacy Video
Date: 1998
Length: 15 minutes
Format: VHS

Produced by International Telecommunications Services (ITS), this is an overview of media literacy designed for middle school students. Explains the importance of media literacy and illustrates how to analyze as well as create media.

Media Education Foundation

Beyond Good and Evil: Children, Media, and Violent Times
Format: VHS and DVD
Length: 39 minutes (VHS) and 35 minutes (DVD)

An examination of "good" and "evil" in entertainment media and the news. Explores how this rhetoric helps dehumanize enemies and justifies their killing as well as treating the suffering and sacrifices of innocent civilians as a necessary evil. Interviews include media scholars, child psychologists, teachers, and children.

The Electronic Storyteller: TV and the Cultivation of Values,
Date: 1997
Length: 30 minutes
Format: VHS

Examines storytelling in today's multinational corporate media environment. Describes cultivation theory and how it differs from traditional studies of media effects and how images of gender, class, and race are critical in today's media. Professor George Gerbner, using this theoretical perspective, describes the role of the media in Americans' conceptions about themselves and the world.

Game Over—Gender, Race and Violence in Video Games
Date: 2001
Length: 41 minutes
Format: VHS and DVD

An educational documentary that explores the representation of race, gender, and violence in video games. The first part of the video looks at sexual and racial representations; the second focuses on images of violence.

The Killing Screens: Media and the Culture of Violence
Date: 1994
Length: 37 minutes
Format: VHS

Examines media violence from the perspective of cultivation theory rather than the simplistic behavioral model that real-world violence is caused by media violence. Professor George Gerbner discusses the psychological, political, and social impacts of growing up in a media environment filled with ritualized and violent images created by multinational media giants.

Rich Media, Poor Democracy
Date: 2003
Length: 30 minutes
Format: VHS and DVD

Explores how today's media environment of large conglomerates lacks competition while providing a homogenization of opinion and formula-driven programming. Professors Robert W. McChesney and Mark Crispin Miller explain how journalism in today's multinational corporate environment typically produces news that is sensational but lacking in information.

Tough Guise—Masculinity and the Media
Date: 1999
Length: 75 minutes (an abridged version is also available)
Format: DVD

An examination of the media's depiction of men and the cultural norms of being a male in today's society. Jason Katz explores sports, video games, school violence, the gun culture, and so on in eleven segments. Some segments include strong violence.

California Newsreel

On Television: Public Trust or Private Property
Date: 1988
Length: 56 minutes
Format: VHS

This video on U.S. television policy examines the Fairness Doctrine, license renewal, and network mergers. It poses the key questions about the electromagnetic spectrum, a scarce public resource. It shows how the Communication Act of 1934 authorized the licensing of commercial broadcasters to develop this resource in exchange for serving "the public interest, convenience and necessity."

On Television: Teach the Children
Date: 1992
Length: 56 minutes
Format: VHS

One of the first documentaries designed to help educators and parents scrutinize television's hidden "curriculum." Using clips from Saturday morning cartoons, situation comedies, and music videos with commentary by critics, scholars, and network executives, this video explores the values television communicates, its role models, and the behaviors it motivates.

On Television: The Violence Factor
Date: 1984
Length: 58 minutes
Format: VHS
On Television Ltd., South Carolina Educational TV

Host Edwin Newman explores the impact of television violence on viewers, especially young children, through interviews with actors, network executives, media analysts, mental health researchers, children, and interested adults.

Race against Prime Time
Date: 1985
Length: 58 minutes
Format: VHS

Explores how African Americans are presented in television news. It focuses on the newsrooms of Miami's three network affiliates during the Liberty City uprising, which left eighteen dead. A classic case study of what people see and don't see in the news. It documents how local television news reporters anoint black community spokespersons, how the news tends to characterize whites as victims and blacks as rioters, and, importantly, how the news fails to place the disturbances within the context of civic neglect.

Additional Producers/Distribution Sources

Beyond the News: Television Violence and You
Date: 1997
Length: 30 minutes
Format: VHS
Mennonite Media Productions
1251 Virginia Ave.
Harrisonburg, VA 22802-2497
Tel: 540-434-6701 or 1-800-999-3534
E-mail: info@MennoMedia.org
Web: http://www.mennonitemission.net/Work/MennoMedia/

George Gerbner analyzes violence in one week of television shows. Television violence is explored in relation to its effects on viewers' perceptions of the world, particularly in relation to violence between men and women and violence at sporting events.

Columbine
Date: 2001
Length: 60 minutes
Format: VHS
CBS Video

    60 Minutes
    524 West 57th Street
    New York, NY 10019
    Tel: 1-800-848-3256

CBS Online store:
http://store.cbs.com/video_category.php?showID=22&collID=21

Originally seen on *60 Minutes, II* (April 17, 2001), this video reexamines the shootings at Columbine High School. It specifically addresses whether the incident could have been prevented or if the police could have done more at the time of the shootings.

Does TV Kill?
Date: 1995
Length: 90 minutes
Format: VHS

PBS Video
Public Broadcasting Service
1320 Braddock Place
Alexandria, VA 22314-1698
Tel: 800-334-3337
Fax: 703-739-5269
Web:
http://www.pbs.org/wgbh/pages/frontline/teach/tvkill-guide.html

An original broadcast of *Frontline,* first seen on January 10, 1995 and produced in conjunction with Oregon Public Television, this video focuses on Leonard Eron's studies on aggression and what we know about television's effects on people, particularly children. The video was prepared as part of the National Campaign to Reduce Youth Violence. Includes interviews with Leonard Eron, Newton Minnow, Barry Sanders, Robert Phillips, and Milton Chen.

Don't Be a TV: Television Victim
Date: 1993
Length: 18 minutes
Format: VHS

Media Watch
P.O. Box 618
Santa Cruz, CA 05061
Tel: 408-427-3169
Web: www.mediawatch.com

Examines biases on television, focusing on gender and racial stereotyping, as well as images relating to violence and sensationalism. Challenges viewers to think about the social roles that television presents.

Media Mayhem
Date: 1994
Length: 29 minutes
Format: VHS

> Northeastern Wisconsin In-School Telecommunications (NEWIST)
> 2420 Nicolet Drive. OS 1040Green Bay, WI 54311
> Tel: 920-465-2599 or 800-633-7445
> Fax: 920-465-2723
> E-mail: newest@uwgb.edu
> Web: http://www.uwgb.edu/newist/

An examination of television, movies, music, and video games by seven teenagers. Shows how media violence is devised to attract audiences rather than reflect reality.

Prime Time Violence
Date: 1994
Length: 47 minutes
Format: VHS
A&E Home Video

> New Video
> 126 Fifth Ave, 15th Floor
> New York, NY 10011
> Tel: 800-314-8822
> Fax: 212-206-9001
> Web: http://www.newvideo.com/

Examines the relationship between television and violence in society. Explores such questions as whether the government should impose guidelines on producers and if such tactics would be constitutional. Includes commentary by Senator Paul Simon, Gene Siske (TV critic), Howard Stringer (president, CBS), Newton Minow (past FCC chairman), and Michael Moriarity (actor).

Social Cognitive Theory
Davidson Films

735 Tank Farm Road, Suite 210San Luis Obispo, CA 93401
Tel: 805-594-0422 or 888-437-4200
Fax: 805-594-0532
Web: www.davidsonfilms.com

A presentation of Professor Bandura's far-reaching theory. It uses archival materials and other visuals to illustrate the major concepts of this important theory in communication and social psychology.

Television and Human Behavior
Date: 1992
Length: 26 minutes
Learning Seed

330 Telser Road
Lake Zurich, IL 60047
Tel: 800-634-4941
Fax: 847-540-0854
Web: www. Learningseed.com

This videotape of a 1991 presentation looks at television in American life and how both individuals and society are affected by television. It explores television addiction, television violence, and the lessons that television teaches about life.

Tell It Like It Is
Length: 15 minutes
Format: VHS

A National Coalition against Censorship Production
Distributed by Carousel Film and Video, New York
250 Fifth Ave, Suite 204
New York, NY 10001
Tel: 800-683-1660
Fax: 212-683-1662
Web: http://www.carouselfilms.com/

Video discussing censorship and its negative implications through the eyes of children and authors.

TV on Trial
Date: 1978
Format: VHS
Length: 119 minutes

> PBS Video
> Public Broadcasting Service
> 1320 Braddock Place
> Alexandria, VA 22314-1698
> Tel: 800-334-3337
> Fax: 703-739-5269
> Web:
> http://www.pbs.org/wgbh/pages/frontline/teach/tvkill-guide.html

Video of the trial of fifteen-year-old Ronny Zamora, who was accused of the murder of his eighty-two-year-old neighbor. The trial was televised and Zamora's lawyer put TV itself on trial because he contended that his client was influenced by violent television programs.

Violence in the Media
Date: 1997
Length: 46 minutes
Format: VHS

> CBS News Productions in association with A&E Network
> New Video
> 126 Fifth Ave, 15th Floor
> New York, NY 10011
> Tel: 800-314-8822
> Fax: 212-206-9001
> Web: http://www.newvideo.com/

Originally broadcast on the History Channel, this program with Mike Wallace examines whether television and movie violence lead to more violence or merely reflect a country filled with violence.

Warning! The Media May Be Hazardous to Your Health
Date: 1990
Length: 36 minutes
Format: VHS

> Media Watch
> P.O. Box 618
> Santa Cruz, CA 05061
> Tel: 408-427-3169
> Web: http://www. Mediawatch.com

Examines media images that glamorize fear, hatred, and violence between the sexes.

9

Print Resources and Annotated Bibliography

Thousands of books and journal articles have been written about media violence. The entries selected for this bibliographic resource are divided into six groups: government commissions and related publications, including government hearings; the media industry; reports from organizations such as the American Medical Association and the Kaiser Family Foundation; a selection of the most important, pertinent, and recent scholarly writings; books generated for a more general audience (trade books); and relevant books and journal articles on video games.

Government Commissions and Related Publications

Baker, Robert. K., and Sandra. J. Ball. 1969. *Mass Media and Violence: Staff Report to the National Commission on the Causes and Prevention of Violence.* Vol. 9. Washington, DC: U.S. Government Printing Office.

A commission organized in response to the racial and political disturbances in the United States during the 1960s as well as the media's coverage of these disturbances. Presents research on the prevalence of violence in television drama in 1967 and 1968 in comparison with real world statistics, violent content in other media, and effects on behavior and attitudes. The task force called for industry support of research and self-regulation of content.

Cater, Douglass, and Stephen Strickland. 1975. *TV Violence and the Child: The Evolution and Fate of the Surgeon General's Report.* New York: Russell Sage.

A history of the surgeon general's Advisory Committee on Television and Social Behavior and its 1972 report. Discusses concerns about media influence voiced during the Senate hearings of the 1950s and 1960s on television and juvenile delinquency as well as the 1974 hearings about the Surgeon General's report. Includes a candid discussion of the politics and the compromises made in completing the report. Summarizes major studies commissioned by the committee.

Cooper, Cynthia. A. 1996. *Violence on Television: Congressional Inquiry, Public Criticism, and Industry Response: A Policy Analysis.* Lanham, MD: University Press of America.

A description of numerous congressional inquiries relating to television violence. The author explains both the response of the industry and public to the testimony of witnesses and the conclusions drawn.

Gerbner, George. 1972. "Violence in Television Drama: Trends in Symbolic Functions." In George A. Comstock and Eli A. Rubinstein, eds., *Television and Social Behavior.* Vol. 1, *Media Content and Control,* pp. 28–187. Washington, DC: U.S. Government Printing Office.

Analysis of violence in weeklong samples (N=281) of prime time and weekend daytime network dramatic programs (1967, 1968, and 1969). Findings illustrate violence as a power hierarchy. Levels of violence remained relatively stable during this three-year period: children's cartoons were the most violent; males were twice as likely as females to be involved in violence; and females, when involved, were more likely to be victims than initiators of violence.

Hoerrner, Keisha L. 1999. "Symbolic Politics: Congressional Interest in Television Violence." *Journalism and Mass Communication Quarterly* 76, no. 4: 684–698.

Examines, over forty-six years, how political, economic, and social factors are related to congressional actions about television violence. Proposes a theory of symbolic politics to explain the relationship. The data revealed that Congress took more symbolic than substantive actions. There was no relationship between the amount of violence on television and congressional interest in the topic.

National Commission on the Causes and Prevention of Violence. 1970. *Final Report.* Washington, DC: Government Printing Office.

Commission's interpretation of sponsored research led to the conclusion that television violence can be imitated by children, particularly if they identify with characters and if the violent behaviors they see are perceived as justified and effective. Young children are particularly vulnerable. The commission suggested that the industry eliminate violent cartoons and reduce violent programming; that the context of portrayed violence be altered; and that research on the effects of televised violence be conducted. Parental supervision of children was also highly recommended.

Pearl, David L., Lorraine Bouthilet, and Joyce Lazar, eds. 1982. *Television and Behavior: Ten Years of Scientific Progress and Implications for the Eighties.* Vol. 1, *Summary Report.* Rockville, MD: National Institute of Mental Health.

Summarizes trends in violent content and results of research about the effects of televised violence on behavior and attitudes, as well as the cultivation of conceptions of violence and mistrust. Outlines methodological issues such as the definition and unitization of violence. Includes a useful bibliography.

Pearl, David, Lorraine Bouthilet, and Joyce Lazar, eds. 1982. *Television and Behavior: Ten Years of Scientific Progress and Implications for the Eighties.* Vol. 2, *Technical Reviews.* Rockville, MD: National Institute of Mental Health.

Technical reviews that update the 1972 surgeon general's report. Includes major studies relating to televised violence—its forms and contributions to the socialization process. The projects discuss differences in research designs and indicate the direction for most current and future research.

Rowland, Willard D. 1983. *The Politics of Television Violence.* Beverly Hills, CA: Sage.

An examination of research on the effects of media violence, focusing on the contributions and roles of researchers, politicians, reformers, and the industry.

Surgeon General's Scientific Advisory Committee on Television and Social Behavior. 1972. *Television and Growing Up: The Impact of Televised Violence.* Washington, DC: U.S. Government Printing Office.

Summary of twenty-three research projects, including field

and laboratory studies, funded by the U.S. government. The Surgeon General's Advisory Committee concluded that the majority of findings supported the view that under certain conditions, television violence causes aggressive behavior among children predisposed to aggressiveness.

U.S. House, Committee on Energy and Commerce. 1993. *Violence on Television*. Hearings before the Subcommittee on Telecommunications and Finance, 103rd Congress, 2nd Session.

U.S. House, Judiciary Committee. 1992. *Violence on Television*. Testimony before the Subcommittee on Crime and Criminal Justice, 102nd Congress, 2nd session.

Media Industry

Lometti, Guy E. 1995. The Measurement of Televised Violence. *Journal of Broadcasting & Electronic Media* 39: 292–295.
   Discusses a possible scenario for measuring television violence. Posits that different types of violence (slapstick, gun shots) need to be assessed differently. The severity or intensity of violent acts should be assessed in addition to a mere count of violent incidents. The context of violence should also be monitored. Samples should consist of composite weeks from both the spring and fall of the year.

Milavsky, J. Ronald, Ronald Kessler, Horst Stipp, and William S. Rubens. 1982. "Television and Aggression: Results of a Panel Study." In David Pearl, Lorraine Bouthilet, and Joyce Lazar, eds., *Television and Behavior: Ten Years of Scientific Progress and Implications for the Eighties*. Vol. 2, *Technical Reviews*, pp. 138–157. Rockville, MD: National Institute of Mental Health. See also J. Ronald Milavsky, et al, "Television and Aggression: Results of a Panel Study." New York: Academic, 1982.
   A lagged, longitudinal quasi-experiment designed to test the hypothesis of a causal relationship between television violence and increased aggressive behavior. The subjects were 2,400 urban elementary school boys and girls and 800 urban high school boys. Exposure to violent television programs was measured by self-reports (how often a list of programs was seen). Aggressive behavior was measured by an index of aggressiveness using peer reports (younger children) and self-reports of the last month's behavior

(high school boys). This study found few statistically significant regression coefficients and concluded that no relationship existed between viewing violence and subsequent aggressive behavior.

Stipp, Horst, and J. Ronald Milavsky. 1988. "U.S. Television Programming's Effects on Aggressive Behavior of Children and Adolescents." *Current Psychology: Research and Reviews* 7, no. 1: 76–92.

Review of the research on the effect of actual television viewing (entertainment) on children and adolescents' aggressive behavior. Few studies exist that are not conducted in a laboratory; the few existing studies do not find significant effects of television viewing. Studies also do not take into consideration recent changes (cable, VCRs) in the viewing environment.

Wurtzel, Alan, and Guy Lometti. 1984. "Researching Television Violence: Television at the Crossroads." *Society* 21, no. 6: 22–30.

Presents the argument that the findings from the NIMH 1982 report do not support the conclusion of a causal relationship between television violence and aggressive behavior because the authors of this article did not see a clear consensus among most researchers. They also argue that the amount of violence on television has decreased and that the research does not support the conclusion that television significantly alters viewer attitudes and conceptions of social reality. Includes a summary of ABC broadcast standards, practices, policies, and procedures (guidelines to ensure responsible depiction of violence in entertainment programming).

———. 1990. "The Television Violence-Viewer Aggression Debate." In R. Surette, ed., *The Media and Criminal Justice Policy: Recent Research and Social Effects*, pp. 23–33. Springfield, IL: Charles C. Thomas.

Contends that findings from the 1982 NIMH report of a causal relationship between aggressive behavior and television violence are not warranted. The authors, researchers with ABC, believe that ABC has a responsibility to put this report and similar studies into perspective.

Organizations and Reports

American Academy of Child and Adolescent Psychiatry. 2000. "Media Violence Harms Children." *Joint Statement of the Impact of*

Entertainment Violence on Children—Congressional Public Health Summit. New York: Lippincott, Williams, and Wilkins.

Statement issued in conjunction with the American Academy of Pediatrics, the American Psychological Association, and the American Medical Association notes the causal relationship between media violence and children's aggressive behavior. Discusses four ways media violence may influence children: suggesting violence as a way to solve problems and conflicts, desensitization, fear of being a victim of violence, and increases in actual aggressive behavior.

American Medical Association. 1996. *Physician Guide to Media Violence.* Chicago: American Medical Association.

Presents the numerous health hazards associated with excessive viewing of media violence and notes the relationship between viewing and negative behaviors, particularly aggressiveness. The guidebook provides suggestions and options that physicians can use, both when seeing children and to pass onto parents. Contains bibliographic references and a list of available resources.

American Psychological Association. 1993. *Violence and Youth: Psychology's Response. Vol. 1, Summary Report of the American Psychological Association Commission on Violence and Youth.* Washington, DC: American Psychological Association.

A description of the environmental factors that may lead to violence in youngsters (typically between three and twenty-two years old) as well as interventions that may help prevent violent behavior.

Annenberg Public Policy Center of the University of Pennsylvania. 2003. *Parent's Use of the V-Chip to Supervise Children's Television Use.* Philadelphia: Annenberg Public Policy Center.

Report of the results of a study that examined whether parents used the V-chip. Some of the problems with using the V-chip are that few parents actually use it, many do not understand how to use it, and the V-chip on the television set typically was hidden and/or difficult to program. Moreover, some parents feel that they do not need a V-chip to adequately supervise their children's viewing. In the study, roughly 100 families received a television set with a working V-chip. At the end of a year, the data indicated that the mothers were typically satisfied with the V-chip and some felt that they would continue to use it. At the same time, some felt that it did not change the way their family watched television but instead was a way to help protect their children from accidentally seeing things the parents would rather they not see. But the V-chip was not seen as a panacea for protecting children from adverse images.

Center for Media and Public Affairs. 1994. *Violence in Prime Time Television: 1992 vs. 1994.* Washington, DC: Center for Media and Public Affairs.

A content analysis that focused on physical violence on ten channels (network, independent, and cable) during one day in 1992 and 1994 and compared findings from the two samples.

Children Now. 2001. *Fair Play? Violence, Gender and Race in Video Games.* Oakland, CA: Children Now.

This report looks at top-selling games, particularly at the types of messages they send about gender, race, and violence. It also explores some of the other unhealthy outcomes related to video games (isolation, obesity, loneliness) and examines how the games could influence children's behaviors, attitudes, and beliefs.

Cole, Jeffrey. 1995. *The UCLA Television Violence Monitoring Report.* Los Angeles: UCLA Center for Communication Policy.

Funded by the broadcast television networks (ABC, CBS, NBC, and FOX), the UCLA Center monitored over 3,000 hours of television programming in the 1994–1995 season and found that network programming had few issues of concern compared to cable and premium channels (e.g., HBO) , although there are still serious issues regarding the scheduling of programs that are violent. Theatrical films, program promotions, and children's television, however, still raise serious concerns and advisories should be applied to these programs more consistently.

———. 1998. *The UCLA Television Violence Monitoring Report, Year 3.* Los Angeles: UCLA Center for Communication Policy.

The report of the UCLA Center's third consecutive year (1996–1997 season) of monitoring television programs. Most of the concerns raised by this project had to do with television specials (often reality programs); these programs had more violence in 1996–1997 than they had in 1994–1995. The violence in movies was relatively stable, and again, the group thought that advisories needed to be provided more regularly. Theatrical films did make some improvement from the first season of monitoring. The most improvement was found for the on-air promotions for the network's future programming.

Federal Trade Commission. 2000. *Marketing Violence to Children.* www.ftc.gov/opa/2000/09/youthviol.htm (accessed August 2004).
Report states that children under seventeen are typically the target of advertising for violent video games, television programs, and movies. The report suggests the violent entertainment rating systems be better enforced and that existing regulatory codes should be expanded to prevent advertising violent media to children.

Federman, Joel. 2002. *Rating Sex and Violence in the Media: Media Ratings and Proposals for Reform.* Menlo Park, CA: Kaiser Family Foundation.
Describes the numerous rating systems currently in use, including ratings for film, television, music, and interactive and coin-operated video games. Proposes a universal rating system.

Huston, Aletha C., Edward Donnerstein, Halford Fairchild, Norma D. Feshbach, Phyllis A. Katz, John P. Murray, Eli A. Rubinstein, Brian L. Wilcox, and Diana Zuckerman. 1992. *Big World, Small Screen.* Lincoln: University of Nebraska Press.
Discussion of the psychosocial effects of television in numerous areas, including how stereotypes of ethnic groups, the elderly, and homosexuals may contribute to the self-image of numerous viewers. Discusses how television can teach and inform, particularly in relation to aggression, callousness, and amorality. Offers suggestions for public policy and research.

Kaiser Family Foundation. 1999. *Kids and Media @ the New Millennium: A Comprehensive National Analysis of Children's Media Use.* Menlo Park, CA: Kaiser Family Foundation, www.kff.org.
A comprehensive study of the media use by over 3,000 children (ages 2 to 18). Looks at how children use the media and whether "new" media are replacing traditional media. Parental mediation of children's use of media is also examined.

———. 2001. *Parents and the V-Chip, 2001: A Kaiser Family Foundation Survey.* Menlo Park, CA: Kaiser Family Foundation, www.kff.org.

Although close to 40 percent of American parents own a TV set equipped with the V-chip blocking device, relatively few use the V-chip to block the programs their children watch. Moreover, more than half the parents did not even know that their TV set was so equipped. More parents are likely to use program ratings to pick programs for their children to watch. Parents felt that a uniform rating system for all types of media (TV, movies, video games) would be more useful than the systems now in place.

———. 2002. *Key Facts: Children and Video Games.* Menlo Park, CA: Kaiser Family Foundation, www.kff.org.
A useful and comprehensive fact sheet about video games. Presents data on the prevalence of games, the amount of time spent playing, and age- and gender-related preferences. Also presents information about video game content and the effects of these games on players. Presents currently available video game ratings.

———. 2003a. *Key Facts: Children and the News: Coping with Terrorism, War, and Everyday Violence.* Menlo Park, CA: Kaiser Family Foundation, www.kff.org.
A useful and comprehensive fact sheet discussing our knowledge of how children may be affected by the horrific images of terrorism and war in the media. Provides guidelines for parents and journalists as well as website addresses for organizations that have addressed this issue.

———. 2003b. *Key Facts: Media Literacy.* Menlo Park, CA: Kaiser Family Foundation, www.kff.org.
A useful, comprehensive fact sheet about media literacy. Presents the issues surrounding both the definition of media literacy and media literacy education. Provides information about the effectiveness of media literacy in relation to aggression and antisocial behavior.

———. 2003c. *Key facts: TV Violence.* Menlo Park, CA: Kaiser Family Foundaiton,www.kff.org.
A useful and comprehensive fact sheet presenting data about the prevalence of violence on television. Presents information from the NTVS, and the UCLA monitoring report as well as summaries of numerous laboratory and field experiments as well as longitudinal studies. Presents views pro and con.

Kunkel, Dale, Wendy J. M. Farinola, Kirstie Cope, Edward Donner-stein, Erica Biely, and Lara Zwarun. 1998. *Rating the TV Ratings: An Assessment of the Television Industry's Use of V-Chip Ratings.* Menlo Park, CA: Kaiser Family Foundation, www.kff.org.

Age-based ratings appeared frequently and were highly cor-related with program content; content-based ratings, although accurate, appeared very infrequently. The rating system will not work particularly well with V-Chip technology because the most programs with objectionable content are not given content-based ratings. The study focused on over 1,000 hours of programming on eleven channels.

Lichter, S. Robert, Linda S. Lichter, and Daniel R. Amundson. 1999. *Merchandising Mayhem: Violence in Popular Entertainment, 1998–99.* Washington, DC: Center for Media and Public Affairs.

A study of violence, sexual imagery, and graphic language in broadcast and cable television, music videos, first-run theatrical movies, and movies specifically made for television in 1998–1999 (N=574). Feature films were the most violent, followed by made-for-TV movies, and most serious violence was aimed at a youth-ful audience. Moreover, acts of violence rarely resulted in physi-cal or emotional harm. Although some violence is necessary and highly rated by critics, such programs are relatively rare (less than 3 percent of films).

National Television Violence Study, Executive Summary. 1994–1995. Studio City, CA: Media Scope.

Summarizes the results of the first year of the NTVS (fund-ed by the National Cable Television Association) in which 2,500 hours (2,693 programs randomly selected from 23 channels over a 20-week period) were analyzed for content. Some of the key findings were that the context of violence poses considerable risks for viewers, perpetrators are frequently unpunished, the negative consequences of violence are not seen, and there are very few programs with antiviolence themes. However, the research found that television violence typically is not graphic or explicit.

National Television Violence Study. 1997. Vol. 1. Thousand Oaks, CA: Sage.

Presentation of findings from the first year of the NTVS, which was funded by the National Cable Television Association.

Begins to focus on the contextual elements of violence. Notes the high levels of violence on television.

National Television Violence Study. 1998. Vol. 2. Center for Communication and Social Policy, University of California, Santa Barbara, ed. Thousand Oaks, CA: Sage.

Report of the second year of the NTVS (funded by the National Cable Television Association) that compares data on the extent and nature of violence from 1995 to 1996. The analysis focused specifically on the context of violent portrayals (reward, punishment, consequences, realism, graphicness, humor, weapons) and how these portrayals might affect viewers.

National Television Violence Study. 1998. Vol. 3. Center for Communication and Social Policy, University of California, Santa Barbara, ed. Thousand Oaks, CA: Sage.

Examines the results from the three-year NTVS (1995–1997, funded by the National Cable Television Association) and compares the findings from year to year, looking particularly at contextual elements of violence and how these elements may affect viewers. The study also examines advisories over three years and shows how the television rating system was initially implemented. Notes specifically those presentations of violence that may pose higher risks for viewers, particularly children.

Rideout, Victoria J., Elizabeth A. Vandewater, and Ellen A. Wartella. 2003. *Electronic Media in the Lives of Infants, Toddlers, and Preschoolers.* Menlo Park, CA: Kaiser Family Foundation.

This survey of 1,000 parents of children from six months to six years old focused on the types of media used by very young children. Children begin watching when very young, and those under six spent about two hours a day watching television and/or videos. Television sets are often left "on" for most of the day, even if no one watches. Parents typically see media as an important educational tool.

Rideout, Victoria J. 2004. *Parents, Media and Public Policy: A Kaiser Family Foundation Survey.* Menlo Park, CA: Kaiser Family Foundation.

This survey of 1,001 parents of children ages two to seventeen found that parents were very concerned that their children were often exposed to inappropriate materials in the media, particularly on television. Parents were most concerned with exposure to sexual content followed closely by violent content and exposure to adult language. Most parents indicated that media content had an effect on children's behavior.

Scholarly Works

Anderson, Craig A., Leonard Berkowitz, Edward Donnerstein, L. Rowell Huesmann, James D. Johnson, Daniel Linz, Neil M. Malamuth, and Ellen Wartella. 2003. "The Influence of Media Violence on Youth." *Psychological Science in the Public Interest* 4, no. 3: 81–110.

Discusses how research on media violence, including violent films and television, music, and video games, provides evidence of immediate and long-term relationships between that violence and aggressive and violent behavior. Although the evidence is consistent overall, it is most compelling concerning television violence. Long-term longitudinal studies provide additional support for the contention that exposure to media violence in childhood is related to aggression, including assault and spousal abuse, later in life.

Ball-Rokeach, Sandra J. 2001. "The Politics of Studying Media Violence: Reflections 30 Years after the Violence Commission." *Mass Communication and Society* 4, no. 1: 3–18.

Presents the author's perspective on the role political forces play in the study of media effects and report writing. Ball-Rokeach was personally involved in the President's Commission on the Causes and Prevention of Violence as the co-director of the Media and Violence Task Force. The author analyzes the types of questions that have been asked in the study of violence and the media.

Bandura, Albert. 2002. "Social Cognitive Theory of Mass Communication." In Jennings Bryant and Dolf Zillmann, eds., *Media Effects: Advances in Theory and Research*, pp. 121–154. 2nd ed. Hillsdale, NJ: Lawrence Erlbaum Associates.

Social-cognitive theory presents a conceptual framework to examine and understand how symbolic communication, such as television viewing, influences attitudes, thoughts, and behavior. Social-cognitive theory looks at the interrelationship among personal, behavioral, and environmental determinants in understanding human behavior and stresses the role of cognitive processes.

Berkowitz, Leonard. 1993. *Aggression: Its Causes, Consequences, and Control.* Philadelphia: Temple University Press.

This book is a discussion of social scientists' work in the area of aggression. It includes chapters that define aggression and discuss emotional aggression as well as the relationship between cognitions and emotions and has a section on violence in society, focusing specifically on violence in the media and how it relates to aggression.

Bryant, Jennings, and Dolf Zillmann, eds. 2002. *Media Effects: Advances in Theory and Research.* 2nd ed. Hillsdale, NJ: Lawrence Erlbaum Associates.

In twenty-two chapters, this book provides an in-depth examination of the most important theories and perspectives in mass communication, including media effects, media consumption, intermedia processes, and prosocial effects.

Bushman, Brad J., and Craig A. Anderson. 2001. "Media Violence and the American Public: Scientific Facts versus Media Misinformation." *American Psychologist* 56, nos. 6–7: 477–489.

Discusses the discontinuity between news reports and scientific knowledge about the relationship between media violence and aggression. Since the mid-1970s, the link between media violence and aggression has been solidly established. The discontinuity is the result of ineffective presentation of the scientific case by researchers as well as the vested interests of reporters.

Bushman, Brad J., and Angela D. Stack. 1996. "Forbidden Fruit versus Tainted Fruit: Effects of Warning Labels on Attraction to Television Violence." *Journal of Experimental Psychology: Applied* 2, no. 3: 207–226.

Experiments compared the tainted fruit theory (warnings will decrease interest) with the forbidden fruit theory (warnings will increase interest). A series of three experiments found that warning labels may increase the number of viewers; the results were consistent with a forbidden fruit theory.

Cantor, Joanne. 1998. "Children's Attraction to Violent Television Programming." In Jeffrey H. Goldstein, ed., *Why We Watch: The Attractions of Violent Entertainment,* pp. 88–115. London: Oxford University Press.

This chapter discusses the evidence that children find media violence attractive and why children experience media violence. The author looks at the results from two recent surveys and makes suggestions for future areas of research.

————. 2002. "Fright Reactions to Mass Media." In Jennings Bryant and Dolf Zillmann, eds., *Media Effects: Advances in Theory and Research,* pp. 287–306. Mahwah, NJ: Lawrence Erlbaum Associates.

A comprehensive examination of fright reactions that result from involvement with the mass media. Focuses on the prevalence and intensity of fright reactions, particularly feelings of fear. Discusses developmental differences in determining what media typically frighten children and what strategies are effective in dealing with children's fear responses.

————. 2003. "Media Violence Effects and Interventions: The Roles of Communication and Emotion." In Jennings Bryant, David Roskos-Ewoldsen, and Joanne Cantor eds., *Communication and Emotion: Essays in Honor of Dolf Zillmann,* pp. 197–219. Mahwah, NJ: Lawrence Erlbaum Associates.

An examination of the communicative and emotional processes involved in the effects of media violence. This chapter also examines possible interventions using interpersonal factors or media-based strategies.

Cantor, Joanne, and Barbara J. Wilson. 2003. "Media and Violence: Intervention Strategies for Reducing Aggression." *Media Psychology* 5, no. 4: 363–403.

Reviews research on media violence and aggression, looking for ways to reduce aggressive behaviors and attitudes. Parental mediation (comments) can sometimes reduce children's aggressive behaviors. The success of the interventions is quite variable with considerable age and gender differences. Some anti-violence productions may boomerang. More research is needed to develop solid parental interventions, strategies for media literacy and the creation of prosocial presentations.

Centerwall, Brandon S. 1989. "Exposure to Television as a Risk Factor for Violence." *American Journal of Epidemiology* 129: 643–652.

Taking an epidemiological approach, this article examines changes in white homicides in three cultures—the United States, Canada, and South Africa. In all three cultures, homicide rates were static until about ten to fifteen years after the availability of television; homicide rates then increased considerably.

————. 1990. "Young Adult Suicide and Exposure to Television." *Social Psychiatry and Psychiatric Epidemiology* 25, no. 3: 149–153.
    A comparison of suicide trends in the United States, Canada, and South Africa between 1949 and 1985 to determine if television viewing is a risk factor for those between ages fifteen and twenty-four. In the United States, the spread of television was unrelated to the increase in young adult suicide rates. South Africa also had increases in suicide rates, even though the society did not have television until 1975. Concludes that nonspecific television viewing is not a risk factor.

Dubow, Eric F., and Laurie S. Miller,. 1996. "Television Violence Viewing and Aggressive Behavior." In Tannis M. MacBeth, ed., *Tuning in to Young Viewers: Social Science Perspectives on Television*, pp. 117–147. Thousand Oaks, CA: Sage.
    Looks at the relationship between watching violence and developing aggressive behavior in relation to three things—the evidence, the processes, and how to intervene to mitigate the influence of violent TV. Focuses on a social-cognitive (information-processing) perspective.

Eron, Leonard D. 1980. "Prescription for Reduction of Aggression." *American Psychologist* 35, no. 3: 244–252
    Early intervention in socializing children can help reduce the level of aggression in society. Children must learn different ways to solve problems so that they are not dependent upon aggressive techniques. Socialization practices should be similar for both boys and girls; in particular, boys need to be encouraged to be cooperative, nurturing, tender, and sensitive, qualities that are often seen as antithetical to aggression.

————. 1982. "Parent-Child Interaction, Television Violence, and Aggression of Children. *American Psychologist* 37, no. 2: 197–211.
    Presents the results of two large longitudinal studies examining the relationship between aggression and television violence in two geographical areas of the United States. The data were similar for boys and girls. The data found that there was a circular causal effect: violence contributed to aggression, but aggressive youngsters typically watched more violent programs. The importance of

intervention was discussed. The children's identification with aggressive television characters emerged as an important intervening variable in the relationship between television violence and aggression.

————. 1987. "The Development of Aggressive Behavior from the Perspective of a Developing Behaviorism." *American Psychologist* 42, no. 5: 435–442.

The description of the theoretical framework that has guided the author's twenty-two-year longitudinal study of the relationship between television violence and aggression. Although the original variables were selected and operationalized because of their relevance to Hull-Spence theory, the data are also relevant to social learning theory and cognitive behaviorism. The author notes that learning theories can now account for the data because they are broader in perspective.

Feshbach, Seymour. 1961. "The Stimulating versus Cathartic Effects of a Vicarious Aggressive Activity." *Journal of Abnormal and Social Psychology* 63, no. 2: 381–385.

Experimental test of the effect of the initial state of arousal on reactions to media violence. Male college students were either (1) angered or (2) treated neutrally before viewing a (1) neutral or (2) aggressive film of a prize fight. Those who were angered and saw the aggressive film exhibited less aggression toward the experimenter than those who were treated neutrally and saw the aggressive film. The author concluded that catharsis occurs for those in a state of arousal before watching violence.

Feshbach, Seymour, and Robert Singer. 1971. *Television and Aggression: An Experimental Field Study.* San Francisco: Jossey-Bass.

The authors examine the relationship between imitative behavior and televised violence. Boys in residential schools watched either violent or nonviolent programs for six weeks. Measures of attitudes and personality were taken before, during, and after the viewing period. The nonviolent viewing groups were more aggressive with peers and school authorities than those who saw violent programs. The authors also examine the role of fantasized aggression as it related to catharsis.

Fowles, Jib. 1999. *The Case for Television Violence.* Thousand Oaks, CA: Sage.

A book-length discussion that shows how television violence has been misinterpreted. Violence on television supports the existing social order by providing a safe outlet for aggressive impulses. Fowles concludes that television violence is the "most recent and least damaging venue for the routinized working out of innate aggressiveness and fear" (p. 119).

Freedman, Jonathan L. 1984. "Effect of Television Violence on Aggressiveness." *Psychological Bulletin* 96, no. 2: 227–246.
Reviews and evaluates the design and results of field experiments and correlational surveys dealing with the relationship between television violence and real-life aggression. Concludes that these studies cannot be interpreted as providing evidence of a causal relationship because the relationships are marginal. Also concludes that there is no clear evidence that those labeled "predisposed to violence" are more likely than other individuals to respond to televised violence with violent or aggressive behavior.

———. 1988. "Television Violence and Aggression: What the Evidence Shows." *Applied Social Psychology Annual. Special Issue: Television as a Social Issue,* no. 8: 144–162.
Asserts that evidence from laboratory, field, and correlational studies does not support the conclusion that television violence causes aggressive behavior in children or adults.

———. 1992. "Television Violence and Aggression: What Psychologists Should Tell the Public." In Peter Suedfeld and Philip I. Tetlock, eds., *Psychology and Social Policy,* pp. 179–189. New York: Hemisphere.
Reviews findings from laboratory and field experiments as well as correlational studies relating to the effects of television violence. Notes that although the evidence cannot be expected to be definitive regarding this complex topic, it should be strong enough that reasonable scientists are convinced that the relationships are valid. Concludes that the evidence does not support the contention that television violence causes or is related to aggressive behavior.

Gadow, Kenneth D., and Joyce Sprafkin. 1993. "Television 'Violence' and Children with Emotional and Behavioral Disorders." *Journal of Emotional and Behavioral Disorders* 1, no. 1: 54–63.
Review of ten years of research on children with emotional disturbances who watch violent programming finds that these

children view considerable amounts of violence, tend to prefer characters who are aggressive, and are likely to believe that fictional content is real. They are, however, no more likely than other children to behave aggressively after watching violent content.

Gerbner, George, Larry Gross, Michael Morgan, and Nancy Signorielli. 1980. "The 'Mainstreaming' of America: Violence Profile no. 11." *Journal of Communication* 30, no. 3: 10–29.

The Cultural Indicators Project, which has monitored broadcast television and examined the relationship between viewing and conceptions of social reality since 1967, supports the hypothesis that television makes specific and measurable contributions to viewers' conceptions of social reality. Violence remained an important thematic element and typically demonstrates power on television. Cultivation analyses show that many of the differences between groups of viewers may be explained by one of two systematic processes—mainstreaming (sharing a relative commonality of outlooks) or resonance (congruence of the social environment with television's messages).

Gerbner, George, Larry Gross, Michael Morgan, Nancy Signorielli, and James Shanahan. 2002. "Growing Up with Television: The Cultivation Perspective." In Jennings Bryant and Dolf Zillmann, eds., *Media Effects: Advances in Theory and Research*. 2nd ed., pp. 43–68. Hillsdale, NJ: Lawrence Erlbaum Associates.

Updates, summarizes, and illustrates the dynamics of cultivation theory. Discusses studies conducted in both the United States and in other countries. Notes how today's media environment of extended delivery systems provides deeper penetration and integration of dominant patterns of media images into everyday life. This in turn lessens the likelihood of fragmentation of the dominant images cultivated by the media.

Gerbner, George, Larry Gross, Nancy Signorielli, and Michael Morgan. 1980. "Television Violence, Victimization, and Power." *American Behavioral Scientist* 23, no. 5: 705–716.

The Cultural Indicators Project, which has monitored broadcast television and examined the relationship between viewing and conceptions of social reality since 1967, shows that violence plays an important role in television's portrayal of the social order. Television programs show a calculus of life chances. They demonstrate the relative distribution of power and the fear of power. Surveys of adults and children show that these lessons are absorbed by cultivating a pervasive and exaggerated sense of danger and mistrust. In the same demographic subgroups, those who watch more television typically exhibit a significantly higher sense of personal risk and suspicion than those who watch less television.

Gunter, Barrie. 1998. "Ethnicity and Involvement in Violence on Television: Nature and Context of On-screen Portrayals." *Journal of Black Studies* 28, no. 6: 683–703.

Content analysis of 1,161 drama programs seen on ten channels in Great Britain. White characters were more likely than black characters to be victims of violence. Both white and blacks were targeted by aggressors who were white. Other Asians typically attacked Asians.

Gunter, Barrie, Jackie Harrison, and Maggie Wykes. 2003. *Violence on Television: Distribution, Form, Context, and Themes.* Mahwah, NJ: Lawrence Erlbaum Associates.

Reports the findings of two large projects studying violence on television in Great Britain between 1994 and 1996 (sampling 56 days that generated 11,000 hours of programming from 8 channels in 1994 and 10 channels in 1996). Although violence was found in programs on all channels, the most excessive quantities were found on the subscription movie channels. Graphic and gory violence was not found very often; when seen, it was on the subscription channels or shown when children were not likely to be in the audience. Provides a comparison of violence on British and U.S. television.

Hamilton, James T. 1998. *Channeling Violence: The Economic Market for Violent Television Programming.* Princeton, NJ: Princeton University Press.

Explores how economics can explain how the self-interest of producers, distributors, and consumers in providing and/or watching violent programs results in problematic social outcomes (children's exposure to television violence). Discusses how television violence is but one possible cause of violence in the United States. Explores how risks from specific violent programs might be assessed and whether policies designed to handle television violence would benefit society.

Hoffner, Cynthia, and Martha Buchanan. 2002. "Parents' Responses to Television Violence: The Third-Person Perception, Parental

Mediation, and Support for Censorship." *Media Psychology* 4, no. 3: 231–252.

Extension of research on the third-person effect (others are more affected by the media than the respondent or their family) on parents' beliefs about the effects of television violence on their own and other children, particularly as related to censorship support and parental mediation. A telephone survey of parents of children aged three to eighteen (N=70) found third-person perceptions viewing the world as dangerous and approving of aggression, particularly aggressive behaviors. Parental mediation and censorship supports were associated with these perceptions of television violence.

Huesmann, L. Rowell, ed. 1994. *Aggressive Behavior: Current Perspectives.* New York: Plenum.

Chapters arranged into five sections present the best current theoretical research on human aggression. Part 1 describes Huesmann's current thinking about human aggression, focusing on a social-cognitive framework. Part 2 discusses the role of gender and peers, noting the particularly harmful influence of peers who exhibit antisocial behavior. Part 3 examines the most long-lasting contextual variables related to aggression, including media violence. Part 4 takes a developmental perspective, looking at data from important longitudinal studies, and Part 5 elaborates two theories relating to group aggression.

Huesmann, L. Rowell, and Leonard D. Eron. 1986. *Television and the Aggressive Child: A Cross-National Comparison.* Hillsdale, NJ: Lawrence Erlbaum Associates.

Results from five studies, undertaken in five countries (United States, Finland, Poland, Australia, Israel) and designed to explain the relationship between television violence/television viewing and aggression. An important study because it looks at the violence-aggression connection outside the United States and North America. Results from all the studies are compared and contrasted. Data from studies conducted in the Netherlands and West Germany are also presented.

Huesmann, L. Rowell, Leonard D. Eron, Leonard Berkowitz, and Steven Chaffee. 1992. "The Effects of Television Violence on Aggression: A Reply to a Skeptic." In Peter Suedfeld and Phillip I. Tetlock, eds., *Psychology and Social Policy,* pp. 191–200. Washington, DC: Hemisphere Publishing.

Refutes Freedman's 1984 article that claims media violence does not stimulate aggressive behavior. The authors make the argument that Freedman's conclusion is unjustified.

Huesmann, L. Rowell, and Laurie S. Miller. 1994. "Long-Term Effects of Repeated Exposure to Media Violence in Childhood." In L. Rowell Huesmann, ed., *Aggressive Behavior: Current Perspectives,* pp. 153–186. New York: Plenum.

Reviews longitudinal research conducted since the early 1980s on children's aggression and exposure to media violence. Research is seen from a social-cognitive theoretical perspective. Media violence is shown to have long-term effects through observational or social learning (viewers learn aggressive behaviors by watching others behave aggressively) as well as short-term effects through the development of cognitive schema of aggressive behaviors (viewers develop outlines or plans about how they could behave aggressively in the future).

Huesmann, L. Rowell, Jessica Moise-Titus, Cheryl-Lynn Podolski, and Leonard D. Eron. 2003. "Longitudinal Relations between Children's Exposure to TV Violence and Their Aggressive and Violent Behavior in Young Adulthood, 1977–1992." *Developmental Psychology* 39, no. 2: 201–221.

Results of a longitudinal study of a sample of men and women growing up in the 1970s and 1980s. The data examine the relationship between viewing violent television for children ages six to ten and aggressive behavior fifteen years later. Exposure to violence as children predicts aggressive behavior of both male and female young adults. Aggression was also predicted by identification with aggressive characters. The relationships withstood controls for socioeconomic status, intelligence, and several parenting factors.

Huesmann, L. Rowell, and Marko M. Skoric. 2003. "Regulating Media Violence: Why, How, and by Whom? In Edward L. Palmer, and Brian M. Young, eds., *The Faces of Televisual Media: Teaching, Violence, Selling to Children,* pp. 219–240. 2nd ed. Mahwah, NJ: Lawrence Erlbaum Associates.

Examines evidence and theories, beginning with the 1997 surgeon general's report linking television violence viewing and aggressive behaviors. The authors discuss several important issues (the formative nature of exposure to violence as a child, long-lasting effects, risk factors, etc.) that should be used to guide regulation. Reviews the history of regulation and offers suggestions for the future.

Kaplan, Robert M., and Rrobert D. Singer. 1976. "Television Violence and Viewer Aggression: A Re-examination of the Evidence." *Journal of Social Issues* 32: 35–70.

An evaluation of the existing body of research on the effect of television violence on aggressive behavior: the validity of the research is in question in relation to elements of methodology, including setting, samples, and aggression measures. Summarizes studies that support three possible effects of media violence: imitation, catharsis, or no effect. The authors say the evidence supporting the null or no effect) hypothesis is the most acceptable.

Krcmar, Marina, and Mark C. Cooke. 2001. "Children's Moral Reasoning and Their Perceptions of Television Violence." *Journal of Communication* 51, no. 2: 300–316.

Experiment focusing on how age (moral development) was related to children's interpretations of television violence and their willingness to use aggression. Children aged four to seven and eight to eleven (N=184) were randomly assigned to one of four viewing groups to watch a violent video clip. The clips had the same violent actions but manipulated provocation and punishment. The dependent variable was the child's judgment as to whether the act was right or wrong and their willingness to use an aggressive solution to a hypothetical conflict. Younger children believed unpunished violence was not as bad as punished violence, whereas older children thought violence was justified if provoked. Selecting a violent story ending was related to experimental conditions for older children only.

Kunkel, Dale, Wendy J. M. Farinola, Kirstie Farrar, Edward Donnerstein, Erica Biely, and Lara Zwarun. 2002. "Deciphering the V-Chip: An Examination of the Television Industry's Program Rating Judgments." *Journal of Communication* 52, no. 1: 112–138.

An examination of the validity of the TV ratings system in a sample of programs on the top ten channels (broadcast, basic cable, premium). Programs were judged for the amount and portrayal of sex (S), dialogue (D), adult language (L), and violence (V) and then compared to the age-based ratings. Age-based ratings gave a reasonable assessment of content, as did the content-based ratings, when used. But many programs were not given content-based ratings. Children's programs contained considerable amounts of violence but were not necessarily identified by the fantasy violence (FV) content rating. The V-chip has limited effectiveness in restricting children's viewing of sensitive and adult content.

Kunkel, Dale, and Brian Wilcox. 2001. "Children and Media Policy." In. Dorothy G. Singer and Jerome L. Singer, eds., *Handbook of Children and the Media*, pp. 589–604. Thousand Oaks, CA: Sage.

Discusses children and media policy, noting that much of this policy is shaped, not by media content but by each medium's specific delivery system. Provides a historical perspective and presents information relating to several genres, such as indecent material, educational programming, and advertising. The review also discusses future challenges to the regulation of programming in regard to children.

Kunkel, Dale, Barbara Wilson, Edward Donnerstein, Daniel Linz, Stacy Smith, Timothy Gray, Eva Blumenthal, and W. James Potter. 1995. "Measuring Television Violence: The Importance of Context." *Journal of Broadcasting & Electronic Media* 39, no. 2: 284–291.

Presents a framework to differentiate between violence portrayals that may be antisocial and those that may be less problematic. Defines and explicates the key elements of violence. Notes how the character's involvement is a critical element. Shows that viewers are less likely to learn or imitate violence if the program illustrates the pain and harm that accompanies violence.

McIntosh, Willaim D., John D. Murray, Rebecca M. Murray, and Sunita Manian. 2003. "What's So Funny about a Poke in the Eye? The Prevalence of Violence in Comedy Films and Its Relation to Social and Economic Threat in the United States, 1951–2000." *Mass Communication and Society* 6, no. 4: 345–360.

An analysis of violent content in the top-grossing comedy films released in the United States between 1951 and 2000. Since 1970, comic violence has been relatively consistent. The comic violence in these films did not show good prevailing over evil, and the aggressors were portrayed somewhat more positively than those who were the victims or targets of violence.

Morgan, Michael 1983. "Symbolic Victimization and Real World Fear." *Human Communication Research* 9, no. 2: 146–157.

An examination of the relationship between relative victimization in television drama and variations in susceptibility to the cultivation of a sense of personal risk in the real world. Using data from a 1979 national probability survey, over 300 demographic subgroups were constructed (combinations of age, sex, race, marital status, and class). Viewers whose fictional counterparts were more likely to be shown as victims of violence exhibited stronger associations between the amount of viewing they did and perceived vulnerability. The relative power hierarchy of television drama strongly matches the real-world hierarchy of susceptibility to violence.

Murray, John P. 1997. "Media Violence and Youth." In Joy D. Osofsky, ed., *Children in a Violent Society*, pp. 72–96. New York: Guilford.
 Discussion of the relationship between media violence, particularly television violence, and children's aggressive behavior. Looks specifically at the research on television violence and those factors that influence its effects.

———. 1998. "Studying Television Violence: A Research Agenda for the 21st Century." In Joyce K. Asamen, and Gordon L. Berry, eds., *Research Paradigms, Television, and Social Behavior*, pp. 369–410. Thousand Oaks, CA: Sage.
 Looking at studies conducted over the past fifty years, this chapter discusses the current state of the study of television violence, noting that the findings, using numerous research paradigms, support the conclusion that television violence influences values, attitudes, and behaviors. The author also notes that we still do not fully understand how these effects occur and that we need to develop strategies to counteract the harmful effects of television violence.

———. 2003. "The Violent Face of Television: Research and Discussion." In Edward L. Palmer and Brian M. Young, eds., *The Faces of Televisual Media: Teaching, Violence, Selling to Children*, pp. 143–160. 2nd ed. Mahwah, NJ: Lawrence Erlbaum Associates.
 Reviews the history of research on television violence and presents research on neurological mediation in relation to watching both violent and nonviolent television. Murray discusses three types of effects (desensitization, fear, and aggression) and notes that the large body of research shows that everyone is affected by media violence.

Paik, Haejung, and George Comstock. 1994. "The Effects of Television Violence on Antisocial Behavior: A Meta-Analysis. *Communication Research* 21: 516–546.
Meta-analysis of studies on television violence and aggressive behavior found a statistically significant and positive relationship. Effects were marginally similar for boys and girls.

Palmer, Edward L., and Brian M. Young. 2003. *Children and the Faces of Televisual Media: Teaching, Violence, Selling to Children*. Mahwah, NJ: Lawrence Erlbaum.
A collection of original essays from the leading scholars in the field. Essays focus on research, trends, and policy issues, specifically television content, effects, comprehension, and viewing patterns in relation to children. Examines children's entertainment programming and advertising directed toward them.

Perse, Elizabeth 2001. *Media Effects and Society*. Mahwah, NJ: Lawrence Erlbaum Associates.
An in-depth examination of media effects focusing on the theories that explain the media's impact on both society and individuals. Comprehensive coverage includes how we learn from the mass media, socialization processes, and violent and sexually explicit content. It shows how theory can guide future research, particularly in relation to new technologies.

Potter, W. James 1996. "Considering Policies to Protect Children from TV Violence." *Journal of Communication* 46, no. 4: 116–138.
Presents the fundamental flaws in the thinking behind the requirement (enacted as part of the 1996 Telecommunications Act) that all new television sets come equipped with the V-chip and that programmers must give programs age-based ratings.

———. 1999. *On Media Violence*. Thousand Oaks, CA: Sage.
A thorough review of forty years of research on media violence in four parts: a review of the literature on media violence, a reconceptualization of many of the key elements and theories, reconsideration of the methods researchers use to study media violence, and a description of a new theoretical perspective (lineation theory for understanding media violence).

———. 2001. *Media Literacy*. 2nd ed. Thousand Oaks, CA: Sage.
A guide for students to use to become more literate consumers

of the media. Potter provides exercises so that readers may examine their own experiences with the media and develop appropriate skills to understand the media and their role in their lives. Shows how the media present multilayered messages and how important it is to have the tools to understand these layers and to maintain control of our perception of the world.

————. 2003. *The 11 Myths of Media Violence.* Thousand Oaks, CA: Sage.
Critically examines and challenges eleven existing myths about media violence to uncover fallacies in both the commonly held logic and beliefs. The book outlines the problem of media violence, presents and analyzes the myths, and finally tries to predict possible solutions to what the author describes as the problems of media violence and misunderstanding.

————. 2004. *Theory of Media Literacy: A Cognitive Approach.* Thousand Oaks, CA: Sage.
Explains how we assimilate the overwhelming amount of information we receive from the media, focusing on how we may process the information incorrectly. Presents a locus to explain media literacy that includes having the skills to interpret what the media present; having sufficient information about media industries, content, and effects; and knowledge about real-world parameters and ourselves.

Potter, W. James. In press. *Encyclopedia of Media Violence.* Thousand Oaks, CA: Sage.
Summary and critical essays covering all aspects of media violence.

Potter, W. James, and Stacy Smith. 2000. "The Context of Graphic Portrayals of Television Violence." *Journal of Broadcasting & Electronic Media* 44, no. 2: 301–323.
Content analysis finds that portrayals of graphic violence are typically found in live action, serious programs with human targets and perpetrators. Posits that highly graphic portrayals are more likely to produce fear effects than disinhibition or desensitization.

Potter, W. James, and Ron Warren. 1998. "Humor as Camouflage of Televised Violence." *Journal of Communication* 48, no. 2: 40–57.

A content analysis of a composite week of television programming found that 31 percent of the 5,970 violent acts presented violence in a humorous context. Although comedy programs had high levels of violence, the violence typically was relatively minor and was trivialized. This article focuses on why viewers may not care about violence in comedies.

Signorielli, Nancy. 2003. "Prime-Time Violence, 1993–2001: Has the Picture Really Changed?" *Journal of Broadcasting & Electronic Media* 47, no. 1: 36–57.

In this examination of violence in prime time network programs broadcast between 1993 and 2001, the author found levels of violence similar to those seen in studies of the 1970s and 1980s. Violence appeared in six out of ten programs at a rate of 4.5 acts per program. Violence was not particularly gratuitous or graphic, and there were few overall consequences for violence. Lack of context teaches that violence is "sanitary" and those who commit violence are not necessarily sorry or punished.

Signorielli, Nancy, and George Gerbner. 1988. *Violence and Terror in the Mass Media: An Annotated Bibliography.* Westport, CT: Greenwood.

Begun as a project for the United Nations Educational, Scientific, and Cultural Organization, the bibliography focuses upon research and scholarly works relating to violence and terror in both the United States and across the world. The studies focus on four areas: media content, effects, terrorism, and pornography. Entries consist of the bibliographic citation and a short abstract.

Signorielli, Nancy, George Gerbner, and Michael Morgan. 1995. "Violence on Television: The Cultural Indicators Project." *Journal of Broadcasting & Electronic Media* 39, no. 2: 278–283.

Presents the way television violence is defined, measured, and analyzed as part of the ongoing, long-term Cultural Indicators Project, which has monitored broadcast television and examined the relationship between viewing and conceptions of social reality since 1967.

Signorielli, Nancy, Larry Gross, and Michael Morgan. 1982. "Violence in Television Programs: Ten Years Later." In David Pearl, Lorraine Bouthilet, and Joyce Lazar, eds., *Television and Social Behavior: Ten Years of Scientific Progress and Implications for the Eighties,* pp. 158–173. Rockville, MD: National Institute of Mental Health.

Focuses on the methodological aspects of assessing violence on television. Describes and provides examples of several content analyses and rating systems. Provides specific information on the Cultural Indicators Project, which has been analyzing trends in television content since 1967, and data on the violence index from 1967 to 1979. Discusses cultivation theory as well.

Singer, Dorothy G., and Jerome L. Singer. 2003. *Handbook of Children and the Media.* Thousand Oaks, CA: Sage.
A handbook of essays from leading media scholars examining the existing research and potential future impact of electronic media on children, focusing specifically on television but also examining video games and the Internet. Part 1 looks at the effects of media on child development and how the media function as agents of socialization. Part 2 explores the media environment, the industry, and the new technology. Part 3 focuses on advocacy and policy issues.

Smith, Stacy L., and Edward Donnerstein. 1998. "Harmful Effects of Exposure to Media Violence: Learning of Aggression, Emotional Desensitization, and Fear." In Russell G. Geen and Edward Donnerstein, eds., *Human Aggression: Theories, Research, and Implications for Social Policy*, pp. 167–202. San Diego: Academic.
Review of the state of knowledge about the harmful effects of media violence on children, adolescents, and adults. Examines viewing habits and violence on television (cable and broadcast), including information about the context of television violence, and discusses the theoretical mechanisms that may be at work. Also reviews research about ratings and advisories and media literacy.

Smith, Stacy L., Amy I. Nathanson, and Barbara J. Wilson. 2002. "Prime-Time Television: Assessing Violence during the Most Popular Viewing Hours." *Journal of Communication* 52, no. 1: 84–111.
Using data from the National Television Violence Study, this article examined the context and prevalence of violence in prime-time programs between 1995 and 1997. Violence was found in more than 60 percent of the programs, and reality programs were seen as the most problematic program genre. The results focused on the channels and genres that would be most likely to result in negative effects.

Sparks, Glenn G., and Cheri Sparks. 2002. "Effects of Media Violence." In Jennings Bryant and Dolf Zillmann, eds., *Media Effects:*

Advances in Theory and Research, pp. 269–285. 2nd ed. Mahwah, NJ: Lawrence Erlbaum Associates.

Discusses what scientific research says about the relationship between viewing and/or participating in media violence and negative outcomes in relation to behaviors, emotions, and cognitions. Addresses where line of research should go in the future.

Strasburger, Victor C., and Barbara J. Wilson. 2002. *Children, Adolescents, and the Media.* Thousand Oaks, CA: Sage.

A comprehensive, research-oriented overview of knowledge on the impact of the mass media on children and adolescents, using a developmental focus. Chapters focus on television violence, advertising, sexuality, music and music videos, video games, the Internet, and media literacy.

Van Evra, Judith. 2004. *Television and Child Development.* 3rd ed. Mahwah, NJ: Lawrence Erlbaum Associates.

A developmental approach to the study of the television and children. Includes chapters on theoretical perspectives, violence and aggression, advertising, cultural diversity, and health-related issues, among others.

Walker, James R. 2000. "Sex and Violence in Program Promotion." In Susan T. Eastman, ed., *Research in Media Promotion,* pp. 101–126. Mahwah, NJ: Lawrence Erlbaum Associates.

An examination of violent and sexual content on both televised and print promotions for prime-time programs. Because promotions typically use extreme program elements, they are very potent. Discusses why such harmful content is used in the promotions.

Williams, Tannis M. 1986. *The Impact of Television: A Natural Experiment in Three Communities.* New York: Academic.

Report of a natural experiment on the impact of television in three towns. One did not receive television at the start of the study (Notel), one town had only one channel (Unitel), and one received multiple stations (Multitel). The solid design used both before and after methods as well as longitudinal analyses. The differences between Notel and the other two towns were more consistent than the differences between Unitel and Multitel. The overall conclusion was that television had a negative impact on viewers in numerous ways, resulting in increased aggression, more gender-biased attitudes, and lower academic performance. The effects of television had more to do with its presence (versus not being available) than what the youngsters actually watched. This book also talks about displacement theory.

Wilson, Barbara J., Carolyn M. Colvin, Stacy L. Smith. 2002. "Engaging in Violence on American Television: A Comparison of Child, Teen, and Adult Perpetrators." *Journal of Communication* 52, no. 1: 36–60.

Content analysis of 2,757 programs broadcast in the Los Angeles area between October 1995 and June 1996 as part of the National Television Violence Study found that younger perpetrators of violence were often found in programs geared for younger children. These perpetrators were typically male and attractive, were seen as good, and were seldom punished for their aggressive behavior; the violence they committed had few negative consequences. Overall, more adults than children or adolescents were perpetrators of violence.

Wilson, Barbara J., Stacy L. Smith, W. James Potter, Dale Kunkel, Daniel Linz, Carolyn M. Colvin, and Edward Donnerstein. 2002. "Violence in Children's Television Programming: Assessing the Risks." *Journal of Communication* 52, no. 1: 5–35.

Content analysis of programming targeted to children under twelve between October 1995 and June 1996 (part of the NTVS). Children's programs had more violence (70 percent) than other shows (60 percent) and the violence was more concentrated, with an average of fourteen incidents an hour. Violence was glamorized but also sanitized and trivialized.

Trade Books

Cantor, Joanne. 1998. *Mommy, I'm Scared: How TV and Movies Frighten Children and What We Can Do to Protect Them.* New York: Harcourt Brace.

Discusses what media content may be disturbing or troublesome for children of different ages. The author provides guidelines for parents and caregivers to make reassuring explanations and offer comfort to children and explains existing television and movie rating systems. Available resources to support parents' efforts are also presented.

David, J. 1991. *Parenting in a TV Age: A CLM Media Literacy Workshop Kit.* CA: Center for Media Literacy.

This book provides aids to help parents learn how to deal with television in their homes and how to make their families, particularly their children, more media-literate.

Dudley, William, ed.1999. *Media Violence: Opposing Viewpoints.* San Diego, CA: Greenhaven.

This anthology of previously published pieces explores opposing views regarding several controversies about media violence and what might be done about it. Chapters include "Is Media Violence a Serious Problem?" and "How Should Society Respond to Media Violence?"

Goldstein, Jeffrey, ed. 1998. *Why We Watch: The Attractions of Violent Entertainment.* New York: Oxford University Press.

An anthology in which authors provide numerous explanations for viewers' attraction to violent television, movies, and sports.

Grossman, Dave, and Gloria DeGaetano. 1999. *Stop Teaching Our Kids to Kill.* New York: Crown.

Discusses how media violence, particularly violent video games, are detrimental for children. Contends that these games make children more aggressive.

Metropolitan Toronto School Board. 1998. *Responding to Media Violence.* Santa Monica, CA: Center for Media Literacy.

Classroom lessons and activities, developed by Canadian teachers, to help children (K to grade 6) understand violence in the media. Examines all genres of media, including sports, news, fantasy, and "real life." Provides ways to integrate school activities with parents and home life. A valuable resource for teachers and parents to help children cope with the media and what it teaches about violence.

Torr, James D., ed. 2001. *Examining Pop Culture: Violence in Film and Television.* San Diego: Greenhaven.

This anthology examining popular culture relating to media violence presents a broad view of this topic. The essays examine violent film genres, research about television violence, the seriousness of the problem, and ways that the issue could be dealt with in society.

————, ed. 2002. *At Issue: Is Media Violence a Problem?* San Diego: Greenhaven.

An anthology that presents all sides of the ongoing debate about media violence on television and in video games, the movies, and rap music.

Video Games

Bensley, Lillian, and Juliet Van Eenwyk. 2001. "Video Games and Real-Life Aggression: Review of the Literature." *Journal of Adolescent Health* 29, no. 4: 244–257.

Examination of the scientific literature published between 1984 and 2000 to assess the relationship between playing violent video games and aggression. Although three out of four studies found increased aggression in young children, the findings were inconclusive for teens and college students. The experimental studies did not find gender differences.

Dill, Karen E., and Jody C. Dill. 1998. "Video Game Violence: A Review of the Empirical Literature." *Aggression and Violent Behavior* 3, no. 4: 407–428.

Reviews the literature on the relationship between aggression and video game playing, noting that the evidence from numerous studies suggests that higher levels of exposure to violent video games is related to aggressive behavior. But there is a solid need for further research because there are several methodological problems and inconsistencies in the existing data.

Espejo, Roman, ed. 2003. *At Issue: Video Games.* San Diego: Greenhaven.

An anthology that addresses numerous issues (pro and con) relating to video games, including concerns about violent content, relationships with aggressive behavior, and whether or not such games can improve children's thinking skills.

Funk, Jeanne B. 2002. "Electronic Games." In Victor C. Strasburger and Barbara J. Wilson, *Children, Adolescents, and the Media*, pp. 117–144. Thousand Oaks, CA: Sage.

Examines the history of electronic games (video and computer) and the existing research. This chapter looks specifically at time spent playing and player preferences, the impact of violent games, physical health risks, addiction, positive uses for games, and the existing classification and rating systems.

Funk, Jeanne B., Heidi B. Baldacci, Tracie Pasold, and Jennifer Baumgardner. 2004. "Violence Exposure in Real Life, Video Games, Television, Movies, and the Internet: Is There Desensitization?" *Journal of Adolescence* 27, no. 1: 23–39.

Study looked for relationships, specifically in regard to desensitization, between real-life and media violence. Fifth graders (n=154) completed measures about empathy, attitudes toward violence, and exposure to real-life and media violence. In the regression analysis, only video game violence was associated with lower empathy, and video games were also related to stronger proviolence attitudes. The authors believe the active nature of game playing may help explain the negative relationships.

Funk, Jeanne B., Geysa Flores, Debra D. Buchman, and Julie N. Germann. 1999. "Rating Electronic Games: Violence Is in the Eye of the Beholder." *Youth and Society* 30, no. 3: 283–312.

Study examining whether existing rating systems reflect consumer perceptions of central game content, particularly violence. Fourth- and sixth-grade students, along with their parents and college students, were the subjects. Agreement existed for both nonviolent games and those with very violent content. Games with cartoonlike violence evoked considerable disagreement.

Griffiths, Mark. 1999. "Violent Video Games and Aggression: A Review of the Literature." *Aggression and Violent Behavior* 4, no. 2: 203–212.

Suggests there is little systematic research to ascertain whether violent video games increase aggressive behavior. The authors review the existing studies and argue that they all have methodological problems and that they only measure short-term types of aggression. The most consistent finding is that young children become more aggressive after playing or watching others play a violent game.

Newman, James. 2004. *Video Games.* New York: Routledge.

Extensive examination of video games, including their history and their rise as popular entertainment and a cultural phenomenon. Chapters also focus on game use, research on their effects, and what researchers may find in the future.

Sherry, John L. 2001. "The Effects of Violent Video Games on Aggression: A Meta-Analysis." *Human Communication Research* 27: 409–431.

A meta-analysis of thirty-two studies from 1975 to 2000 looking at the effects of violent game playing on aggression in children, teens, and young adults. The effects of video game playing were less significant than those of watching violent television programs. Games with fantasy violence or those with violence against humans were more likely to affect aggression than games with sports violence. Aggression was less with longer playing time.

Index

About the Author

Nancy Signorielli (Ph.D., University of Pennsylvania, 1975) is Professor of Communication and director of the M.A. program in Communication at the University of Delaware. Beginning with her dissertation research, an in-depth methodological examination of television characters, she has conducted research on images in the media and how these images are related to people's conceptions of social reality (cultivation analysis) for the past thirty years. An original member of the Cultural Indicators Research Team, she published one of the very first (and most frequently cited) studies of characterizations on television ("Patterns in Prime Time," *Journal of Communication,* 1974). She has also published extensively on television violence and health-related images on television.

Professor Signorielli is a member of the National Communication Association, the International Communication Association, Broadcast Education Association, and the Association for Education in Journalism and Mass Communication. She testified in May 1993 at the U. S. House Energy and Commerce committee's subcommittee on telecommunications and finance oversight hearings on television violence and its impact on children.

She has written or edited several books including *Mass Media Images and Impact on Health* (1993) and *Women in Communication: A Bibliographic Sourcebook* (1996). Her research has appeared in numerous journals as well as in edited books on mass communication. Her most recent publications include "Prime-Time Violence 1993–2001: Has the Picture Really Changed?" in *Journal of Broadcasting & Electronic Media* (2003), and "Aging on Television: Messages Relating to Gender, Race, and Occupation in Prime-Time" also in *Journal of Broadcasting & Electronic Media* (2004).